SWAHILI
PORT CITIES

᪥ ᪥ ᪥

SWAHILI
PORT CITIES

THE ARCHITECTURE OF ELSEWHERE

PRITA MEIER

INDIANA UNIVERSITY PRESS   *Bloomington & Indianapolis*

This book is a publication of

Indiana University Press
Office of Scholarly Publishing
Herman B Wells Library 350
1320 East 10th Street
Bloomington, Indiana 47405 USA

iupress.indiana.edu

The paper used in this publication
meets the minimum requirements
of the American National Standard for
Information Sciences—Permanence
of Paper for Printed Library Materials,
ANSI Z39.48–1992.

Manufactured in the
United States of America

Library of Congress
Cataloging-in-Publication Data

Meier, Prita, author.
  Swahili port cities : the architecture of
elsewhere / Prita Meier.
    pages cm — (African expressive
cultures)
  Includes bibliographical references and
index.
  ISBN 978-0-253-01909-7 (cloth : alk.
paper) — ISBN 978-0-253-01915-8 (pbk. :
alk. paper) — ISBN 978-0-253-01917-2
(ebook) 1. Architecture and society—
Africa, East. 2. Stone buildings—Africa,
East. 3. Port cities—Africa, East. 4.
Islamic architecture—Africa, East.
I. Title. II. Series: African expressive
cultures.
  NA2543.S6.M48 2016
  720.1'03—dc23

2015033413

1 2 3 4 5   21 20 19 18 17 16

Für Mädi Richter, in Liebe

CONTENTS

ACKNOWLEDGMENTS

This book took shape in many places, with the help of many individuals. At its center stand the exceptional people of Mombasa and Zanzibar. Mombasa remains a place I call home, and I continue to be inspired by the compassion and wisdom of my colleagues and friends there. First and foremost among them are Mohamed Mchulla, his wife Rukiya Abdulrehman, and their wonderful children. Aunty Rukiya lights up the world and her hospitality is unsurpassed. Mchulla's willingness to help, integrity, and quick wit are unrivaled. I owe an enormous debt of gratitude to them. I also remain grateful to Mzee Mohamed Matano, who shared his remarkable life experiences and knowledge unreservedly, making this project possible. His passing in 2008 was a great loss to many. His relatives, especially Mohammad Ahmed and Mohamed Abdallah Mohamed, also kindly offered essential guidance. Mama Hubwa and her extended family have been welcoming me to Mombasa since 2003, and her granddaughter Sharazad "Sherry" Mohammad, her husband, and their children continue to amaze with their kindness and generosity. Mzee Hamid Ahmed Al Baloushi, who passed away in 2015, was the grandest of father figures and his wise counsel will always be missed and appreciated. I am also thankful to his family members, including those living in the UK, Zanzibar, and Dubai. His daughter, Naila, is a wonderful friend; her passion for life continues to make every day with her an adventure.

The people who patiently shared their knowledge of Swahili coast history and culture are listed in the appendix, but I want to thank in particular Mzee Mohamed Shalli and Msellem Amin for many hours of provocative conversations. I am also indebted to Professor Abdul Sheriff, who kindly facilitated my access to various places and institutions when I first arrived in Zanzibar. I have learned much from his scholarship and fascinating stories about life in Zanzibar. I am obliged to the leadership and staff of the National Museums of Kenya (NMK), Kenya National Archives, Mombasa Old Town Conservation Office, and the Zanzibar National Archives. During his tenure as Head of Coastal Archaeology, Athman Lali Omar advised me countless times, and he continues to do so in the present. I benefited from many discussions with Athman Hussein, NMK Assistant Director of Museums, Sites, and Monuments, whose knowledge and friendship have had a tremendous impact on this project. I very much appreciate the help and support of Salum S. Salum, Acting Director of the Zanzibar Department of Archives and Records. Many others in Zanzibar and Mombasa have been extremely kind, including Zeineb Mohamed, Noor Sood Mohammad Shikely, Abdulwahid Hinawy, Mariam Abubakar, Masoud Riyami, Chama Al Baloushi, and their families.

In North America I am especially grateful to Raymond A. Silverman. His principles, intellect, and care have inspired and nurtured me for almost two decades. His influence is evident in every part of this book, and my gratitude to him and the lovely Mary Duff-Silverman runs deep. Allen F. Roberts has also been an important influence over the years. His and Polly Nooter Roberts' work was what first drew me to Africanist art history, and I am thankful for all they have shared with me, including their unflagging support.

I first began working on the subject of this book during my studies in the Department of the History of Art and Architecture at Harvard University, where I was part of a wonderful community of students and scholars. Suzanne Preston Blier shaped my thinking in innumerable ways. She is a brilliant scholar, generous mentor, and dear friend; her sharp insights always manage to jolt me out of states of stasis or confusion. Thomas B. F. Cummins, Carrie Elkins, Gülru Necipoglu, and David Roxburgh also provided essential guidance during my years at Harvard. I learned much from fellow students Ladan Akbarnia, Makeda Best, Chanchal Dadlani, Miguel Debaca, Mark DeLancey, Miraj Dhir, Brendan Fay, Emine Fetvaci, Hallie Franks, Cécile Fromont, Rachel Goshgarian, Genevieve Hyacinthe, Aden Kumler, Michelle Kuo, Leora

Maltz-Leca, Jacob Proctor, Gemma Rodrigues, Jennifer Pruitt, Dalila Scruggs, Ruth Simbao, and Suzan Yalman. The friendship of Kristina van Dyke and Sarah Rogers was especially important; their support and love made all the difference.

During my time as a postdoc at Johns Hopkins University I benefited from the support and counsel of a number of people, including Sara Berry, Stephen Campbell, Don Juedes, Pier Larson, Herica Valladares, and all the faculty and students associated with the Africa Seminar. Gaby Spiegel's incisive ideas and close reading of my work enriched this project in fundamental ways. I am particularly grateful to Herbert Kessler, who remains a tremendously generous supporter and friend. Fellow fellow Bibi Obler was a delightful office mate, and I rely on her wisdom and friendship still.

A residential fellowship at Cornell University's Society for the Humanities in 2009–2010 provided me the opportunity to work through important conceptual challenges and complete key sections of this book. The scholars I met there pushed my thinking in new directions. Most important in this respect were the Society fellows: Seeta Changani, Peter Dear, Maria Fernandez, TJ Hinrichs, Mary Jacobus, Ruth Mas, Martha Schoolman, and Stephanie Tsai. Thanks also to Annetta Alexandridis, Judy Byfield, Iftikar Dadi, Elvira Dyangani, Ramez Elias, Reem Fadda, Renate Ferro, Cheryl Finley, Sandra Greene, Nidhi Mahajan, Fouad Makki, Natalie Melas, Tim Murray, and Viranjini Munasinghe for making my time in Ithaca so much fun and intellectually rewarding. Also, I am grateful to Salah M. Hassan, whose support and pioneering approach to the study of African modernities have been essential to my work.

I spent two rewarding years teaching at Wayne State University, where I was surrounded by wonderful colleagues and students. I want to express my sincere thanks to Dora Apel for being such a superb mentor and friend during my time in Detroit. It was she who first recommended I include "the Elsewhere" in title, and I benefited greatly from our lively conversations. John Richardson was the coolest department chair, which made everything easy. Marie Persha, who passed away in 2015, was an exceptionally dedicated colleague; she is deeply missed by many. At Wayne and in the wider community I made lifelong friends who have all left a lasting impression on me. Thank you especially to Jeff Abt, Danielle

Aubert, Iris Eichenberg, Bill Ferry, Jonathan Flatley, Fanny Gutierrez, renée hoogland, Todd Meyers, Richard Oosterom, Scott Richmond, Grace Vandervliet, and Greg Wittkopp.

My current colleagues, students, and friends at the University of Illinois at Urbana–Champaign have been a great help on many levels, and I am delighted to be part of such an amazing group of artists, activists, and scholars. I cannot name them all, but I must express my sincere thanks to fellow art historians Anne Burkus-Chasson, Jennifer Burns, Jennifer Greenhill, Areli Marina, David O'Brien, Amy Powell, Kristin Romberg, Lisa Rosenthal, Oscar Vázquez, and Terri Weissman for creating such a nurturing and inclusive community. Lisa has also been the most wonderful junior faculty mentor. Thank you also to Jim Brennan, Anita Chan, Lauren Goodlad, Kevin Hamilton, Patrick Hammie, Heather Minor, Michael Rothberg, and Yasemin Yildiz. I am especially grateful to Allyson Purpura and Jesse Ribot for the joys of their friendship. They make Illinois feel like home, and Allyson is my closest interlocutor in all things relating to the Swahili coast.

Several institutions provided invaluable support during the research and writing stage of this book. Initial fieldwork and research funding was provided by the US Department of Education Fulbright-Hays Research Abroad Program and by Harvard University, including its Department of the History of Art and Architecture, Aga Khan Program, and Committee for African Studies. The University of Illinois at Urbana-Champaign's School of Art and Design and Office of the Vice Chancellor for Research also provided financial support for research trips and the image program in this volume. I also must thank the curators, archivists, and librarians who helped me access their collections and who showed me how to get things done in so many different countries and their unique bureaucracies. I am particularly thankful to those who have also generously lowered or waived image reproduction fees.

At Indiana University Press I had the opportunity to work with great people, for which I am grateful. My editor Dee Mortensen is a delight, and her suggestions proved vital to my work. Darja Malcolm-Clarke and Sarah Jacobi shepherded me through the final stages of publication with care and patience, and Candace McNulty's expert copyediting greatly improved this text. I thank them.

I wish to express my sincere thanks to many others who have shared their friendship, ideas, or experiences along the way. Among them: Ned Alpers, Kelly Askew, Cynthia Becker, Aimée Bessire, Anne Biersteker, Randall Bird, Daniela Bleichmar, Bill J. Dewey, Anouk de Koning, Henry Drewal, Andrew Eisenberg, Darby English, Jesús Escobar, Chris Geary, Elizabeth Giorgis, Erin Haney, Shannen Hill, Paola Ivanov, Joan Kee, Dominique Malaquais, Meredith Martin, Jessica Levin Martinez, Karen Milbourne, Eileen Moyer, Steven Nelson, Sylvester Ogbechie, Ikem Okoye, Costa Petridis, Robin Poynor, Victoria Rovine, MacKenzie Ryan, Kerstin Pinther, Barbara Plankensteiner, Peter Probst, Nasser Rabbat, David Rifkind, Dana Rush, Gitti Salami, Michelle Sheldrake, Barbara Thompson, Nancy Um, Monica Visonà, Iain Walker, Heghnar Watenpaugh, and Luise White. I am also especially grateful to Jeffrey Fleisher and Isabel Hofmeyr, whose feedback and criticism have been extraordinarily helpful.

As is apparent from these acknowledgments, I took my sweet time writing this book. In fact, I would still be working on version 102 of the introduction if Kenny Cupers had not appeared in the cornfields, waving his magical to-do list. He patiently explained the importance of life on a schedule, told me to get up before noon, and never tired of chanting "just send it off!" morning, noon, and night. He also read and reread what I wrote, always offering great suggestions and new insights. And so his vision to see his friend get a move on finally became a reality, slightly off schedule, of course. I am very, very grateful to him.

I end with a big, loving shout out to my wild and wondrous family. My parents, Sarjano Lynch, Coleman Lynch, and Thomas Meier, took me on many fun and splendid trips (some lasting years), which are my favorite memories to this day. Without Sarjano's and Coleman's hunger for adventure and transformation I would still be sitting in German Siberia (also known as Upper Franconia), likely collecting potatoes under a rock. My mother's strength and determination are especially remarkable; she makes amazing things happen. My brothers Gyani and Nito Meier, my sister in-law Jenna Meier, my niece Anya Meier, my nephews Tristan and Ashton Meier, and uncle Klaus Heinritz and his partner Rainer Lang have given me so much love and joy. Without them life would be drab and dull, and I am very lucky to have them. I regret that my grandfather Ludwig Richter, who passed away in 2011, did not see me finish this thing; his gentle and steadfast loyalty has always meant so much to me. Finally, my deepest thanks and love to Jeanne Lawler, who has shared so much with me over the years. She is my oldest friend and she will always be family.

This book is dedicated to Mädi Richter, my beloved and fabulous grandmother, whose dangerous pastries and loving care have sustained me my entire life. Oma, Du bist mein bestes Stück!

SWAHILI
PORT CITIES

ᦂ ᦂ ᦂ

Introduction

The Place In-between

On the Swahili coast of east Africa, monumental stone demarcates the border zone between the African continent and the Indian Ocean. Since at least the twelfth century locals have built luminously white coral stone houses, tombs, and mosques to transform wild coastlands into ordered civilization. Kilwa, a powerful port city in the fourteenth century, was famous for the glowing whiteness of its stone façades. Its harbor palace complex, known as Husuni Kubwa (figure o.1), once dominated the coast of east Africa, its vaulted pavilions, domed halls, and hundred-plus rooms covering nearly a hectare on a promontory overlooking the Indian Ocean. A luminous white lime plaster, made of shells and coral, covered its walls, reflecting the light of the sun so that its grandeur could be seen from great distances by incoming ships. Kilwa's networks connected the societies and economies of mainland Africa with the maritime world of the western Indian Ocean, and a key function of its waterfront architecture was to structure the exchange of ideas, goods, and also people across vast distances. It was an architecture of mercantile mobility whose style mirrored the built form of oversea emporia, especially those of the Arabian Sea.

Kilwa and many other Swahili city-states have long since been destroyed or abandoned, their stately ruins scattered all along the coastal territories of present-day Tanzania and Kenya. Yet such thriving coastal

1

FIGURE 0.1. The gleaming white buildings of the waterfront of Husuni Kubwa, thirteenth–fourteenth centuries. Reconstruction of the eastern promontory as seen by incoming *dhows* (Indian Ocean seafaring vessels). Illustrated in Peter Garlake, *Early Art and Architecture of Africa*. Oxford: Oxford University Press 2002, illustration 101, page 172; by permission of Oxford University Press.

towns as Mombasa, Zanzibar, and Lamu (plate 1) still dress the structures of their historical harbors with a pure white finish. While today Lamu is no longer a major center of global trade but instead the focus of tourism and pilgrimage, its architecture continues to function as a symbol of cosmopolitan power and transnational convergence, giving material force to an age-old Swahili desire—the desire to claim belonging to a range of elsewheres. The ornate verandahs and pointed arches of Lamu's seafront are not particularly ancient; they largely date to the nineteenth and twentieth centuries, when British, South Asian, and Arabian ornament and style interpenetrated each other with unprecedented speed. As a result, today's Swahili cities are simultaneously chronotopes of modernity and memorials to ancient histories of global connectivity. Like the grand monuments of Kilwa's waterfront, the transoceanic style of Swahili cities today is local and supralocal all at once. In fact, Swahili architecture revels in being familiar and exotic to locals and newcomers alike. Yet, while new decorative elements are always being added to the surface of buildings, the weighty mass of white stone continues to order one's experience of the Swahili waterfront. The tradition of marking the edge of Swahili cities with gleaming white stonework remains, conveying a sense of enduring timelessness. Thus, the expansive materiality of the Swahili waterfront also embodies a striking paradox: an aesthetic of unyielding permanence defines an anything-but-static littoral society. Diaspora, migration, and constant travel characterize this African mercantile society, even as its architecture expresses a sense of immobility and austerity.

This book explores the significance of this contradiction. It tells the story of why a society that celebrates the mercurial nature of coastal life and embraces bricolage and appropriation also attributes extraordinary power to seemingly immobile and unchanging stone monuments. As this book will reveal, this tension reflects a defining feature of Swahili society, namely an ongoing concern with reconciling the need for mobility and mixing on one hand and fixity and rootedness on the other hand. Indeed, one of the central arguments of this book is that stone architecture plays a central role in mediating shifting ideas of what it means to be fixed or mobile on the Swahili coast. These shifts are reflected in changing meanings, discourses, and representations projected onto the form of coral stone masonry architecture by diverse people throughout Swahili coast history. In order to throw the mobility of immutable stone into high relief I emphasize its transformation over the last two hundred years. A focus on how architecture works in relationship to the politics of modern empire allows us to gain new insight into how artifacts, such as built form, can compel people to experience personhood and community in new and even contradictory ways.

My study untangles this web of contradictions, revealing how the past and the present constantly interpenetrate each other within the walls of coastal architecture. It is a historical ethnography of related buildings and neighborhoods in east Africa's still-thriving port cities, including Mombasa, Zanzibar, and Lamu. I attend to the way life is lived and meaning is made in relationship to the materiality of city life. I offer a genealogy of architectural meaning, showing how a seemingly stable form—coral architecture—became a palimpsest of multiple and even oppositional claims over the last two hundred years. By focusing on the enduring power of the Swahili culture of stone to affect people's daily lives in the present, the book draws attention to the way Swahili worked stone is a dense material that gathers into itself a multiplicity of experiences and meanings.[1]

It is important to remember that there is nothing "natural" or "typical" about the Swahili coast emphasis on stone architecture, although many other societies share similar ideas and traditions. But houses and structures can take many forms, and permanence is not at all a defining feature of civilizational order. For example, the tent architecture constructed by transhumant societies, such as Muslim Tuaregs living in the Sahel region of western Africa, is not at all about material permanence. Here the flexible nature of textiles, the ease with which they can be shaped, folded, and layered, is celebrated. Tuareg homes are made up of mobile segments that can be assembled again and again, allowing for the seasonal movement of entire families. Even the famous architecture of the medieval cities of Djenne and Timbuktu, which are also Islamic cities like Zanzibar and Mombasa, is a masterful exploration of the transience and organic fluidity of adobe as a building material.

In contrast, the imposing stone mansions and the austere silhouettes of mosques on the Swahili coast materialize the "difference" of the Swahili city: it is a permanent place, unlike the "pagan" impermanent earthen settlements of the mainland. This understanding of architecture constitutes a defining feature of local worldviews. Stone is significant to Swahili coast residents because it embodies the desire to claim belonging to the civilizational order of urban Islam. Whitewashed stone masonry links the Swahili coast to other Islamic cities in the local imaginary. Islam has been a defining feature of coastal life since at least the ninth century, and by the twelfth and thirteenth centuries the coast was a central node in the global *umma,* or the worldwide community of Muslims. Exactly at this time the built environment of local cities began to feature elaborate stone architectural structures. Rather than seeing themselves as marginalized communities, Swahili coast residents claimed (and continue to claim) full membership in the umma. Building recognizably "Islamic" cities gives material form to that claim. Strikingly, locals have long emphasized that stone architecture is essential to creating an Islamic sense of place. This emphasis on stone architecture constitutes a Swahili understanding of the cultural order of Islam. Muslims throughout history have often viewed Islam as a practice linked to urban life, but these ideals are not always predicated on the permanence of stone.

A MATERIAL HISTORY

This book is about the power of built form and its attendant material culture to mediate human experience. Such a focus is useful because it emphasizes how things and people are enmeshed and constitute each other. Why the substance of things matters is often left unanalyzed because scholars usually focus on how objects or spaces are representations of human experience. This leaves us without fully appreciating why physical matter, such as masonry stonework, informs the choices people make in shaping their environment in the first place. It is this oversight that I address; in a sense this book is a material history of Swahili lived experience.

Clearly the affective power of coral stone figures prominently in Swahili ideas about why coastal east Africa is different from other places and societies. In local worldviews, constructed stone can create new horizons of possibilities. But does coral stone has a life of its own? Poststructuralist critical theory, with its emphasis on discourse analysis, would have us focus on how things work as social constructs. But in recent years "new materialist" thinkers, including Jane Bennet, Graham Harman, and Bruno Latour, have focused on the ontological status of things, or the essential being of nonhuman objects. They have also suggested that both subjects and objects are active agents in a network of relationships.[2] From this perspective, then, it becomes possible to think about how inanimate objects, like tables, transportation networks, and even global warming, have agency. The ideas of these new materialists are varied and complex, but their admirers in the humanities have often used their work to return to studying "things themselves." For example, art historians have embraced such thinking to reemphasize the "real" of artifacts, those aspects that exceed the discursive or representational. Many are especially keen to have us see objects as significant forms again, as sculptures or paintings that are constituted by their own autonomous logic of being.[3]

I have been very much inspired by new materialism's capacity to trouble the boundaries between the physical, mental, and cultural. Ascribing agency to buildings, or even tables or glaciers for that matter, does allow one to imagine that things are more complex than what we make of them. Many also hope that such a perspective will inspire us to treat the world with more care and justice. But I believe that reorienting the study of culture toward the ontological is fundamentally problematic: it elides the historicity of all our accounts of objects in the world. Further, such a focus tends to erase questions of power and politics, deeming them irrelevant to understanding the essential truth of the object. Wanting to give an ontological account of man-made objects is especially misguided exactly because they are just that—things created and sustained through the actual work of people—and therefore they are always objects *in* history, even when they help shape history. This book therefore argues that the imperative to historicize people's entanglement with matter is more important than ever. Whether stone, tables, or artworks might have an autonomous life is not my concern; what fascinates me are the reasons for which people desire or even need to see agency in things. What activates their awareness that the material world around them might be vibrant matter? In the case of the Swahili coast, the enduring physicality of stone architecture was reanimated in moments of sociopolitical crisis.

Questioning why certain objects become subjects in the eyes of people has long been the focus of scholars of non-western material culture. For example, Suzanne Preston Blier's book *The Anatomy of Architecture* is a groundbreaking exploration of the animated dimension of the Batammaliba built environment.[4] Carolyn Dean has established that the ancient Inka saw their rockwork as a vital energy on a continuum with plants, animals, and also human beings.[5] And most recently, David Doris's work on Yoruba aesthetics has focused on how seemingly ordinary materials, such as trash, become *aale,* or objects with "affecting power."[6]

Most closely related to this present book is the work of Peter Pels and William Pietz, who have reenlivened the problematic concept of the fetish to talk about a radically new understanding of materiality that first emerged in the littoral trading enclaves of west Africa during the sixteenth and seventeenth centuries.[7] As their ethnohistorical work shows, in its original formulation *fetish* did not designate an African thing, but rather a new transcultural awareness "of the capacity of the material object to embody—simultaneously and sequentially—religious, commercial, aesthetic and sexual values."[8] The fetish was an attempt to come to terms with difference in the face of unprecedented change, when European capitalism and colonial expansion reshaped the global world order. Faced with each other's radically different beliefs, social systems, and economies, Africans and Europeans became aware that some aspects of objects resisted translation and abstraction even as many objects (and people) were forced to act like commodities, whose value was interchangeable and therefore abstract.[9] Commodification could also lead to an emphasis on materiality. Both Africans and Europeans came to see an object's irreducible materiality—or what Pels calls the spirit *of* the matter, not *in* the matter—precisely because encountering the values of others revealed something of the material world that had remained invisible beforehand. As objects continued to move across increasingly vast distances and came to enter different cultural contexts, their ability to compel people also manifested itself in new ways.

Interestingly, the Swahili coast shares certain crucial characteristics with coastal western Africa: both were transoceanic long-distance trading systems whose material culture helped diverse societies translate between different commercial, social, cultural, and also aesthetic systems. There exists no single conceptual category, such as fetish, that captures the way in which different worldviews merged on the Swahili coast. Instead, it was the material form of the port itself that structured an array of transcultural practices. The coral mosques, merchant palaces, and customs houses of the Swahili seafront were where people who traveled along the networks of the Indian Ocean could meet and exchange ideas, commodities, and cultural traditions. In that sense, then, these buildings can be understood as spatial objects that manifest what Walter Mignolo has termed "border thinking," or a set of interrelated ideas and practices that emerge at and from the borders of various world systems.[10] But in contrast to Africa's Atlantic coast, the Indian Ocean coast was shaped by a long history of encounter not only with the west, but also with other parts of the so-called Global South, especially the Middle East and present-day India; the Swahili coast was, and is, a fulcrum of South-South relations.

THE INDIAN OCEAN CONTEXT

The unprecedented scale of the enslavement and forced migration of millions of Africans to the Americas beginning in the sixteenth century forever altered the course of world history. In drawing attention to the fact that Africans transformed almost every society in the so-called New World—even in the face of unspeakable violence and degradation—African diaspora studies has profoundly shaped how we think about the global repercussions of capitalist modernity. Today, the "Black Atlantic" not only denotes a period in African or African American history, but also the complex effects of globalization all over the world. Also, because scholars of the African diaspora take the Atlantic Ocean as a unit of analysis, they have long worked beyond the boundaries of the nation-state; our current efforts to think transnationally are very much indebted to them. But a shift toward the Indian Ocean has recently reconfigured our understanding of the role of Africa in the making of the modern world. East Africans regularly traveled and migrated—both as free and enslaved persons—across the Indian Ocean since the early modern period, and the shared practice of Islam created a sense of unity across the different littoral communities of the Indian Ocean.[11] Most significantly, Africans living in the Indian Ocean realm did not develop a sense of African diasporic belonging as many in the Atlantic world did, where the western category of race has played a major role in identity formation since the transatlantic slave trade. While social categories of difference were certainly also about being "black" in the eyes of others, being from Africa meant something very different in the Indian Ocean than in the Atlantic world, especially before colonization by western empires.[12] The view from the Indian Ocean, then, offers a very different vantage point from which to understand the African experience and the relationship between Africa and the rest of the world.

The Indian Ocean has also taken center stage in "global" accounts of our changing world order. Now that India, the countries of the Arabian Peninsula, and China are recognized as economic superpowers, the Indian Ocean is often seen as the future center of geopolitical power.[13] In fact, Indian Ocean studies, along with world literatures and oceanic studies, is now one of the emerging "global" disciplines. Instead of specializing in either African or Asian studies, for example, scholars emphasize transoceanic and multi-sited research. Indian Ocean research has produced rich work on macro-scale economic and political developments, revealing the complexity of the long-distance trading and migration patterns.[14] It has been especially popular to characterize the Indian Ocean as the "cradle of globalization" because it can be viewed as a world system long before the rise of North Atlantic capitalism.

Scholarship on the cultures of the Indian Ocean realm has emphasized the bonds between societies separated by great physical distances. Tracing the history of Islam and the role of Muslims—as traders, slavers, and scholars—in the Indian Ocean realm has resulted in rich work on the cultural dimension of transoceanic connectivity.[15] Most recently scholars have also explored how the maritime circulation of handwritten and printed texts created a complex web of interconnected reading, quoting, and writing publics.[16] In a sense, all Indian Ocean research can be seen as questioning established notions about cultural difference. If we realize, for example, that members of the Hadhrami diaspora have been living, working, and marrying in Mombasa, the Comoros, Cape Town, and Indonesia for over a millennium, we can hardly think about them as being fundamentally different from their various host communities.

Yet it is striking that despite being one of the most vibrant interdisciplinary fields today, few scholars of the Indian Ocean have focused on the arts of this transcultural system. The material realm has been largely ignored in favor of questions about how modes of reading, writing, and recitation—or even consumption patterns—create translocal imaginaries and subjectivities. While objects such as fashions and house decorations are often considered as examples of the kinds of commodities that circulated in the networks of the Indian Ocean, little has been said about the kind of actual places and lived experiences such material flows create.[17] This book, then, seeks to address this lacuna. It asks what happens to things once they stop being mobile commodities and come to rest on specific bodies, and in specific buildings. The larger material landscape of port cities, their mosques, merchant mansions, and even the houses of people who are not powerful traders are not just the backdrop for diaspora and migration, for trade networks and imperial formations; rather they actively create tactile and embodied experiences of these phenomena. Monsoons, long-distance commerce, and even faraway places are not just symbolic imaginaries but very much the physical matter of life on the Swahili coast.

Why do people living in coastal east Africa prefer to create a trans-oceanic material world, in which houses and their decorations seemed moored to some distant locale across the sea? What does this material world do for people whose daily experiences are in fact shaped by the region's terrestrial exchanges and migrations from inland Africa just as much as by their maritime ones?[18] This book seeks to answer these questions, ultimately suggesting that things, houses, and even people on the Swahili coast are relational loci, brimming with all sorts of different cultural traditions that cannot be traced back to one place or society—even when they *look* distinctly "Middle Eastern" or "foreign." The Swahili coast asks us to reconsider where Africa, Asia, and Europe begin and end.

ARCHITECTURES OF CONTESTED MEANINGS

My study shows how Swahili coast architecture is multilayered, the focus of constantly changing ideas and experiences. Until the nineteenth century, stone structures functioned as transactional spaces, where merchants from all over the world met, traded, and competed with each other in the context of the coast's thriving mercantile economy.[19] Because of the emphasis on mercantile worldliness in local worldviews, people valued and collected imported luxury goods for display on their bodies and in their homes. Exotic objects fulfilled a desire to possess and amass the materiality of the faraway. This culture of things encapsulated the port city itself, and these objects paid tribute to mobility and the ability to make the exotic one's own. Great distances separated the ports of east Africa from other cities across the sea, but having direct access to the objects of those faraway places endowed the port with an aura of worldly sophistication. In a sense, then, the stone architecture of the waterfront and its ornament played a vital role in surmounting distance.

Today the architecture of the waterfront is a symbol of past glories, when Swahili coast people actively participated in complex networks of exchange across vast distances. In fact, the merchant house with its simple square form (figure 0.2) is one of the most symbolically significant buildings in any coastal town that claims to be part of this global trading and migration history. Most of the extant Swahili coast merchant houses date from or were renovated in the nineteenth century, when Arabian Peninsula architectural ornament became popular all along the coast. For example, by the 1870s the merchant structures of Zanzibar's waterfront all featured crenellated parapets (figure 0.3). These rooftop rows of pointed merlons mirror the defensive architecture of desert forts in inland Oman, but on the Swahili coast they are purely decorative, their original function as battlements long forgotten or even unknown. In the nineteenth century such newly ornamented houses were signs of modernity and social mobility, but today these structures are associated with the ways of the "ancients" or the traditions of the precolonial period. No matter how old or new, the merchant house encapsulates a "cosmopolitan" utopian ideal.[20] To be truly cultured means one has the power to create networks of affinity across great distances—like the great merchant families of the past.

But stone architecture not only embodies romanticized interpretations of the past; it is also very much linked to painful family rivalries and contests over rights to, and in, the city. All Swahili towns are mixed spaces, in the sense that traditional architecture shares the same space as corrugated-steel and concrete homes, British-built government offices, and Dubai-inspired neo-Orientalist mosques and shopping centers. Yet only the material form of precolonial stone architecture carries the burden of being a symbol of struggle, anchoring painful memories of subjugation and the rise of racialized nativism. Rather than receding into the background as a distant icon of a bygone era, stone architecture came to be an almost overdetermined sign from the colonial period onward, as diverse peoples sought to control the material and symbolic fabric of Swahili city life. Local narrations about what it means to be a modern citizen, an African, an Arab, and a Swahili, are all bound up with stories about the material fabric of "stone town."

While today the beautiful coral architecture of the coast is certainly also celebrated as a traditional art form that belongs to the national heritage of Kenya and Tanzania, it is also a policed and contested space of exclusion and embattled social rights.[21] To claim the historic stone structures of the Swahili waterfront as one's heritage means that one seeks recognition as a rights-bearing free member of society. To live in stone town carries great significance because of the kind of power

FIGURE 0.2. Whitewashed stone houses on the waterfront of Zanzibar Town, 1870s. Photograph courtesy of the Zanzibar National Archives.

FIGURE 0.3. View of Zanzibar Town's waterfront with crenellated rooftops in the foreground. Photograph taken by Sir John Kirk in July 1884. Photograph courtesy of the Trustees of the National Library of Scotland.

wielded by those families who once presented themselves as the rightful patrons of the celebrated monuments of the past. It means one is intimately connected to an ancient world of privilege and autonomous selfhood. To this day Lamu, Mombasa, and Zanzibar are symbolically divided into "stone" and "*makuti*," or impermanent, neighborhoods. The permanence of stone architecture is seen as the cultured opposite of the makuti thatch-roofed earthen architecture, which in fact housed the majority of the local population until the 1920s (figure 0.4). While in reality stone and earthen structures intermingle and are part of the same spectrum of building technology, conceptually stone is linked to the sea and earthen houses to mainland Africa. Historically, most people, even the most ancient indigenous families, were farmers, craftsmen, and fishermen who did not have the means to trade and travel across great distances. Stone architecture was the prerogative of the patrician elite, or *waungwana*. To own or control a stone house endows one's family with the aura of respectability and patrician gentility and the ability to network freely across diverse places and societies.

Many grapple with the history and legacy of stone architecture because it gives material form to cosmopolitan longing but also to histories of racialized violence and objectification. In coastal Kenya, for example, many families—even those whose ancestors were not elites—see the refined lifestyles associated with grand stone mansions as their rightful tradition. But the austere and imposing walls are also linked to recent histories of brutality and ethnic violence. In fact stone architecture is connected to the coast's most contested and unresolved questions: Who enslaved whom in the nineteenth century, and who colluded with colonialists? Because the most powerful slavers and beneficiaries of slavery also claimed the Swahili culture of stone as their own, from a mainland or non-elite perspective stone mansions memorialize the unfolding of plantation slavery in the nineteenth century.[22] When the first Busaidi sultan moved his capital to Zanzibar in the 1830s, the institution of plantation slavery became widespread in the region to produce cash crops, such as cloves, for export to Europe. While institutions of bondage and slavery had existed in the past, the unprecedented scale and dehumanizing cruelty of modern hereditary slavery forever changed the social landscape of the region.[23] The financiers and owners of plantations also built the

FIGURE 0.4. A typical Swahili coast house constructed from coral-rag and other earthen materials. The front façade is defined by a large verandah (*baraza*). This photograph was taken in the Ng'ambo neighborhood of Zanzibar Island in the 1880s. British colonial administrators called Ng'ambo the native quarter. Photograph courtesy of the Ethnologisches Museum, Staatliche Museen zu Berlin—Preußischer Kulturbesitz.

largest stone structures ever seen on the Swahili coast. Today many are abandoned ruins, their crumbling edifices often defining the landscape. Populist histories describe how the patrons of these structures sacrificed and entombed countless enslaved Africans within the walls of their mansions before the abolition of slavery in Zanzibar in 1897 and on the Kenyan coast in 1907. Many locals today remember histories told by their parents and grandparents about the inhumane cruelty of those who built and owned the most imposing mansions and palaces of the coast. While one might question the accuracy of these accounts, Luise White's masterly analysis of rumor has shown us that it is precisely such shared stories that give us insight into how non-elites experienced the violence and upheavals of empire building in Africa.[24] Indeed, no physical evidence has yet been collected suggesting that people were entombed in walls, but such stories function as allegorical scaffolding for very real experiences of suffering. Stone therefore acts as an important witness on the Swahili coast. Disallowing erasure and forgetting, it stands as a permanent sentinel of truth, especially since the descendants of plantation owners often deny the horrors of plantation slavery. Thus the very same structures celebrated by some as monuments of a great civilization are seen by others as evidence that the elite once built their wealth on the bodies of the enslaved.[25]

But many, including mainland Africans, embraced the culture of the port to make a new life for themselves in the city during the colonial period. While the former elite looked down upon these newcomers, they also quickly lost control over who could claim those artifacts of culture once only the purview of the elite. Many erased the mark of enslavement from their family's past by decorating their more humble homes like the interiors of stone mansions. While this process was by no means easy or uncontested, the formerly marginalized could reinvent themselves as urbanite Muslims by claiming the visual culture of stone town. Dressing and living like a member of stone town therefore gave one the sheen of having always been part of the ancient Swahili coast culture of stone. As a result, today there is no unified local opinion about the significance of stone masonry or what it means for the production of Swahili heritage. Many are proud to see it as part of their heritage, understanding it alternately as an Arab, African, or simply Islamic cultural form. Others question why it should be celebrated at all when, in the eyes of many, it is linked to violence and violation and to the elite snobbery of people whose families benefited from slavery and colonialism.

STORIES OF STONE

One of the main aims of this study is to show how stone architecture came to be so contested in the local imaginary. Building on work that focuses on the transformation of social identities during the colonial period (when "Swahili" first became an identifiable ethnic category), I argue that to understand the meaning of stone architecture we must understand how imperialism and modern state-building radically reconfigured local life.[26]

When Zanzibar became the seat of the Arab Omani sultanate in the 1830s and a British protectorate in 1895, local networks were increasingly connected to the North Atlantic world system.[27] Said bin Sultan al Busaidi, the first Omani sultan of Zanzibar, was able to establish a new empire on the Swahili coast by first forging alliances with and then displacing local polities. With support from the British, the Busaidi dynasty of Oman began to act like an imperial state, making territorial claims on the Swahili coast and drawing on European models to change the economic systems of the region. By the mid-nineteenth century, Zanzibar became the center of an African consumer market that was directly connected to the North Atlantic economic system. East and central African consumption patterns affected merchants, financial markets, and factories as far away as London, Bombay, and Salem, Massachusetts.[28] Merchant vessels from all over the world—from Turkey, Europe, North America, and even Latin America—docked in Zanzibar and Mombasa to sell their wares. The leaders and financiers of the sultanate also began to control the existing export economy of central Africa. While in the past ivory and agricultural goods were brought to the coast, now an important "export" was enslaved Africans.[29] Furthermore, with the opening of the Suez Canal in 1869, travel time between Europe and east Africa decreased significantly, and by the 1870s east Africa was connected to an international web of steamship routes. By this time slave-labor plantations that produced cloves for export also became the cornerstone of the sultanate's wealth. These technological, economic, and political revolutions also forever changed how people lived their lives and related to their environment.

From the 1890s onward, the meaning of permanent masonry work was increasingly submitted to the logic of empire and nation building. The ability of local stone architecture to mirror the elsewhere in a myriad of ways is exactly what made it so amenable to reinterpretation. Because it looked vaguely familiar to newly arrived Arabs and Europeans, it became the object of keen scrutiny beginning in the nineteenth century. Newcomers first came to covet these structures simply because they also seemed to reflect the civilizational codes of Europe and other urban places in "civilized" Asia. Zanzibar, Mombasa, and even the more remote Lamu hosted an ever-growing influx of immigrants from the 1850s onward. Would-be colonialists, businesspeople, migrant workers, and missionaries—among many others—all wanted to make a new life for themselves in these thriving coastal towns. Mombasa and Zanzibar especially saw their populations expand dramatically in the nineteenth century. South Asian financiers came to Zanzibar on the invitation of the sultan because he needed them to connect Zanzibar to the currency markets of Bombay. European and North American merchants, especially from Salem, Massachusetts, and the port cities of present-day Germany, established permanent offices in Zanzibar and Mombasa for the first time. The Hamburg company O'Swald and Co. was particularly successful in procuring favorable trade agreements from Seyyid Majid al Busaidi in the 1840s. William O'Swald and his Zanzibari employees oversaw a complex triangulation of trade between western and eastern Africa and the North Atlantic world, and he became incredibly wealthy during his tenure as the chief agent of his family's company in Zanzibar. Like all European merchants, he wanted to live and work in a stone merchant house on the edge of the sea. O'Swald rented two stone mansions from the Busaidi family and made a point to paint and photograph (plate 2) each of the houses in his memorabilia album. While German merchants were already living in local stone houses in Zanzibar by the 1840s, by the 1880s South Asians, Europeans, North Americans, and Arabs from all over the world rented or owned the best houses on the waterfront in Lamu and Mombasa as well.

As European intervention in the area became more intense and more about the politics of empire, the architecture of the waterfront was also annexed into European systems of signification. British colonial urban planning schemes, archeological research, resettlement programs, and taxation policies all had an impact in remapping the meaning of the Swahili coast built environment.[30] Stone architecture was forced to correlate with new racial taxonomies, and Europeans attributed its origin to some distant Arab colonizer, effectively delegitimizing local claims to this architecture and the way of life associated with it. The transoceanic character of these structures was therefore used to exclude locals from a significant part of their heritage. It is tragically ironic that the ability of locals to build spaces that mirror the built environment of other port cities also led to their marginalization in their own cities.

THE ROLE OF ARCHITECTURE IN
SWAHILI COAST SCHOLARSHIP

This study focuses on monuments and built structures that have not received much scholarly attention, largely because they are still part of daily practice today or because they do not conform to what is known as classic Swahili coast architecture. For example, small neighborhood mosques such as the Basheikh mosque and Mandhry mosque (plate 3) of Old Town Mombasa have long been the most important public monuments in this ancient port city, their form structuring people's communal religious and political practices, but they are mentioned only in passing in general surveys of eastern African Islamic architecture.[31] During the colonial period they became the focus of intercommunal rivalries, as locals struggled to understand how best to respond to being absorbed into the Omani Sultanate of Zanzibar and then the British Empire. Stories of complicity with and resistance to the new regimes are anchored in the material fabric of these mosques. Beyond their role as sites of social history production, their architectural form has also evaded explanation. In fact, their unusual minarets, which take the form of starkly white tapering pillars, do not belong to any recognizable Islamic architectural type.

By focusing on the recent past and noncanonical monuments, I seek to counter the prevailing view that the so-called Swahili Golden Age of the fourteenth through sixteenth centuries represents the apex of Swahili coast creativity and originality. It is no surprise that most popular accounts of Swahili heritage focus on this period. In fact the study of local architecture is largely the purview of archeologists, who have produced major studies of the grand ruins dotting the coast. The remains of Kilwa and Gedi feature massive stone complexes and beautiful mausoleums that have long captured the public imagination both in eastern Africa and abroad. In recent years several documentary films have celebrated the ancient architecture of the Swahili coast, and tourists from abroad and Kenyan and Tanzanian schoolchildren regularly visit the most accessible monuments, which are all maintained by the national government as heritage sites. The continued focus on the distant past has tended to reinforce the general opinion that after the Portuguese first invaded the region in the sixteenth century its cities became a stagnant backwater or the stage for outside colonizers. I argue the opposite, pointing out that the nineteenth and twentieth centuries represent pivotal moments in Swahili coast architectural history. Like other port cities connected to capitalist networks of trade (such as Dakar, Bombay, and Cairo), the breakdown of distances increasingly defined daily life in Zanzibar and Mombasa. Locals had to contend with colonial aggression, but also could access once-distant places and cultures more easily. During this period of heightened connectivity and conflict, the past and the present interpenetrated each other in surprising ways. The somber façades of old merchant mansions and mosques and the delicacy of hand-carved orna-ment suddenly existed in the same space as massive cast-iron balconies and industrial commodities from overseas.

The resultant spectacle was not simply an example of the remaking of local space in the west's image. Instead, it represents the intensifi-cation and even reification of locally constituted practices. I therefore untangle how the old and the new engulfed and transformed each other during this transformative period in the spaces of daily life. A perfect example of this process is the original House of Wonders (figure 0.5) of Zanzibar, whose structural core was a monumental whitewashed man-sion encased in mass-produced cast-iron verandahs imported from Eng-land. Designed by a German adventurer, paid for by the third Omani ruler of Zanzibar, Seyyid Barghash al Busaidi (r. 1870–1886), overseen by South Asian masons, and constructed by enslaved Africans, the struc-ture stood at the intersection of ancient and new ways of making an architecture of power. It also occupied the site of the former stone palace of a famous indigenous or Shirazi queen, whose descendants are still seen by many as the legitimate rulers of Zanzibar. Barghash wanted to remake the entire waterfront of Zanzibar not only to signal to the west that he too could be a modern colonialist and capitalist, but also because he needed to appropriate and suppress the indigenous symbolic land-scape of stone architecture.

Scholars interested in Swahili material culture have largely ignored globalization and colonization because modernity is seen as the water-shed that marks the loss of local authenticity. Only the still-extant ar-chitecture of the more remote towns of the Lamu Archipelago has been studied, because it is readily seen as authentically Swahili.[32] In fact,

FIGURE 0.5. The House of Wonders before it was damaged during the Anglo-
Zanzibar War of 1896. Photograph courtesy of the Melville J. Herskovits
Library of African Studies Winterton Collection, Northwestern University.

Lamu stone mansions from the eighteenth century are now celebrated
as representative of Swahili tradition, even though their style and layout
were radically innovative when they were first built. Indeed, scholars
have presented these structures in rather romanticized and ahistorical
terms, as signs of the refinement and good taste of the waungwana elite.
Linda Donley-Reid's vision of the Lamu stone house being the "structuring structure" of the waungwana way of life has been especially powerful in this regard. Her work has allowed us to imagine that the meaning of Swahili coast stone architecture has remained constant over the
centuries.

Conversely, historians, who are not burdened with issues of cultural
authenticity and originality, have focused on Mombasa and Zanzibar
precisely because they are sites of intense sociopolitical revolution from
the nineteenth century onward. For example, Frederick Cooper, Laura
Fair, Jonathon Glassman, Jeremy Prestholdt, Abdul Sheriff, and Justin
Willis (among others) have demonstrated the importance of under-

standing how urban life during the colonial period was shaped by the interpenetration of European and local ideas and practices.[33] Yet the built environment plays only a minor role in their accounts of Swahili coast revolution and transformation, largely because it is seen as the backdrop for the making of history. I am very much indebted to their work, but instead I focus on the active role of the material world in shaping history. I consider architecture not only as it expresses social meanings, but also through its effect on history. From my perspective, architecture came to mediate relations between people in novel ways during the colonial period.

Urban geographers, on the other hand, have emphasized the making of the colonial city. But they have largely focused on large-scale mapping and planning projects to reveal how the colonial state attempted to control urban life through laws and administrative policies.[34] By focusing on the racist remains of colonial governance—such as building codes, zoning regulations, and property laws—geographers have foregrounded the ways British administrators hoped to fix racialized hierarchies into place through "writing" the colonial city. For example, William Bissell has explored how urban planners and their "modern dreams of total design" created a largely imaginary Zanzibar on paper that had little to do with the "indigenous and everyday powers of urban design."[35] I draw upon this important body of work, but I argue that a focus on individual buildings and people's stories about their individual experiences in specific spaces tells a very different story about Swahili coast port cities.

In many ways *Swahili Port Cities* is first and foremost in dialogue with the field of Swahili coast archeology. At first glance it might seem odd to seek connection to a discipline that focuses on the study of ruins and the distant past to study the haptic experience of globalization and empire, but archeologists such as Jeffrey Fleisher, Abdurahman Juma, Adria LaViolette, and Stephanie Wynne-Jones have recently emphasized that the built environment reveals something unique about how Swahili coast place-making strategies have changed over the centuries.[36] Archeology was also central in debunking some of the central myths proffered by the British government to justify colonial rule. Between the 1970s and 1990s archeologists, including George Abungu, Felix Chami,

Mark Horton, Chapurukha Kusimba, Athman Lali, Mohamed Mchulla, and Thomas Wilson, shattered the assumption that only Arabs could be credited with building the great Swahili coast cities of stone.[37] Their focus on the African identity of Swahili coast cultural heritage was also important for the nation-building project of the postindependence era. Their work encouraged mainland Kenyans and Tanzanians to see their coastal countrymen and women as part of the national fabric. Further, their deep commitment to comparative archeological work provided us with a much more nuanced view of the deep histories and interconnections between mainland and coastal African building technologies. We now know that stone architecture represents just a small fragment of the Swahili built environment; most urban residents have always lived in much humbler wattle and daub structures. Thus the notion that Swahili cities are "stone towns" must be understood as an ideological tactic or utopian imaginary, rather than the "real" nature of urban space.[38] I extend the study of Swahili architecture into the present, showing how ancient ideals and imaginaries are transformed, reimagined, and also rejected.

THE CHAPTERS

This book comprises four chapters, each focusing on a small number of buildings or a series of interconnected spaces within a specific city. Investigating the micropolitics of architectural space, I trace the intricacies of everyday life while remaining mindful of larger sociopolitical processes. The first step in understanding the complex ways stone architecture works on the Swahili coast is to look at its long history and its many reinventions from the fifteenth century until now. Accordingly, the first chapter focuses on the region's oldest continuously inhabited port city, Mombasa. It narrates its founding by people from the African mainland in distant past and the many ways its residents have always had to deal with how outsiders made sense of their way of life. In this chapter I investigate how Mombasa's oldest communities experienced shifting categories of belonging and difference. It charts what happens to precolonial ways of being when its material form—its architecture—is linked to putative hierarchies of racial difference.

The second chapter examines the way memory and religious practice intersect with politics. During the colonial period stone architecture was increasingly important to claims to land and territory. Colonial overlords argued that building in stone was not a local tradition, but an import brought by ancient Arab colonizers. This tactic was an attempt to delegitimize local claims to the cities and civilizations of the Swahili coast. A built environment that Europeans had to recognize as "civilized" presented a problem to colonial governance: it was difficult to dismiss to the extent that it makes visible, in western worldviews, claims to territories, people, and resources. As a result the practice of religion was ever more linked to struggles over social and economic power. To be an "ancient" Muslim meant one could demand being recognized as a rights-bearing citizen and owner of property, even in the eyes of the British. Who owned and built recognizably Islamic architecture on the Swahili coast was a hotly contested issue, because these facts were seen as evidence of true ownership. To untangle how Islam, architecture, and claims to territory became intertwined, I consider the many afterlives of two premodern mosques in Old Town Mombasa, the Mandhry and Basheikh mosques—sites that became the center of heated battles over the "true" history of Islam in east Africa. Their enigmatic pillar minarets, mentioned above, have evaded scholarly explanation; to this day their presence in Mombasa is seen as a mystery. Oral history and archeological evidence suggests multiple strands of influence, linking both mosques to other monuments. Their elusive and composite history allows diverse peoples to use them as symbols of their heritage. In fact, today painful memories of personal and communal betrayal are anchored in their forms as people recall and retell how during the colonial period Mombasa's Old Town leaders policed access to these mosques on racial terms. The battle between "Arab" and "Swahili" ownership of Mombasa was fought in the prayer halls of both mosques, for to claim the most ancient emblems of Islam as one's rightful heritage meant one "owned" the city.

The third chapter explores the transformation of Swahili coast architecture in relationship to the material and technological artifacts of modernization. I focus on the much-reviled House of Wonders and its patron, Sultan Barghash, whose large-scale building projects transformed Swahili merchant architecture into an emblem of capitalist empire. Barghash intentionally inscribed the House of Wonders with multiplicity. Built in 1880s as a ceremonial palace, it was the largest architectural project ever completed on the Swahili coast and featured imported European balustrades, South Asian filigree work, and calligraphic wall panels from Egypt. Its structure is essentially a colossal version of a typical merchant mansion, yet its ornamentation, as a seeming pastiche of foreign styles, has resulted in it being dismissed as being "out of place" and therefore not relevant to the study of Swahili culture. This chapter argues that House of Wonders is in fact central to the narration of local culture—precisely because, as a monument to bricolage, it manifests the fact that coastal architecture has always been about making claims to cultures and places that are not entirely "local."

Chapter four develops an intimate reading of the aura of life at the edge of the sea, focusing on the interior architecture of the stone house. Domestic design programs prominently feature imported porcelain, mirrors, furniture, and other objets d'art, producing an accretive aesthetic of mercantile wealth. These spaces were carefully constructed exhibitions of being at home in the world. This chapter documents the origins of this practice in the fourteenth or fifteenth century and its subsequent reinvention with the impact of capitalist globalization. The chapter also tempers the recent celebration of consumption as a liberating process of self-making. Diverse peoples, including the urban poor, did increasingly dress their bodies and homes with exotic commodities once beyond their means, but the Swahili coast relationship to capitalist modernity is not simply a wonderful spectacle of reinvention. Not everyone became more self-realized because they could consume exotic things more easily once European traders flooded the region with cheap commodities. The impact of the North Atlantic world did lead to loss and erasure.

This book primarily concerns itself with local experiences of architecture, but it does not purport to give an authentically local view; the architecture itself would make such a project impossible. The strategies of appropriating and fragmenting the faraway define Swahili coast material practices. This is a cultural space that exists between what western observers often call the local and the global. Further, while I do focus on the experience of colonial and postcolonial modernity, I am also mindful of the fact that the modern period does not represent a radical break from what came before. The foundational character of Swahili coast architecture was already in place long before empire-building reshaped the region. North Atlantic and Omani colonial cultures certainly have had significant impacts, but the material fabric of Swahili coast cities has been defined by bricolage and eclecticism for centuries. Swahili stone monuments have always been about creating networks of affinity with faraway places; these networks are necessary in intensely competitive and mercurial places such as Swahili coast port cities. From the vantage point of the Swahili coast, the current fascination with transnationalism is simply the newest iteration of a complex struggle to control the crossings of people, ideas, and things in a globalized world.

Difference Set in Stone

Place and Race in Mombasa

Architecture has a powerful impact on how culture is experienced. The very notion that people "belong to" or can claim a certain territory is constituted by culturally variable politics of *inhabiting,* in which the built environment plays a central role. Examining how these spatial processes unfold in such fluid borderlands as the Swahili coast is an especially clarifying exercise because its port cities are fundamentally nonterritorial cultural landscapes, shaped by the constant movement of peoples and things across great distances. Here the relationship between identity and place is particularly mercurial and in constant flux.

For centuries permanent stone architecture occupied an important place in the civilizational order of Mombasa. Founded sometime in the early second millennium, this ancient Swahili city was the site of an important port long before it became part of the British Empire. In contrast to Lamu and Zanzibar, whose global connectivity is a fairly recent phenomenon, Mombasa has nurtured direct connections with inland Africa, Europe, and Asia since at least the fourteenth century. Great Zimbabwe, Portugal, and Ottoman Turkey were among the major empires that had regular contact with the city. Mombasa Town stood at the edge of intersecting worlds; its vibrant mercantile culture drew peoples from the African mainland, South Asia, Europe, and the Middle East. Merchants, diplomats, and even attacking armies came to Mombasa because it provided access to the markets and resources of inland

Africa. As a result Mombasa figured prominently in the consciousness of foreigners. This long history of transcultural contact also influenced the worldview of Mombasans. Locals learned to appropriate faraway objects, styles, and technologies in the making of their city. Yet the nineteenth century marks a major watershed moment in this long history of transregional engagement, when industrial capitalism and colonization changed a range of preexisting systems and traditions. I chart this process of transformation by showing how stone architecture once embodied the Swahili ideal of the "elsewhere" and how it came to stand for racialized difference. What becomes clear is that the revolutionary circumstances of the nineteenth century forced Mombasans to reconstitute how they made their sense of place useful to themselves and legible to others in the world.

SWAHILI COAST IDENTITY POLITICS

Today Mombasa is the second largest city of Kenya, with municipal boundaries embracing all of Mombasa Island (an area of six square miles) and parts of the adjacent mainland. Its historical center, Old Town (plate 4), is situated on the southeastern side of the island, overlooking a protected creek that still serves as a harbor for regional and overseas ships carrying foodstuffs and commodities from other western Indian Ocean ports. Before the colonial period the city exported grain and timber from the neighboring mainland and ivory and also enslaved persons from more distant places in central Africa.[1] Overseas imports were largely confined to manufactured goods such as cloth, metalwork, porcelain, and beads from South Asia, the Middle East, and as far away as China. The fifteenth century is often celebrated as Mombasa's "golden age," when it was an independent city-state overseen by a local oligarchy.[2] During this period powerful polities, including the Portuguese empire, increasingly took an interest in the city and its transcontinental trading networks. Mombasans also gained a reputation for being intensely competitive and unpredictable at this time. Indigenous leaders constantly negotiated a complex web of alliances and counteralliances throughout the city's history in an attempt to garner protection, but also autonomy, from others.[3] As a city-state without an army or other

FIGURE 1.1. "Mombasa Swahilis" lithograph, 1856. Illustrated in Charles Guillain, *Documents sur l'histoire, la géographie et le commerce de l'Afrique Orientale, recueillis et rédigés* (Paris: A. Bertrand, 1856), insert.

defenses, Mombasa depended on cultivating good relationships with powerful allies.

The oldest community of Mombasa, the *Thenashara Taifa,* or Federation of Twelve (figure 1.1 and plate 5), continue to be a strong sociopolitical force in Old Town. Until the colonial period the Taifa functioned as a series of loose and expanding alliances, absorbing peoples from diverse places, including from inland Africa and the Middle East. Strict social hierarchies characterized Taifa membership even before the colonial period. Before the abolition of slavery, and even long afterward, one's status within the Taifa was measured in terms of how long one's immediate family was *watumwa* (enslaved or bonded) or *waungwana* (freeborn, not bonded). By the second half of the nineteenth century the waungwana of the Taifa began to lose their authority and power. In response, they attempted to foreclose the incorporation of newcomers into their community in order to consolidate whatever authority they had left.

Arab cultural markers also became desirable in Mombasa during this period. Because, by the 1830s, Muslims from the Arabian Peninsula controlled the economic institutions and trading networks of the region, dressing in Omani fashions or using Arabic words came to signal prestige in new ways. For example, Thenashara Taifa is an Arabic appellation likely coined sometime in the early nineteenth to make the local political system mirror categories familiar to Omani newcomers. But while some lineages within each moiety elected to Arabicize their names, by adding "al," for example, the twelve moieties that make up the Thenashara Taifa all still carry ancient Swahili place-names. Ten of the twelve lineages belonging to the federation are in fact named after settlements on the African continent, while two are named after places on Mombasa Island.[4] Thus the umbrella polity, the Thenashara Taifa, evokes overseas connections to the Middle East, while the more intimate social matrix of familial relations ties each member of the Taifa to the African continent.[5]

Today those Mombasans associated with the Taifa will also use a range of modern identities, calling themselves—depending on context—Swahili, Kenyan, Shirazi, or African. These narrative shifts in belonging and selfhood are in part a response to the identity politics of the colonial and later postindependence periods, when modern citizenship was increasingly linked to ethnicity. One of the defining aspects of the nineteenth century was the emergence of ethnoterritorial categories of identity. Yet coastal Muslims never fully embraced a single identity or one place of belonging, although the British colonial administration wanted *Swahili* to be a clearly demarcated African tribe.[6] But coastal peoples remained strangely "hybrid" to the colonial administration. Coastal Muslims posed a threat to the logic of colonial governance because they always attempted to detribalize themselves by claiming to be nonnatives (by sometimes calling themselves Arabs or Persians). Living in a border zone between land and sea has allowed locals to cultivate concepts of affiliation and belonging that still confound newcomers who are more familiar with identities linked to one territory or one place.

Yet Swahili was not just a modern or colonial category. The term originates in a distant moment of encounter and translation. It is derived from an Arabic word meaning *edge* or *border*. Originally the term encapsulated an Arabic-speakers' perspective, and traders and immigrants used it describe the coast and its inhabitants. In the nineteenth century, upcountry Africans also started calling themselves *Mswahili*, or a Swahili person, to connect themselves to the wealth and power of the distant coast.[7] Similarly, recently arrived immigrants to the coast who converted to Islam would call themselves *Waswahili* (the plural of Mswahili), to claim the rights and opportunities accorded to city-dwellers. Thus, while the British and local use of Swahili were interrelated, ultimately it had very different meanings.

Until independence (and sometimes today), families belonging to the Taifa Thenashara largely rejected the ethnic marker Swahili, emphasizing instead their Muslim heritage and ancient pedigree as patrons of an urban civilization. To Mombasans it was always more important to be *wamiji*—peoples of the city—since urban citizenship offered an entirely different spectrum of opportunities and advantages compared to the social networks of the non-Islamic mainland. In fact, coastal residents often still do not "make sense" to mainland Kenyans, who often comment that "Swahili is not a real tribe," meaning that their Kenyan citizenship is suspect. This is because contemporary Kenyan nationhood emphasizes the rights of natives, who are presented as having a fixed and primordial connection to the physical geography of Kenya. Clearly this definition of citizenship runs counter to the notion of wamiji, and as a result coastal Muslims also often feel that they are a marginalized minority in Kenya, whose rights are not fully recognized because they are oriented toward the global Muslim community (this also takes on sectarian dimensions because they are Muslims in a largely Christian nation).

A CITY WITH MANY NAMES

Since its independence from Britain and separation from the Arab Sultanate of Zanzibar in 1963, the Indian Ocean–oriented world of Mombasa Island has been confined to Old Town, although no physical boundaries separate it from the high-rises, markets, stores, and traffic congestion of the abutting business district developed during the colonial period. During the day the frenetic energy of international commerce extends into Old Town, where stores specializing in Middle Eastern and Indian imports draw a diverse clientele. Yet Old Town gradually unfolds as a distinctly Muslim place as one moves from the business district toward the historical waterfront. Here the five calls to prayer and minarets visually and aurally distinguish the space from the rest of the city. Swahili, Arab, Baluchi, Mijikenda, Hadhrami, Barawa, Ithnasheri, and Bohra families have resided in Old Town for generations, and their visibly Islamic expressive and material culture seems rooted in time-honored practices.[8] Yet, new waves of immigrants, aesthetic choices, and political and religious ideas are constantly adding to the existing fabric of the town—making it a perpetually changing place. For example, over the last decade large numbers of Somali Muslims have moved into Old Town, creating new tensions among its many different Muslim communities. "Neo-Orientalist" style mosques, often funded by Saudi patrons or members of the city's diaspora living abroad, have replaced old mosques. Imams from across the Middle East become new leaders of old religious institutions, sparking heated debates and intergenerational conflicts regarding the appropriateness of locally established Islamic practices.[9]

Outsiders see Old Town as a place apart from the rest of Kenya. European tourists and mainland Kenyans take short tours of Old Town in the hope of glimpsing an exotic culture. Prepared by the popular images presented on postcards and tourist memorabilia, visitors expect to see veiled women, "Arab" architecture, and other oriental vistas. For them the physical layout of Old Town has the characteristics of an unplanned maze, where few real streets exist and one easily loses one's bearings. Old Town also continues to frustrate the municipal government of the larger city, which strives to gain oversight over the urban fabric of Old Town for census and taxation purposes. For residents, the Town's interwoven web of small unpaved alleys and interconnected spaces between houses are a practical matrix of pedestrian passages, making moving between abutting houses and neighborhoods quick and easy (plate 6). In contrast to outsiders, Mombasans conceptualize the city as a flexible and logical space whose topography is easily understood as a series of named places. In Mombasa—as in many other coastal cities—the designations of neighborhoods, or *mitaa* (pl.) in Swahili, do not describe a series of streets or the boundaries of areas, but memorialize patterns of migration and significant historical events. The *mtaa* (sg.) system is

a kind of palimpsest of communal memories and shared experiences.[10]
In Old Town Mombasa, where one mtaa ends and another begins is
not physically inscribed onto the city, but is rather embodied in its residents as a form of oral knowledge. Residents are very much aware that
to outsiders Old Town is disorienting, which in their eyes enhances the
city's reputation as a place of the subversive and uncanny, a place that is
ultimately unknowable to outsiders since they cannot *see* the ordering
logic of the city.

Even today visitors cannot quite decide whether Old Town is an "African" or "Middle Eastern" place. In contrast, Mombasans see their city
as a fulcrum in motion, a great hub where peoples, ideas, and practices
merge and converge to create a mercurial and multilayered landscape.
Local conceptions and interpretations of Mombasa are defined by a
heightened sense that the city is not fully knowable to outsiders. According to wamiji elders, Mombasa is not a territory or stable place, but
a zone of mobility constituted by a unique relationship to the sea. As
Mzee Muhammad Ahmed explained, "The essence of the city is not seen
by many, you must know the secrets the ocean brings to Old Town."[11]

To this day apocryphal accounts of the city emphasize that the city's
visible structures are mirrored by a hidden city that lies beneath the
watery depths of the bay in front of Old Town, in the creek separating
Mombasa Island from the mainland. This city beneath the sea is ruled
by *majini* (pl.), or Muslim spirit beings.[12] Those who take an interest in
such matters believe that majini regularly move between the ocean and
Old Town, where their presence shapes the daily life of residents. They
are believed to have come from the Middle East to Mombasa in the
distant past because of the city's central position in trade and migration
networks of the larger Islamic world. Mombasa was *interesting* to these
beings because this is where power, wealth, and ambition converged.
According to accounts given by some elders, local Mombasans once cultivated close relationships with majini (and some continue to), bringing
them into their homes and families.[13] In fact, the oral histories of specific
lineages in the Taifa recount that the family begins with the marriage of a
human and a *jinni* (sg.), making all descendants hybrid beings.

Connections to majini also had a practical side. Elders state that majini helped their ancestors foresee the dangers that lay ahead on long

trade expeditions and to understand the true intentions of distant trading partners. Merchants and caravan traders also always worried that they could lose their competitive edge to others.[14] In these narratives Mombasa's true significance lies in its role as an ancient intermediary between land and sea, which also makes it a particularly dangerous place: its state of in-between-ness leads to constant instability and uncertainty. Interestingly, mainland Kenyans also recount stories of Muslim majini, usually characterizing them as dangerous and mischievous beings who use their powers to seduce unsuspecting Christian mainlanders.

Locals also inscribe the city with names and foundational histories not recognized or understood by foreigners. Elders emphasize that Mombasa is not the "real" name of the city, but simply a name invented by outsiders.[15] One account presents "Mombasa" as a nonsensical word, the result of a classic moment of intercultural misunderstanding. When the British first arrived at the edge the city, they asked a passing Mijikenda man, "What is the name of this place?" He responded in Giryama, "What are you saying?"—which sounded something like "Mombasa" to British ears.[16]

According to Taifa accounts, the original name of the city is *Mvita*, which means "place of war." It encapsulates the conflict-ridden history and desirability of the city. The stanza below from a famous local epic poem conveys the city's significance in the local imaginary:

> Kongowea belongs to Mwana Mkisi, Mvita is the ancient city.
> Do not exceed its bounds, but tread respectfully therein.
> Cast down your head, and do not look straight, with your eyes wide open—
> It is an abyss of deep gloom; even those who are well informed comprehend it not.[17]

The poem, which recounts the many battles fought over the island, was composed by Muyaka bin Hajj in the 1830s, when the Omani sultan of Zanzibar began to make claims on Mombasa. Muyaka is Mombasa's most celebrated Swahili poet. In this stanza he was exhorting his listeners (such poetry would have been originally recited to an audience) to remember the importance of Kongowea and Mvita, the ancient settlements of the island. Also, by asserting that Kongowea belongs to Mwana Mkisi, the poet was supporting Thenashara Taifa claims to Mombasa Island; Mwana Mkisi was the original ancestor of the oldest lineages within the Taifa. She was a pagan queen who founded Kongowea, the first center of urban civilization on the Island. Mvita is also the proper name of an important Taifa ancestor, but unlike Mwana Mkisi, Shehe Mvita was a man and a Muslim. His arrival marks the beginning of the Islamic history of Mombasa. He is believed to have been a great Muslim mystic from somewhere "overseas," who came to build the first permanent stone mosque in Mombasa in the distant past. By evoking these ancient names of power in the face of Omani Arab aggression in the 1830s, Muyaka was insisting on the fundamental alterity of Mombasa. No matter Mombasa's transoceanic connectivity and its status as an Islamic city, the poet reminds his audience of the fundamental distance between Arab newcomers and local inhabitants. Ultimately, Muyaka's stanza is a warning, reminding all with claims to Mombasa that "even those who are well informed comprehend it not."[18]

Today's wamiji still remember Kongowea as the most ancient urban settlement on Mombasa Island and the original center of Taifa, or "Swahili," power. Many elders insist that old Mombasan families are all "children of Mwana Mkisi." Most significantly, the names Mwana Mkisi and Kongowea evoke a sense of place that connects Mombasa to central Africa's great empires and kingdoms. These names create a symbolic landscape that is not oriented toward the Middle East or Indian Ocean. *Mkisi* is the personification of *ukisi*, which means "the holy" in Kongo contexts. In central African religious thought, this referred to the essential life-giving and healing power of the divine. *Kongowea* can also be understood as the Swahili locative of *kongo*, a term that denotes the essence of civilizational order in central Africa. Thus, while today Mombasans emphasize belonging to the umma, the global community of Muslims, these ancient and still active concepts remind us that Mombasa is still connected to non-Islamic systems of signification.

Most families living in Old Town also cultivate a sense of distance from their immediate coastal neighbors. Their ancestry is "African," but they do not align themselves with Mijikenda communities living in the coastal hinterland.[19] Many are even Mijikenda descendants who moved to Mombasa Island over the last two centuries. Yet Mombasans often elide this fact, instead emphasizing their "ancient" histories and connections to Kongowea and Mwana Mkisi because they constitute a powerful "elsewhere," which is so essential to Swahili personhood. In fact, locals do not specify the exact origins of Shehe Mvita or Mwana Mkisi. What is important in their roles as Mombasa's founding father and mother is that they were not local, but mysterious individuals who came from *very* "far away" to remake the civilizational order of the region. Thus Swahili coast townspeople see themselves as having connections to distant communities, while simultaneously obfuscating their exact origins.

This penchant for valorizing "distance" is often misunderstood as expressing the denial of townspeople to be African. Certainly, locals coveted, and continue to, associations with distant places. Marriages with Muslim families from the Middle East also brought great social prestige and strengthened alliances with overseas centers of Islam. It is also true that many believe their ancestors came from Shiraz (a port city in present-day Iran), but I would argue they do because Shiraz exists largely as a symbolic place of distance. Unlike Arabs, Shirazis never came in large numbers to the coast, and therefore they did not represent a direct threat to the independence of local polities. In fact, it has been suggested that claims to Shirazi ancestry are not corroborated by historical evidence; instead, coastal patricians created these stories because of "the prestige foreign origins so often bring" in littoral societies.[20] As a faraway place with little direct impact on the coast, Shiraz worked as an interstitial imaginary for people living on the Swahili coast.

Today it is almost a postmodernist truism that social and cultural identities are constructed imaginaries.[21] In many ways Swahili identity is just as situational and fabricated as any other modern ethnic category or national identity. Swahili narratives of belonging are not only constructed or situational, however. They fundamentally exceed received ideas about communal identification because, especially in their precolonial iteration, Swahili coast cultural codes emphasize indeterminacy. Swahili coast selfhood is not the same as contemporary ideals of cosmopolitan placelessness, which are celebrated by such theorists as Michael Hardt and Antonio Negri as an alternative to nativist parochialism or as a tool of resistance against contemporary globalization.[22] Rather, it is a heightened awareness of the potential malleability and translatability of all notions of self and belonging, an awareness shaped by the mercurial character of coastal life. The ability to move between and inhabit

FIGURE 1.2. Whitewashed stone houses on Mombasa's waterfront, circa 1890s. Photograph courtesy of the Melville J. Herskovits Library of African Studies Winterton Collection, Northwestern University.

multiple locales and worldviews lies at the heart of a Mombasan's sense of place. Code-switching and multilingualism are essential, but newcomers or outsiders are also always reminded by long-term residents that they are not in command of the city's multiplicity.

The Civilizational Order of Stone

For centuries permanent stone architecture was an icon of culturedness and freeborn mobility on the Swahili coast.[23] According to Linda Donley-Read, the stone mansion was the most important space for the performance of elite social identities and gender roles. In her elegant phrasing, it was the "structuring structure" of waungwana civilization.[24] Similarly, James de Vere Allen saw stone architecture as a representation of the longevity of the waungwana moral order.[25] In Mombasa stone architecture also played a role in its economic life (figure 1.2). The lime-plastered façades of its waterfront reflected the light of the sun, making it visible from great distances. Since it looked like a typical Islamic port city, it was instantly recognizable and felt familiar to travelers and traders of the western Indian Ocean. The built environment of the port facilitated networks of affinity with powerful overseas partners and allies.[26] Newcomers were hosted in the homes of waungwana families, they were invited to pray in the Friday mosque, and business deals were cemented in the customs house.

Archeological research suggests that stone architecture became a privileged space of local civilizational discourse sometime between the twelfth and fourteenth centuries. Increasingly locals built tombs, mosques, homes, and public monuments using coral masonry technology. Some coral structures reached up to four stories. Imported commodities from overseas, such as Chinese ceramics and luxury goods from South Asia, ornamented the interiors and exteriors of elite architecture. It was not the case, as British archeologists assumed during the colonial period, that "Arab colonizers brought" stone architecture and urban civilization to the Swahili coast. Locals—who of course also had overseas connections and relations—developed the Swahili coast built environment. However, certain local ornamental forms and building technologies also clearly exhibited influences from overseas, including from the Red Sea area and South Asia. For example, the mosques and palaces at Gedi and Kilwa featured barrel vaults, domes, and pointed arches that mirrored forms found in Muslim South Asia.

Local architects focused on developing building technologies that exploited the unique qualities of coral stone. Coral, abundantly available since it is the bedrock of much of the coast, was transformed into a range of building materials and ornamental forms. Both living (porites) and dry coral served a range of uses. Porites coral was cut from living reefs into large blocks and structural elements, such as load-bearing pillars. While still soft it was also carved and incised to create elaborate doorway, niche, wall, and window decorations. For example, sometime in the eighteenth century it became fashionable to cover the entire surfaces of walls with low-relief geometric and floriated patterns and with

FIGURE 1.3. Ruins of an eighteenth-century stone mansion in the Lamu Archipelago, circa 1885. This interior lime plaster wall is covered with dozens of miniature niches (*zidaka*). Photograph courtesy of the Trustees of the National Library of Scotland.

rows upon rows of miniature niches (figure 1.3). Dry coral rag was also mixed with limestone cement to build walls. All stonework was dressed with white lime plaster, produced by burning coral rock and specific sea shells. The production of fine and lustrous lime was one of the hallmarks of Swahili building technologies. Once applied to the surface of walls, lime plaster endowed Swahili waterfronts with a shimmering whiteness that could be seen from far away by people arriving via caravan roads or dhows and other ships.

In the early nineteenth century stone structures belonged only to a small minority of elite merchants and caravan leaders, who saw themselves as living apart from the majority of the local population who labored on the land. Elite families patronized this culture of stone, presenting their stone homes as symbols of their rights as the freeborn and patrician "owners" of the city. They claimed to be the authors of the city's ocean-oriented heritage. Although in the late nineteenth century formerly enslaved persons who became rich caravan managers did buy the houses of declining patrician families, in theory such houses were never to be sold—especially to nonpatricians—but were passed down from generation to generation. The stone house also often belonged to female members of an elite family.

Stone architecture did more than reflect or produce elite status, however. One did not have to own a stone mansion to claim its aura. Living in Mombasa meant one belonged to its culture of stone. In local worldviews, stone architecture gave material form to the very difference of Mombasa: it was a Muslim urban society. Today oral histories, as given by respected community elders, repeatedly return to stone architecture as evidence of Mombasa's worldliness and international connectedness.[27] Along with others, Mwalimu Mohammad Matano, a local historian of Mombasa's Thelatha Federation, conceptualized stone-built architecture as part of a continuum of cultural forms marking Mombasa as a distinct from mainland settlement, noting that "these things have always been here because of the ocean."[28] Conceiving of stone architecture as part of a dialogue with places beyond one's physical location is still characteristic of Mombasan strategies of self-fashioning. Today, families associated with the Thenashara Taifa will insist that building in stone is evidence of their ancient status as true wamiji—people of the city.

As scholars of the Swahili coast have pointed out, the cultural codes encapsulated by stone buildings represent an ideal. In reality the majority—even many freeborn waungwana—lived in earthen homes not dissimilar to those found across central and east Africa. Even today the "Swahili" architecture of the masses is much more humble and consists of single story buildings with *makuti* (palm frond) or corrugated iron roofs. In fact, many elders are aware that their ancestors did not live in grand lime-plastered mansions, but they argue that their homes belong to the larger spectrum of Islamic stone architecture. They point out that the walls of their homes have had right angles since the very founding of their cities on the coast. Ironically, such stories reproduce colonial-era stereotypes that Africans who live in the "deep bush" build only circular single-room "huts," whereas non-Africans built square buildings.

In the nineteenth century, stone houses, *nyumba za mawe,* also embodied a distinct body of knowledge. Unlike *nyumba za miti* (buildings in wood), stone masonry was a specialized technology and art mastered only by a select few. To become a stonemason required years of training and apprenticeship, and *wahusi wa mawe,* or specialists of stone, were likened to blacksmiths and herbalists because they could control supernatural forces and manipulate the natural world. Ludwig Krapf, a missionary living in Mombasa in the 1830s and 1840s, attempted to describe their unique role in local society: "The Wahunsi are supposed to be great sorcerers, who know the secrets of Nature and can perform wonderful things by witchcraft."[29] Oral histories explaining how ancient stonemasonry "worked" also emphasize its danger and volatility. A stone house required an offering when its foundation was laid, lest it cause the death of a worker or future resident. It was common practice to conduct a ceremony to honor and protect a stone structure. Such ceremonies were public and accepted by Muslim religious leaders of the community until around the 1950s. Also, to this day rumors of secret human sacrifice are associated with most large-scale building projects. The interred bodies of enslaved persons are understood to have functioned as protective emblems in the distant past, although no material evidence suggests such practices actually occurred. It was indeed a local Swahili tradition to sacrifice an ox upon the completion of a stone house. This was considered to be an Islamic religious ceremony, performed by a respected Muslim scholar. Most important, narratives about the "ancient days" continue to emphasize that the waungwana were beholden to no one and that they could build majestic structures because they had the will and ability to protect them with the bodies of humans. For example, Mwalimu Mohammad Matano presented an extended exegesis on the subject: "When they [waungwana] were building great structures they still had much *heshima* [respect, honor]. It wasn't seen as something bad, to sacrifice a slave . . . It reflected certain abilities if someone could sacrifice a slave, it was their *uwezo* [power, capability] that allowed them to do such things. There are many houses where slaves were sacrificed and put in the walls."[30] Matano presented this as a horrific and unjust practice, but insisted on its historical veracity because it clarified why stone architecture was more than just a material form that expressed social prestige. To him, the key truth about stone architecture was that it existed outside the realm of the mundane, embodying supernatural power and the ability to transgress the ethics that structure society. Stone architecture created a spectacle beyond the confines of acceptable behavior, and only those with great heshima had the means to mark the landscape with what were essentially transgressions against the laws of nature and society.

A Relational Built Environment

While Mombasa is an ancient stone town, its built environment is a palimpsest of local and international developments. It major buildings and urban layout facilitated the circulation of commodities, peoples, ideas, and values. It therefore is not a useful endeavor to attempt to classify what is local or foreign in the city. In the early modern period the built environment of the waterfront was already a kind of imbricated place, where Portuguese overlords, overseas Muslims, and locals fashioned spaces that emphasized transcultural translation and oceanic mobility. During this period stone architecture was not linked to a distinct ethnicity or even a single cultural identity. Rather, all who wanted to associate themselves with the wealth and culture of the port desired it.

Well into the 1880s only the waterfront and an abutting narrow causeway featured stone structures.[31] This long narrow street, described as a foxhole by the Portuguese in 1606, ran parallel to the harbor.[32] This "foxhole," now called Mbarak Hinawy Street, survives today. It is still the main thoroughfare of Old Town, defining the urban character of the city's Swahili core, stretching on a north-south axis along the eastern waterfront. It connects the interior of the city to the large plaza facing Fort Jesus, the military citadel built by the Portuguese in 1593. This emphasis on a single causeway is a characteristic feature of Swahili coast urban space. To this day many of the humble coastal towns surrounding Mombasa feature one main street bifurcating the town. Mombasa is the only Swahili city that also became an international port whose core is still defined by such a classic causeway. New settlements and buildings radiated in a west- and northward direction along the street's narrow expanse. In the nineteenth century another causeway, running parallel to Hinawy Street, began to take shape. Simply called Ndia Kuu, or Main

Street, it is broader than the very narrow Hinawy Street. Both connect the large plaza in front of Fort Jesus to a small square at the gates of the harbor and customs house, allowing for the easy movement of imports and exports to their respective destinations. By the 1890s Ndia Kuu was dominated by large stone mansions and commercial houses (figure 1.4). During the height of the city's economic boom in the late nineteenth century, agents, missionaries, hoteliers, and "curiosity" dealers built or appropriated large structures along both streets. Here chartered trading companies specializing in ivory trade processed and auctioned their merchandise before loading them onto vessels destined for South Asia, Europe and North America.

The waterfront was clearly radically transformed by the mid-nineteenth century. Yet in many ways this was an ancient phenomenon. Mombasa had to contend with overseas incursions from 1505 onward, when Portugal began to seek control over the city and its trading networks. Although the Portuguese were violent colonial overlords, sacking the city several times, they also depended on the city's indigenous built environment. Duarte Barbosa's 1517 description of Mombasa evokes a majestic city comparable to the prosperous cities of Europe. He celebrated the architecture as "very grand and beautiful, and built of high and handsome houses of stone and whitewash, and with very good streets."[33] Another Portuguese account described Mombasa as a city of over nine hundred houses and a dense web of narrow streets flanked by stone buildings up to three stories high. The exterior of the buildings featured stone benches, which were protected by palm-thatch porches. The smooth surface of the lime-plastered exteriors was decorated with "beautifully worked wood."[34] Portuguese chronicles also represent the earliest written documentation of Swahili lime plaster technologies, and they commented on the striking whiteness of the gleaming façades of the waterfront.[35]

Portuguese overlords did seek to transform Mombasa's urban landscape to reflect their will to control the city. Between 1593 and 1596 they built Fort Jesus, the monumental military citadel from which they launched attacks on the local population whenever they feared an uprising throughout their century-long occupation. Churches and monasteries also dotted the waterfront, signaling that in their view Mombasa now belonged to Christendom. By the sixteenth century heavy fortifications

FIGURE 1.4. Whitewashed façades of Ndia Kuu (Main Street) of Old Town Mombasa, circa 1900. Photograph courtesy of the Melville J. Herskovits Library of African Studies Winterton Collection, Northwestern University.

separated the Portuguese settlement, the area still known today as *Ga-vana* (government, in Portuguese), from *mji wa kale* (old town, in Swahili), which had its center slightly to the north of the harbor. This area is still seen as the ancestral heart of Swahili Mombasa. When Richard Burton visited Mombasa in 1857, the remnants of the wall separating Gavana from "Black town" was still visible.[36] The Portuguese clearly wanted to separate themselves from locals, but throughout their rule of Mombasa they also continued to be impressed by Mombasa's ancient urban civilization. For example, a 1505 account describes Mombasa's mji wa kale as grand and beautiful. Here the "king had his palace, built in the style of a fortress, with towers and turrets and every kind of defense."[37]

Mombasa existed as a cosmopolitan place in the European imagination since the sixteenth century. Images of the city represented Mombasa akin to a European Renaissance "stone town." A colored engraving (plate 7) from the first volume of the Georg Braun and Franz Hogenberg's city atlas, *Civitates Orbis Terrarum* published in Cologne in 1572, visualizes the city as an idealized place of civic order and prosperity, complete with towers and multistoried stone houses with shingled roofs. This idealized vision of the city followed cartographic conventions of the time, in which illustrations did not purport to represent how the city would have looked to a visitor, but rather it gave viewers a stock image of a type of urban space. Mombasa was simply imbued with markers of beautiful "city-ness." Any sense that Mombasa was "different" is obscured by the stock imagery employed for "civilized" cities.

Images of Mombasa began to change subtly as Portugal became the dominant military and economic power in the Indian Ocean. The 1646 *Livro do Estado da India Oriental* contains an image of the city that still endows Mombasa with a sense of civilized urban order. Tiny single-story houses with red pitched roofs arranged in parallel lines still stand for urban space in these depictions. But now the city looks more like a provincial Portuguese military outpost. This image (not pictured) too is largely a symbolic mapping of the city. It hovers between being a map and landscape, where the miniature houses function largely as pictographs or symbols of urban life, not as actual representations of individual structures. Ignoring the conventions of perspectival illusionism, the artist drew sight lines akimbo so that such details as the towers of the largest structure on the map, Fort Jesus, are rendered pointing toward each other on a flat plane, while houses are stacked on top of each other.

In fact, in most Portuguese visual representation of Mombasa, only Fort Jesus is rendered with some detail. Usually the citadel is pictured as a gigantic monument, fantastically dwarfing the rest of the city. Fort Jesus was largely a defensive structure, protecting Portuguese trading monopolies in the Indian Ocean and those Portuguese living as besieged and unpopular colonial overlords in the city. Under Portuguese patronage Gavana had become militarized zone, where stone buildings first and foremost functioned as defensive and surveillance structures; but as time progressed Fort Jesus was unmoored from its association with Portuguese rule. Many local oral histories and narrative poems focus on the importance of Fort Jesus to local residents.[38] Even today elders recall the dramatic battles fought within its walls. Fort Jesus is often presented as the very reason why the indigenous name of the city, Mvita—place of war—is more apt than Mombasa. For example, when the Yarubi dynasty of Oman sent Mazrui and Baluchi forces to help the Thenashara Taifa oust the Portuguese at the end of the seventeenth century, they had to lay siege to the citadel for three years.

After the Portuguese left Mombasa, the Mazrui expropriated all their property, including Fort Jesus, parts of which they converted into living quarters and public reception halls. Mazrui leaders also annexed the stone structures built by the Portuguese in Gavana. None of these structures retain their Portuguese identity today, but in 1846 a French explorer, Captain Guillain, documented the extant structures of an Augustinian monastery and two Portuguese churches, which, much to his horror, had been turned into domestic quarters by the Mazrui. Mazrui patrons also introduced new forms to the extant built environment of the waterfront. Once more, as Omani Arabs began to settle in the city in the 1700s, it became fashionable to add pinnacled crenellations to the roofline of buildings. Also, Mombasa's merchant mansions began to feature a single central courtyard, a typology that seems to have been prevalent in the coastal cities of Oman; this is discussed in detail in the next section of this chapter.

It was not until the 1820s that Europeans began to return to Mombasa. These newcomers translated their experiences by constantly referencing earlier Portuguese written and pictorial interpretations of the city. For example, Richard Burton and Carl von der Decken, whose travelogues were widely read, depended on early Portuguese publications to anchor their own descriptions of Mombasa and the Swahili coast. Duarte Barbosa's emphasis on the glory of its stone structures was quoted or referenced by many visitors. When the missionary Charles New moved to Mombasa in the second half of the nineteenth century, he also emphasized the stone buildings of the waterfront in his description of Mombasa, noting that "in the front [facing the harbor] there are several stone houses, glaring white in plaster."[39] He also was the first westerner to document the local Mombasan term for stone architecture, nyumba za mawe. New images of the port also began to circulate in the western media of the time (figure 1.5). They too emphasized the stone structures of the port; their main purpose was to illustrate reports about the city's potential usefulness to Europeans.[40] They construct an image of the city for European audiences that they would receive as picturesque. Mombasa is represented as a pleasing vista, a city of tropical breezes and mysterious ancient monuments. Yet such images and descriptions are not just the visualization of preexisting ideas. They do not only represent self-enclosed or totalizing western constructions or "imaginary geographies." Instead, Swahili and western ideals regarding the meaning of local building cultures intersected each other even more, creating new material and conceptual landscapes.

In the nineteenth century, stone architecture continued to signify the pinnacle of culturedness in local systems of signification. Mombasa's merchant mansions always had austere and unadorned exteriors, even in the nineteenth century, when South Asian immigrants began ornamenting the façades of their homes with lavish woodwork. Mombasa's mansions mostly featured only molded bands of unbroken stringcourses, indicating the level of each floor along the façade, and rows of rectangular windows with wooden shutters (figure 1.6). The only exterior decorative flourish, the only visual hint of the wealth and sophistication to be found within, was the addition of a wooden doorway on the main entrance façade (figure 1.7). Its size and the intricacy of its carving program indicated the wealth and social status of the mansion's owner.

FIGURE 1.5. "Town of Mombasa" etching, *Illustrated London News*, 7 May 1875.

ARCHITECTURE IN TRANSLATION

It was during the late nineteenth century, when elites of stone towns lost their status and autonomy, that the stone house began to gradually demarcate a new politics of exclusion. Since colonialism's rule of difference depended on racial hierarchies, whether Swahili coast architecture was "African" and "indigenous" or "Arab" and "foreign" became a pivotal issue, because such definition seemed to offer the possibility of fixing racial identities into place.[41] As the colonial project progressed, Europeans, in an attempt to master space and people, sought to segregate and police the complex heterogeneity of Swahili urban life by instituting a hierarchy of architecture based on racial and evolutionary models. According to this schema Africans build and live in perishable or semipermanent "huts," and only "higher races," such as "Arabs," create permanent stone architecture. These assumptions racialized the cultural prestige associated with stone architecture, and its historically variable form became typed as "Arab."

European racial taxonomies depended on external visual signs, such as architecture, precisely because all populations are always already

FIGURE 1.6. Stone mansions near the waterfront of Old Town Mombasa. Photograph courtesy of the National Museums of Kenya.

FIGURE 1.7. Intricately carved doorway of an old stone mansion on
Ndia Kuu (Main Street), Old Town Mombasa. Members of the Church
Missionary Society rented the house in the 1880s; it became known as
the Ladies House because most of the missionaries were women.
Photograph courtesy of the National Museums of Kenya.

"mixed" and the human body is not a stable marker of difference. Especially in the diasporic milieu of the Swahili port city, where most residents had relatives from diverse places, social hierarchies constituted
by the external appearance of the human body could not be sustained.
Because the process of grouping artifacts and buildings based on their
formal morphology was understood to be unquestionably objective, the
seeming indexical stability of material culture offered a more secure
system of fixing ethnic or racial difference.[42] From the late eighteenth
century onward, the western "exhibitionary complex" endowed material culture with an authority to stand for peoples.[43] The built environment became the primary framework for anchoring the cultured body in
place—it was used to create a "natural" relationship between territories
and social bodies. As we shall see, by the height of the colonial period it
was accepted, even self-evident, to see a link between the characteristics
of people, geography, and the physical form of housing.

     Colonizers used such racialized discourse across the globe for an ar-
ray of reasons. On the Swahili coast it facilitated the European annexation of existing cities. When the Imperial British East Africa Company
leased Mombasa as a concession from the Sultan of Zanzibar in 1887, the
city's extensive trade networks with western Indian Ocean and inland
African markets were absorbed into the North Atlantic economic system. Especially the unprecedented demand for ivory in North America
and Europe attracted newcomers from all over the world to Mombasa,
where its merchants had long specialized in overseeing and managing
ivory caravans. Europeans, Arabs, and South Asians gradually began to
appropriate the city's economic infrastructure and its attendant material
landscape.[44] Featuring a built form, layout, and infrastructure similar to
other Indian Ocean port cities, the architecture of the waterfront was
comfortingly familiar to South Asian and Arab newcomers. Europeans
also found the existing waterfront appropriate for their own way of life;
in their view it belonged not to the African but to the Arab cultural
sphere, which they imagined to be closer to theirs. Thus, rather than spa-
tially distancing themselves from local life, as was the municipal policy
of the high colonial period, European newcomers inserted themselves
into the preexisting cityscape. Newcomers adapted these local spaces
for their own uses, all within the context of being foreigners in the city.

Westerners also liked living in the stone houses of the waterfront to signal their sophisticated "insider status" and deep knowledge of local culture. Like certain travelers and researchers today, nineteenth-century Europeans valued and performed a particular form of "going native," one that privileged having access to the spaces and aesthetics of the local ruling classes. In a rare occurrence in the history of European encounters with Africa, female members of the Church Missionary Society (CMS) created a photographic record of their lives in the patrician spaces of Mombasa Old Town during the late nineteenth century. The photograph in figure 1.7 shows CMS women and a pupil proudly posing in front of "their" Swahili doorway in Mombasa Old Town. Its size and ornamentation, which represents the most intricate of the Indo-Zanzibari designs that became fashionable in the mid-nineteenth century, indicates that this was indeed a grand mansion, the kind only owned and patronized by the wealthy freeborn members of Mombasan society. The Ladies House, as it was known, stood in the most coveted area of Ndia Kuu, the stone town area of Old Town, close to the waterfront. The women operated a school for local children and lived in this structure, the only presence Christian missionaries maintained in Old Town Mombasa. Like all missionary organizations along the Swahili coast, all other CMS headquarters were located on the mainland, beyond the purview of Muslim communities. CMS women seemed to partially embrace the social life and cultures of the coast both in their private lives and in the educational curricula for their pupils. Their school and home in Old Town focused on secular knowledge; one teacher recorded that "the boys are mainly instructed in Arabic, Ki-Swahili and English" and the girls in "Zanzibari mat braiding."[45]

Another photograph, part of the memorabilia album of Sibbie Bazett, a CMS missionary who lived and worked in the Ladies House in the 1880s and 1890s, shows her and a friend posing for the camera dressed like Mombasan freeborn nobles (figure 1.8). In fact, the same album contains photographs of such women, who Bazett and her companion mimicked, especially in the ways they arranged their garments and shawls. Both CMS women are signaling their understanding of local politics of dressing. Their carefully arranged tableau includes the silver anklets and the high wooden sandals that only highborn waungwana women were allowed to

FIGURE 1.8. Sibbie Bazett (right) and companion pose as "Swahili patricians." The photo was likely staged in the upper gallery of the Ladies House. Photograph courtesy of the Gladys Beecher and Hollis Collection, National Museums of Kenya.

wear before slavery was outlawed. Bazett herself was more ambitious in presenting a "complete" image of local fashion by also wearing a nasal septum ring, as was the height of Swahili fashion in the 1890s.[46]

The photographer also took care to find the appropriate *in situ* backdrop to document this moment of intercultural cross-dressing: the image shows the women standing and sitting in a "native" space, most likely one of the second-story galleries of a stone mansion, the traditional domain of female members of a patrician Swahili household. Singular in the photographic records of missionary work in Mombasa, these photographs hint at the personal play, humor, and perhaps transgression found in the unofficial spaces of daily life in Mombasa at the turn of the century. Certainly these images document the women's fantasies attached to their encounters with local female spaces and ways of being, but also record an intimate level of shared lives in the social and physical spaces of Old Town. Although such encounters leave few archival traces, in 1904 the *Mombasa Times* commented on a lecture by a CMS female missionary about an "Arab lady's abode." The missionary had become friends with local patrician women and so could give a rare glimpse into the domestic sphere of Muslim families, which few Europeans had access to at the time.[47]

FROM MERCHANT MANSION TO "WHITE" HOUSE

An example of architectural acculturation allowing us to trace the transformation of a merchant house into a space of European whiteness is the Hinawy House (figures 1.9–1.11), which still stands on Mombasa's waterfront. Although its foundation date is unknown, it was one of many stone structures situated along the waterfront in the nineteenth century. In 1889 the house entered the Sultanate of Zanzibar administrative records for the first time, when Tharia Topan bought it from a local man named Nasir bin Salim.[48] Topan, Zanzibar's chief of customs, spearheaded the redirection of the entire coastal economy, connecting Mombasa and Zanzibar to the financial markets of the British Raj. He and his patron, Sultan Barghash, transformed the architectural fabric of Zanzibar's waterfront by building the most modern of structures: Topan's Jubilee

FIGURE 1.9. This 1884 photograph is the only image of the Hinawy House (as it is known today) before a verandah and balcony were added to it by Tharia Toban in the 1890s. The Hinawy House is the stone mansion on the far left. Photograph courtesy of the Trustees of the National Library of Scotland.

FIGURE 1.10. Tharia Toban's stone house (today known as the Hinawy House) with an added verandah, circa 1890. Illustrated in Mary Sheldon, *Sultan to Sultan: Adventures Among the Masai and Other Tribes of East Africa* (Boston: Arena [publishing company]; Saxon, 1892), page 102.

FIGURE 1.11. Toban House with an intricate cast-iron verandah on the second floor, circa 1880s. From an Ismaili family photography album now at the Fort Jesus branch of the National Museums of Kenya, Mombasa. Photograph courtesy of the National Museums of Kenya.

Hospital and Barghash's House of Wonders (see chapter 3). Both buildings celebrated modernization, as the most technologically advanced
European cast-iron mass-produced ornaments and hand-carved fret-
work from India were imported for the decoration of the ostentatious
exterior balconies.

Topan, like many Ismaili financiers, easily moved between European,
indigenous, South Asian, and Arab communities, providing diverse con-
stituents access to the expanding credit networks of the Indian Ocean.[49]
Although he never spent any extensive time in Mombasa, the purchase
of an old merchant house on the waterfront allowed Topan to permanently establish a presence in the city. A ground plan of the building
exists from 1903 (figure 1.12), when Walter Rössler leased it from the
Topan estate to establish the German vice-consulate in Mombasa (the
consulate was in Zanzibar). Rössler described how the "stately" structure
could be seen by all ships arriving in the harbor. He assured his superiors
in Berlin that the building's "Arab style" made it suitable as the residence
and office of the vice-consul. Rössler also struggled to make sense of the
interior layout, which he described as "inefficient" and "useless" because
in his view so many of the rooms seemed too small and not connected to
the rest of the building. The fact that British had also occupied it at some
point somehow assured him that it was the right building to establish a
German presence in Mombasa, although he did complain that this fact
made the lease more expensive.[50]

Yet from the perspective of local practice, rather than being useless,
the building's plan clearly manifests a specifically Swahili coast spatial
and social logic. The plan still embodies the local architectural practice of producing a graduated and controlled movement from public
to private space. Significantly, no doors are on axis, emphasizing the
compartmentalization of each section. The large inner courtyard is also
recessed within the folds of the outer rooms, indicating its function as
a semi-private transitional space between the reception areas of the
ground floor and the domestic area of the upper floors. This inwardness
of Swahili social life becomes a minor obsession for European visitors.
For example, nineteenth-century travelers described their frustrated
attempts to peer into the domestic areas of merchant houses from the
roof of neighboring buildings.[51] The second and third stories and upper

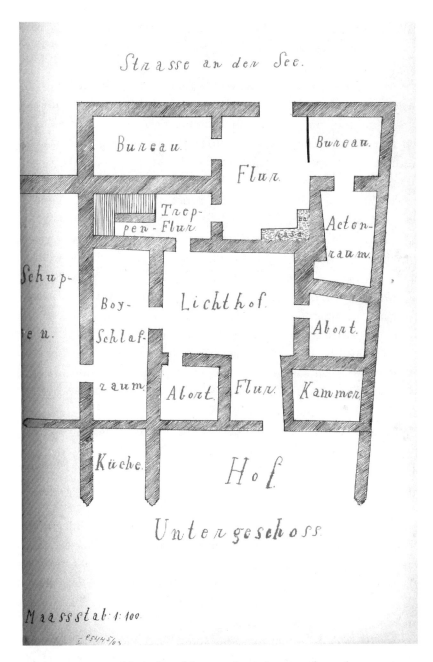

FIGURE 1.12. Ground floor plan of the stone house known today as the Hinawy House (plan hand-drawn in 1903). Courtesy of the Political Archives of the Federal Foreign Office of Germany, Berlin.

galleries functioned as the true domestic space of the house; here women and children moved about freely, and the matriarch of the house was in complete control of this area.

Other key Swahili features are indicated on the plan. The drawing includes only one Swahili word, *baraza,* which labels the built-in sitting area of the front section of the building. Every Swahili coast home, whether a humble single-story makuti house or a stately stone mansion, features a public space of reception and sociability, always called a baraza (see figure 0.4). The physical form of a baraza can vary; depending on the size of the building, it can be a simple bench or porch, but also a grand verandah or a hall lined with benches. It is often not connected to the rest of the building, serving as a kind of public stage where guests await entrance to more private spaces or one comes to rest for long conversations. The baraza is conceptualized as belonging to the public domain of the city, where male members of the neighborhood gather to socialize, since the interior is the domain of women. First and foremost it is the physical locus of an important Swahili cultural ideal: the ability to converse fluently and wisely in Swahili. To be a true wamiji means one can participate in urbane conversation and sophisticated argumentation. Having the right to come to rest on a baraza means one can speak and act like a true citizen of the city.

Once newcomers appropriated the mansion in the 1880s, the front half of the ground floor, including the baraza, continued to function as a semi-public space. Its German residents used the spaces directly connected to the baraza as administrative spaces, where the official business of the consulate was conducted. The building's exterior fabric was completely transformed and seemingly delocalized by means of integrating the exterior into the decorative language of other places of modern empire-building. It was redecorated along the latest British Raj styles with the addition of a grand seaside colonnade and a second-floor balcony (figure 1.11).[52] The balcony, most likely imported directly from Bombay and assembled by itinerant South Asian craftsmen, featured a cast-iron mass-produced balustrade. Balconies and verandahs extended the space of living and ownership beyond the austere surface of the whitewashed façade. This addition to the local architectural vocabulary in turn transformed the aesthetic qualities of surface and volume of the city's public space. Perforating and extending the surface of the building to create various platforms for exterior-oriented ocular pleasures and surveillance becomes the hallmark of later colonial architecture all along the coast.

Other patrician stone houses on the waterfront were successively transformed throughout the nineteenth century. The Imperial British East Africa Company (IBEAC) rented or expropriated several "large white buildings."[53] The house occupied by the IBEAC's first administrator, George Mackenzie, had also been occupied by William Owen during his short-lived Mombasa Protectorate of 1824–26.[54] Today it is still called the Leven House, named after the main ship of Owen's fleet. The structure was leased to Owen in 1823 by a man associated with the Mazrui clan, and according to one lieutenant's descriptions, it was originally a large two-story stone building with seven rooms.[55] Subsequently the sultan of Zanzibar lent the house to Reverend W. S. Price of the Church Missionary Society, who also significantly altered its exterior by hiring two "artisans from Bombay" and "English mechanics" to add prominent second-story verandahs to the building.[56] Most notably, continuous verandahs united two separate buildings. When Mackenzie acquired the building he promptly ordered more mass-produced architectural components from the Iron and Steel Fencing and Buildings Company's mail catalogue, in order to add "more modern wide and open verandahs all round the house."[57]

Yet ownership of the house was contested throughout this transitional period. In the 1880s Mazrui descendants disputed the legality of the sultan's claim to the house and his subsequent leasing of it to the CMS. The Mazrui argued that the sultan did not have legal rights to the structure because his father had simply expropriated all Mazrui property in Mombasa when he ousted them from the city in 1837.[58] Mazrui family members, who had retreated to the neighboring town of Takaungu, sought to regain ownership of the Leven House in the 1880s. They ultimately failed, but their claim was nominally recognized by the British Protectorate government; the CMS was required to pay $2,000 to Salim bin Hamis Mazrui (the governor of Takaungu) once he agreed to "relinquish all and every claim and right that he has or might have in the house."[59]

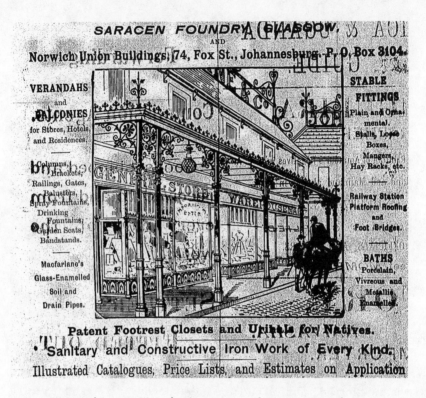

FIGURE 1.13a–b. (*above and facing*) Advertisements for Saracen Foundry in the *Mombasa Times*, 1890s.

As Mombasa became an official British protectorate in 1895, imperial modernity was firmly imposed onto Mombasa's cityscape and local
citizens soon faced further marginalization in their own city. Europeans
living in other Indian Ocean ports came to Mombasa seeking business
prospects. For example, the Feldmann family, originally from Germany,
moved from Aden to Mombasa in the 1890s to establish the Afrika Hotel
in Old Town.[60] During this period "poor whites" arrived daily in Mombasa, looking for new opportunities when construction on the Ugandan
Railway and Kilindini Harbor began on the other side of the island.[61]
Portuguese citizens, mainly Christian South Asians from Goa, soon
established shops in Old Town, their signage dominating the streetscape
of the two main commercial arteries of the waterfront, Ndia Kuu (Main
Street) and Mbarak Hinawy Street. The British administration in turn

praised Goan immigrants for "look[ing] after the wants of the first European residents."[62] European governmental representatives also increasingly dominated the waterfront. Portugal, Germany, Italy, Belgium, and the Austro-Hungarian Empire established consular and business offices in Old Town, "internationalizing" its space.[63]

Manufacturers of ornamental ironwork, such as the Scottish Saracen Foundry, increasingly distributed their "oriental" mass-produced cast-iron balconies and architectural embellishments all over the British Empire, including Mombasa and Zanzibar. The company's advertisements were the first pictorial components of the local newspaper, the *Mombasa Times* (figure 1.13a–b), and their fantastical designs, based on the fusion of Middle Eastern and Victorian ornamental forms, inspired the latest architectural projects along the Swahili coast. For western residents and visitors, Mombasa Town became an area marked by familiar architectural ornaments and decorative arts, vaguely "tropically colonial" in

FIGURE 1.14. The store of a textile merchant with an elaborate second-floor verandah imported from England. Illustrated in Playne and Gale, *East Africa (British): Its History, People, Commerce, Industries, and Resources* (London: Foreign and Colonial Compiling and Pub. Co, 1908), page 10.

style (figure 1.14). Mombasa Town was remapped as a celebratory space of British capital. Significantly, during this period the local population also rearticulated their understanding of the waterfront, which was re-named *mtaa ya mzungu* in the local parlance, meaning "white peoples' quarter."[64]

Coloniality and the City

By the second decade of the twentieth century, Europeans began to dis-engage from the historical waterfront. A new administrative center was constructed south of Old Town, on the higher grounds of Ras Serani Point. The neoclassical façade of the Law Courts became the center point of a new wave of building activity just outside Old Town, where a "modern" city began to take shape. Authoritatively positioned next to,

but outside of, Old Town, the Law Courts supplanted the previous structures and systems of governance. Yet Old Town still remained an active
hub of the Indian Ocean dhow trade. Goods destined for local consumption still came through its port. As late as 1907, a local British resident
reported on the vibrancy of the Old Port, observing, "Dhows from the
Persian Gulf, Bombay and Somaliland are arriving daily in Mombasa . . .
Their cargos being considerably mixed: Bombay chairs, dates, tin trunks,
earthen pots, cattle, horses, sheep, carpets, etc."[65]

Old Town was also increasingly forced to "look like" a properly segregated city, at least on paper. Colonial urban planning reports and maps
of the city created a racially segregated image of the city. One map from
1917 (plate 8), which represented an ambitious plan to completely remake
the city's urban layout, visualized a cityscape in which communities
styled as European, better-Arab, Indian, and African lived in separate
neighborhoods. The British administration also began to emphasize that
Mombasa was the possession of the sultan of Zanzibar, and therefore was
part of an "Arab" state. Even when the Kenya Colony was established in
1920, coastal residents were administered as "British Protected Persons,"
not as subjects of the Kenya Colony.[66] Omani Arabs dominated the political life of Mombasa's waterfront during this period. The Arab Administration and the British colonial government made concerted efforts to
categorize Mombasa's oldest communities as the "Swahili tribe," even
while their Muslim identity allowed them to maintain an ambiguous position in the racial hierarchy of the colony, where they hovered between
being categorized as "low-class" Arabs and "native" Africans. The stone
architecture of the waterfront became the purview of Arabs who worked
for the colonial government and South Asian families.[67] Rich Arab families lived in the most luxurious merchant houses. For example, the stone
mansion once owned by Topan and leased by the German government
became the property of a prominent Omani family, the Hinawy, whose
most famous member was Sir Mbarak Hinawy, the *liwali* (governor)
of Mombasa in the 1940s and 1950s.[68] By this time the area was also no
longer described as mtaa ya mzungu by Swahili-speaking residents, but
simply renamed *baghani*, the waterfront.

By the 1910s the European government also took an interest in the
marketability and imageability of Old Town. Europeans visited the

historical waterfront to encounter picturesque vistas of "houses old and
new built in the Arab style."[69] Colonial-period guidebooks and postcards presented the waterfront as a tableau vivant of the past, evoking
the romance of the "ancient Orient."[70] Such images presented Old Town
as self-contained aestheticized space and spectacle for consumption.
Old Town was allowed to exist as a temporary destination of leisure or
as a stock image in memorabilia album, but it became irrevocably *distant*
from the rest of the city in the colonizer's imaginary.[71]

Mombasa's municipal administrators also started drawing comparisons between Zanzibar Town and Mombasa Old Town in the hope
that Zanzibar would serve as a model for improving Mombasa.[72] In 1905
the Mombasa Public Works Department praised Zanzibar for "slowly
dressing itself up" in a "new restful golden ochre" instead of continu-
ing to plaster the façades with the "crude whitewash so glaring to the
eyes." It was hoped that Mombasans would do the same: "After the rains,
when the white-washing brush usually becomes active, we hope public
spirit will assert itself among private householders and the new pigment
brought into more general use."[73] Also, according to Mombasa's administrators, Zanzibar City had always existed as a "properly" segregated
city, in contrast to Mombasa. While in reality Zanzibar was also a heterogeneous and mixed urban space, colonial officials presented its stone
town as the Arab quarter and Ng'mbo as the African quarter.[74] To make
the city more like Zanzibar, Mombasa's administrators wrote municipal
zoning laws and building ordinances to also create a properly segregated
city.[75] New laws strictly regulated who could build stone structures.[76] By
the turn of the twentieth century, "Swahilis" could only build "wattle
and daub huts with makuti (palm fronds) roofs," since this was "the native manner."[77]

In reality such ordinances could not be enforced, and after World
War I Old Town morphed into an alarming place of disease, social disorder, uncontrollable migration, and Muslim agitation in the British
imagination. Old Town was increasingly described as a lost cause in
Mombasa's Public Work's Department annual reports. In 1919 the Municipal Health Officer noted that "it is impossible to do much toward
improving the Old Town and that the best course would be to let it die
a natural death."[78]

Old Town certainly did not die; it survives today as a vibrant community. Yet its reformulation during the early years of the colonial period irrevocably changed the everyday experience of place in Mombasa. In fact, the recent urban preservation program implemented by the National Museum of Kenya (NMK) is largely an attempt to return Old Town to the garb of Empire. For example, the National Museum's Mombasa Old Town Conservation Office (MOTCO) has so far restored the Leven House and a merchant house that features an intricately carved balcony on the second story.[79] Both structures have been reordered to create an imperial spectacle, their new Victorian-style verandahs, wooden window-shutters, and external decorative additions returning the cityscape to the tropical colonial style of the late nineteenth century. The reason for this is simple. Transforming Old Town into an important tourist destination, like Zanzibar Stone Town or Lamu, is seen as key for securing the city's future. The colonizer's image of and presence in Mombasa is thus revitalized as a monument of national heritage.[80] Certainly, the use of the Leven House is multivalent and much more complex than its style of architecture. For example, the dedicated leaders and staff members of the MOTCO and NMK work in the Leven House every day, creating a range of programs and projects meant to engage the local community in meaningful ways. Yet at the same time, the reconstructed Leven House is meant to produce an image easily consumed by tourists, in the hope that the city will conform to the current western taste for picturesque panoramas of the colonial past. Preservation ordinances have also been passed by the national and municipal government that stipulate which materials can be used to alter the exterior architectural features of structures in Old Town Mombasa, ironically recalling the regulations of the colonial period.

TWO

A "Curious" Minaret

Sacred Place and the Politics of Islam

While stone architecture in general is important in local worldviews, only one type of masonry structure is essential for creating sacred place on the Swahili coast: a mosque. Port cities, such as Mombasa, Lamu, and Zanzibar, can claim being true stone towns precisely because their histories begin with the building of stone mosques. For example, Mombasan origin stories recount how founding father Shehe Mvita constructed the first stone mosque on Mombasa Island with the help of three mysterious men from "the North." Their help came in the form of a new building material: lime mortar, the binding agent that makes stone masonry possible.[1] The earliest written documentation of this event presents lime as miraculous matter: "The lime which the three strangers presented to Shehe was sufficient for building a mosque in a few days, whereupon these remarkable persons departed and constructed mosques in other places."[2] Transforming the architectonic order of Mombasa from earthen impermanence to stone permanence marks the beginning of Islamic time on Mombasa Island.

This narrative also endows the foundation of a mosque with sacred significance; to this day families connected to ancient mosques are revered. Until the colonial period only the wealthy patrician families of coastal cities built and endowed congregational mosques as public monuments, giving visual force to their Muslim piety and signaling their political power and cultural leadership in city. Constructing and supporting a mosque is considered one of the greatest acts of Islamic charity and civility; such an act blesses and memorializes the patron and his or her family. Patrons of mosques also shape the daily religious and cultural life of a community. In the past Swahili waungwana families financed the maintenance of mosques and madrasas and also financially supported the mosque's imam and muezzin. Mosques were the most important centers of Islamic education, scholarship, and jurisprudence on the Swahili coast. Patrons of mosques invited itinerant scholars from overseas to teach at their mosques, and they supported local Muslim scholars and jurists: a mosque that became famous as a center of Islamic learning also helped enhance the wealth and reputation of the patron family and the city. Muslims from abroad, including scholars and business people, would be attracted by a city's aura of religious piety and righteousness. It made the city "trustworthy." In this way the prestige and prosperity of the port were directly linked to the reputation of its mosques.

Mosques carried the names of their patrons, but lineages lost the right to name and patronize mosques if their political and economic power waned. To this day once-powerful families link their erasure from official history to their inability to maintain their families' mosques during the colonial period. Nowhere is this more evident than in Mombasa. Unlike in Zanzibar, Mombasa's ancient lineages (the Thenashara Tăifa) still actively demand recognition of their rights as owners of the city by claiming that they are the rightful heirs of Mombasa's Islamic heritage. These claims are highly contested, however, because of the shifting nature of Swahili identity politics and the transformation of religious practice in Mombasa over the last two centuries. In particular, Mombasa Island's most ancient mosques are the focus of fraught intercommunal struggles and a complex politics of remembering and forgetting. The Mandhry mosque (figure 2.1) and the mosque now known as the Basheikh (formerly called Tangana or Mnara) mosque (plate 9) both have the "pillar" or *mnara* minaret, an architectural form considered indigenous to Mombasa.[3]

Other mosques are periodically reconstructed to keep pace with contemporary architectural styles, and many mosques now feature heavy cement additions, neo-orientalist façades, or other contemporary elements that connect them directly to the mosque architecture of the Arab

FIGURE 2.1. Mandhry mosque, founded circa sixteenth century.
Photograph by the author, 2013.

Gulf states. In contrast, the basic character and architectural vocabulary of the Mandhry and Mnara mosques, established in earlier periods, is never altered. Only an annual whitewashing is permitted on both
structures. In a sense, the classic iconicity of the conical minarets and
their stark whitewashed surfaces separate them from the fluctuations
of time. As actively used religious spaces, however, they are seen not
as the remnants of a waning past, but as irrefutable markers and sites
of the continued presentness of the past. However, as explained in the
rest of the chapter, the ability of these monuments to overcome temporal
distance was increasingly politicized and racialized from the colonial
period onward.

MOSQUES AS TRANSLOCAL SPACE

Islam has been part of the social, political, and cultural landscape of the
Swahili coast since the end of the first millennium. Historians have suggested that Muslims from southern Arabia, or from present-day Ethiopia, Somalia, or Iran first introduced the faith during its formative years,
between the ninth and twelfth centuries. Archeological excavations at
such sites as Shanga in the Lamu Archipelago of present-day Kenya
document the existence of stone mosques as early as the ninth century,
and the still extant Kizimkazi mosque on Zanzibar Island has an 1107
foundation inscription. Certainly, the presence of such ancient mosques
does not necessarily mean all members of a settlement were practicing
Muslims, but by the thirteenth century the towns and villages of the
coast claimed belonging to the *dar al-Islam,* or the global House of Islam.
Muslims from far and near regularly visited and even immigrated to the
coast's most prosperous port cities. For example, the famed Moroccan
scholar and traveler Ibn Battuta visited Mombasa and Kilwa in 1332 because extensive pilgrimage and trade routes linked the coast to the holy
sites of Medina and Mecca. Battuta recognized himself and his values in
the sociocultural landscape of Mombasa; he even praised Mombasans
for their particularly pious practice of the faith.

Yet contrary to popular assumptions, locals did not simply receive the
faith. Certainly, itinerant Muslim scholars and merchants from abroad
influenced how people understood Islam and its institutions. But locals,

familiar with both overseas and mainland African religious and cultural codes, shaped its daily practice on the coast. In many ways, the mobility encapsulated in Islam strengthened local desires to reach out to distant others. East Africans embraced Islam because its claim to universalism gave them the conceptual and political tools to imagine themselves as part of a planetary social order.[4] To be a Muslim meant one was part of the umma, an extraterritorial community dispersed across the globe. In fact, a sense of constant movement between multiple locales is at the heart of the faith. As noted by Barry Flood," The idea of mobility is . . . intrinsic to the history and prescription of Islam, a religion whose year zero is measured not from the birth of the Prophet but from the migration of the nascent Muslim community from Mecca to Medina."[5]

Islam allowed Swahili coast residents to expand extant networks of reciprocity, to symbolically collapse distance, and to engender new patterns of relations with the world. They deployed the universalism of the faith as a means to strengthen partnerships with other societies. Its doctrines, jurisprudence, and cultural codes facilitated familial alliances across the Indian Ocean. Islam gave shape to and was shaped by the importance of long-distance trade in the social and economic lives of local people. In fact, the dhow (figure 2.2), the sailing vessel of the Indian Ocean that made sea trade and travel possible, is to this day seen as an emblem of the Islamic heritage of the region.[6]

The architecture of a mosque, its sensuous materiality, transforms this imaginary into a real place of bodily experience. Historically, Swahili coast port cities each had one large congregational mosque on the waterfront, announcing the Islamic identity of the city to incoming ships. The pillar minaret of Shela Town's waterfront mosque still defines the cityscape from afar, although a new hotel now stands in front of its once-imposing whitewashed walls (figure 2.3). Most other waterfront congregational mosques were obscured from view long ago by the expansion of port facilities during the colonial period. For example, Mombasa's Mandhry mosque was once the most visible monument on the waterfront, but now newer buildings dominate. Mombasa's elders recount that in the past one of its main functions was to help newcomers find their bearings in the city. Any Muslim visitor could rest and even sleep in the prayer hall of the Mandhry mosque upon arrival in the city.

FIGURE. 2.2. Dhow sailing in the Lamu Archipelago, Kenya.
Photograph by the author, 2014.

In this sense the mosque acted as a threshold, helping newcomers orient
themselves in a different place. Yet, since the mosque was built by the
local stewards of the city, this process of transition was also controlled
and in a sense authored by them. As the agents of Muslim hospitality,
locals orchestrated and managed how newcomers perceived them and
their city.

All Swahili coast mosques also structure an experience of the elsewhere. A mosque is not a consecrated space, like a church, and Muslims
do not focus on something inside it. Instead it directs their attention to
something located across the ocean. That is, the main ritual purpose
of a mosque is to orient the body, mind, and spirit toward the Kaaba in
Mecca, the material axis mundi of the faith. The mosque's most important architectural feature is therefore the *mihrab,* the semicircular niche

FIGURE 2.3. The minaret of Shela Town's oldest congregational mosque is still visible from the sea. Photograph by the author, 2014.

that is set into the *qibla,* the wall indicating the direction of Mecca. For example, when Muslims face the beautifully carved mihrab of the Shela Town pillar mosque (figure 2.4) they are surmounting their physical distance from the Kaaba.

ISLAM AS A SPACE OF CONTESTATION

During the early years of the colonial period, mosques became intensely politicized spaces. Locals used Mombasa's role as an Islamic city—its "Islamicity"—as a site of resistance against the British and Arab ruling elite. When the Busaidi dynasty of Zanzibar first claimed Mombasa as part of its mercantile empire in 1837, a significant faction of Mombasa's leadership accepted the sultan as the official figurehead of the town.[7] The representatives of his government claimed the right to manage the

FIGURE 2.4. Trifoliate mihrab of the Shela Town waterfront congregational mosque. Photograph courtesy of Raymond Silverman, 2005.

customs house and thereby began to control the economic prosperity of the port. But the Thenanshara Taifa was still the rightful "owner" of Mombasa Island and its immediate hinterland. A treaty was ratified between Seyyid Said, the first Busaidi sultan of Zanzibar, and the most powerful *matamin* (titled leaders) of the Taifa. This document enshrined their religious and judicial independence. This was in part because, belonging to a different school of Islam than the local population, Omanis could not impose their authority in matters of Islam. Omanis traditionally follow the Ibadi school, while Swahili coast Muslims follow the Sunni Shafi'i school; in effect they belong to two distinct religious communities. But the Omani sultan was accepted as the highest-ranking Muslim leader of Mombasa, although he lived in Zanzibar. This endowed him with quasi-religious authority, which was publicly acknowledged every Friday all along the coast when his name was evoked in noon congregational prayers.

This began to change when Barghash, the second son of Seyyid Said to ascend to the throne, became sultan in 1870. Mombasa and other coastal cities actively critiqued Barghash because of his increasing dependence on the British, and many wanted to rebel against his rule.[8] Mosques played an important role in this development. The first public rebellion against the sultan occurred when Mombasans refused to name him as the leader of the community during Friday prayers. In doing this, Mombasa symbolically repudiated the authority of Zanzibar. This act of revolt was precipitated by Barghash's apparently imminent defeat by a man many viewed as a more pious and acceptable Muslim leader, the khedive of Egypt (also a Sunni Muslim). In 1875 Khedive Ismail Pasha sent an army toward Mombasa to take control of the Sultan's east African dominions. Once Mombasans believed the arrival of Egyptian troops was imminent, they named him during Friday prayers instead of Barghash.[9] Coastal peoples also critiqued Barghash's "un-Islamic" ways.[10] Questioning his religious integrity gave them an acceptable platform from which to renounce their allegiance to Zanzibar. This was not only a matter of indigenous Swahili coast families rising up against their Arab overlords. Arabs who had lived and married locally also began to reject the sultan. Many converted in unprecedented numbers from Ibadism to the Shafi'i beliefs during Sultan Barghash's reign. In fact, some

of the most respected Ibadi religious scholars of Zanzibar and Mombasa
converted to Shafi'ism and began to embrace the populist teachings
of Sufism, which the sultan sought to suppress.[11]

Once the Imperial British East Africa Company (IBEAC) leased Mombasa and its associated mainland from Barghash in 1887, symbolic acts
of rebellion became violent insurgencies, although Mombasans also
accepted lavish gifts from the IBEAC.[12] In 1888, after German officers
desecrated a congregational mosque in the port town of Pangani in present-day Tanzania, uprisings destabilized the entire coastal region.[13] In
the same year armed men attempted to oust the leader of the IBEAC,
George S. Mackenzie, from Mombasa.[14] These uprisings continued into
the last decade of the nineteenth century. Some of Mombasa's leaders
embraced exile in neighboring towns rather than accept the authority
of the IBEAC. Some exiles, such as Hamisi bin Kombo and Mbaruk bin
Rashid, became famous for repeatedly attacking British and Zanzibari
caravans around Mombasa. Under their leadership the towns of Gazi,
Takaungu, and Mtwapa became communities of resistance, where disaffected peoples from all over the region, but especially from Mombasa,
sought refuge and joined efforts to disrupt British and sultanate rule
in the region. Local peoples saw these rebellions in religious terms, as
righteous attempts to install a truly just form of governance in Mombasa. The British dismissed their actions as a form of religious hysteria,
describing the rebels as "fanatical native elements . . ."[15]

When Mombasa was made into a British protectorate in 1895, British
forces spearheaded a series of punitive expeditions in the hope of gain-
ing full control of the coast. Even then Mombasans continued to support
the rebels, at least covertly. For example, in 1896 a Mombasan elder,
Mwenye Jaka, who was commissioned by the British to assist in finding Mbarak bin Rashid, helped the rebels ambush the British instead.[16]
Mtwapa, the stronghold of Hamisi bin Kombo, held out against the British until October 1895, when another British punitive expedition burned
it to the ground because Hamisi bin Kombo refused to acquiesce to
British demands.[17]

Once rebel authority was crushed, protectorate officials sought to
present themselves as a new pro-Islamic government, mindful of the way
rebels utilized the ideal of Islamic governance to reject foreign authori-

ties. Upon arriving in Mombasa, the protectorate's first commissioner, Arthur Hardinge, assured local leaders that "the laws, customs, and religion of their people would be scrupulously respected by the new ruling powers."[18] But in effect a new judicial and administrative system was instituted. Hardinge had served several years in the British colonial government of Egypt, where he became familiar with the Ottoman imperial system. He was intent on recreating the administrative logic of British-controlled Ottoman Egypt in Mombasa. Accordingly, the region was recast as the Seyyidieh Province of the British East Africa Protectorate. The province was further subdivided into *wilayets*, an administrative category derived from the Ottoman imperial system, where the term designated frontier districts within the Ottoman Empire.[19]

It is precisely through the implementation of European colonial governance based on Middle Eastern models that local laws became more "Arab" on the Swahili coast under British rule. While the Swahili coast was shaped by contact with overseas centers of Islamic learning for a long time, Islamic practice on the coast existed in a dialectical relationship to other African religious and judicial systems until the nineteenth century.[20] This was especially the case in regard to the way territory and property was conceptualized and managed on the Swahili coast. Islamic and non-Islamic laws of land tenure and property ownership coexisted and intermingled in the production of Swahili place. However, from 1895 onward local practices were increasingly remapped to conform to British and Omani conceptions of Islamic law. Hardinge created the position of chief kadhi (*sheikh ul Islam*) in 1897 and founded the Wakf Commission in 1899. The chief kadhi became the paramount authority on Islamic law in the protectorate, and the Wakf Commission was invested with the authority to oversee all religiously endowed monuments and properties on Mombasa Island. In effect, the new rulers sought to consolidate control over Mombasa by inducing locals to accept a state-managed version of Islam.

Yet Old Town, an ancient center of Islamic learning and heritage, presented a serious challenge to the colonial government. Here the British and Omanis confronted a deep history of local Islamic practice that could not be simply remade to conform to British or Omani understandings of Islamic law. Especially the physical fabric of the city's

Islamic heritage resisted an unencumbered erasure. While the city's municipal council implemented various township ordinances in an attempt to remake Old Town into an orderly and picturesque colonial city, religious structures proved to be especially challenging because of their permanence and impenetrability. Simply put, locals often refused British officials entrance to their mosques, asserting it was against Islamic law.[21] In fact, "Islamic law" was often evoked to resist a range of colonial commands.

In 1915 the protectorate's commissioner Charles Hobley and the Conservancy Department attempted to alienate several plots of land in Old Town by arguing that the mosque and cemetery located on these plots were "heaps of rubbish [that] form refuges and breeding places for rats" and therefore presented a violation of hygiene and cleanliness laws.[22] Responding to protests mounted by the townspeople, some Wakf Commission members refused to support plans to demolish the mosque and cemetery. In the eyes of the local citizenry it was an affront to Islamic law and religiosity to change or alter these monuments, even if they were partial ruins. The Wakf Commission informed Hobley that it was forbidden to remove even one stone from such sacred sites.[23] Enraged, Hobley cited the city's Township Ordinances, threatening to prosecute the commissioners for their intransience. They in turn threatened to resign. He requested support from the colonial administration in Nairobi, but the governor forbade him to pursue the issue, warning him that "now is not the time"; the government saw Mombasa as a center of renewed religious agitation since the outbreak of World War I. The Ottoman Empire had entered World War I in 1914, and coastal Muslims expressed their support for Turco-German forces precisely because some hoped the Ottomans would liberate them from British rule. Throughout the war colonial authorities feared Mombasans would repeat their revolts of the 1870s and 1880s. In fact, during World War I the British enjoined the Sultan of Zanzibar to write an open letter to Muslims of the protectorate, reminding them that "Great Britain is the greatest Mohammedan Power in the world, and her care for Moslems and our faith has never failed."[24] As this proclamation indicates, the British wanted to present themselves as not only accommodating but even embracing the faith as their own, at least on a symbolic level.

THE MANDHRY AND MNARA MOSQUES: THE
POLITICS OF "INDIGENOUS" ARCHITECTURE

Thus, while the rest of the city was increasingly submitted to colonial
control as a series of township ordinances authorized the Conservancy
Department to implement plans to reshape peoples' domestic space and
modes of living, religious monuments continued to represent the one
space off limits to the colonial government. In turn, Muslims expanded
the material landscape of Islam. Hundreds of new mosques were built
along the coast after the British took control from the Busaidi dynasty.[25]
For example, most of the fifty-one mosques standing in Zanzibar Stone
Town today were constructed during this period.[26] Indigenous polities,
such as Mombasa's Taifa, built and renovated over thirty mosques in and
around Mombasa Old Town during the early colonial period, between
the 1870s and 1920s.[27] Yet it was not the new mosques of the city but
the most ancient structures that anchored the most fraught struggles to
define and claim the city. Chief among these are the Mnara (alternately
known as the Tangana or Basheikh) and Mandhry mosques. The oldest
mosques still in use in the city, they became terrains of inclusion and
exclusion, anchoring intercommunal struggles to define what it means
to be Muslim and a citizen in east Africa. Although both mosques have
been in continuous use for hundreds of years, little is known or remembered about their early histories. The Mandhry mosque has a firm sixteenth-century foundation date, and the Mnara mosque was built even
earlier, perhaps as early as the fourteenth century. Although modest
in size, both are congregational (Friday) mosques. Prominent families
would compete to become the stewards of each mosque because great
social prestige, political power, and religious authority are associated with
overseeing the community's Friday mosques.[28]

It was particularly for the Sunni community that these were the most
important congregational mosques of Old Town until 1927. Each mosque
would alternate hosting Friday noon prayers on a weekly basis.[29] Mombasa's Taifa, who represented the Sunni majority, acquiesced to having them function as congregational mosques only after the Mandhry
mosque was converted from an Ibadi to a Sunni space sometime in the
seventeenth or eighteenth century.[30] It is important to note, however,

that some Taifa members today claim that the Mandhry was originally
a Taifa Sunni mosque, and that it was given to the Mandhry (who are
originally from the Arabian Peninsula) by the Taifa to encourage them
to settle in Mombasa.[31] Regardless of these issues of original ownership,
until around World War I the Mnara, because it was recognized as the
oldest Friday mosque in Old Town, had always played a more prominent
role in the local community. This changed as the mechanisms of colonial governance solidified in Mombasa. Through its Arab Administration, the British Protectorate government increasingly communicated
to "pure" Arabs its characterization of the "Swahili" community of Old
Town as inferior.

During this period the Mandhry mosque also became more important in both the local and international imagination.[32] Its minaret was
often commented on in travelogues, where it was described as "curious"
because it seemed somehow "odd," or different from minarets seen in the
Middle East.[33] The Mandhry mosque's visibility was also in part due to
its location on the waterfront. In contrast, the Mnara mosque is located
in the Mkanageni mtaa, or moiety, which lies in an area described by
the British and Omani Arabs as the native quarter of Old Town during
the colonial period. Accordingly, as it symbolized the city's "Arab" or
"oriental" charm and demarcated the city as an extension of the Arab
Sultanate of Zanzibar, it was the Mandhry mosque that became the most
photographed monument of Mombasa Old Town during the colonial
period. It figured prominently in countless travel accounts, postcards
(figure 2.5), guidebooks, and government publications. As visual frag-
ments of the colonial imaginary, such images present Mombasa as the
ideal colonial city, where the touristic picturesque and modern progress
meet in benign ways.[34]

From a local perspective the two mosques are not examples of "oriental" charm at all. Instead they work as active sites of religious embodi-
ment and make present the ancient roots of Islam in Mombasa; they
are twin monuments that constitute the making of local community
and religiosity. Both mosques are examples of an architectural style that
developed along the coast from circa 1100 onward. The basic plan of both
(figures 2.6 and 2.7) is typical of pre–nineteenth-century Swahili coast
mosque architecture and their general layout shares certain affinities

FIGURE 2.5. Undated colored postcard of Mandhry mosque on Mbarak
Hinawy Street (formerly Vasco Da Gama Street). Courtesy of the Friends
of Fort Jesus Collection, National Museums of Kenya.

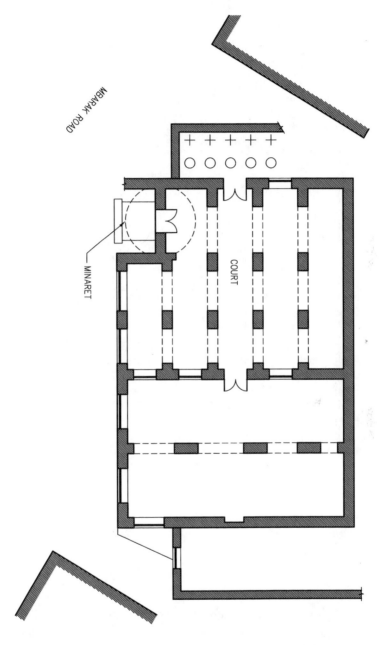

FIGURE 2.6. Ground plan of Mandhry mosque, before the 1988 and 1992 renovations (not to scale). Based on a plan provided by Mombasa Old Town Conservation Office. Drawing by Tait Johnson.

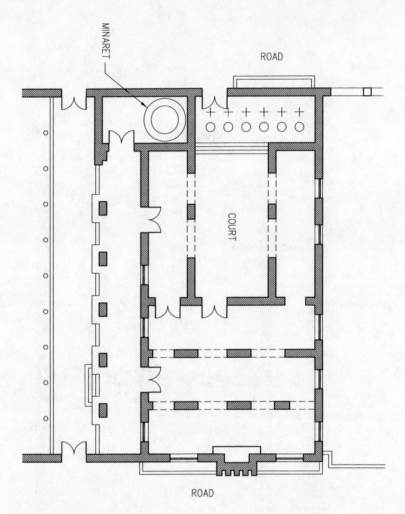

FIGURE 2.7. Ground plan of Mnara mosque (not to scale). Based
on a plan provided by Mombasa Old Town Conservation Office.
Drawing by Tait Johnson.

with mosques found throughout the western Indian Ocean.[35] Like the
stone mansions discussed in chapter 1, their exterior walls are unadorned
and dressed with a fine lime plaster. At the height of the midday sun,
the stark whiteness of their plastered surfaces to this day dominates the
streetscape.

FIGURE 2.8. Mandhry mosque interior, showing the transverse arcade in the front half of the prayer hall (parallel to the mihrab). Photograph by the author, 2013.

Both are simple rectangular flat-roofed structures, raised on a plinth and built of local coral stone and hardwood timber. Neither mosque is designed in a formal sense. Few exact right angles exist and the width and distance between various structural elements are not consistent throughout the space. In both cases the prayer hall is divided into a series of bays by stone piers that support a superstructure of arches. The Mandhry mosque prayer hall features rectangular piers, a single transverse arcade in the front half of the prayer hall parallel to the mihrab (figure 2.8) and four longitudinal arcades in the back.[36] The Mnara mosque is more elaborate than the Mandhry in terms of its structure and ornament.[37] It features octagonal columns instead of simple square piers (figure 2.9) and it has an external colonnade, whose arcades mirror the arcade system of the interior (figure 2.10).

Both mosques have relatively low ceilings and wide and thick ogee arches with a notched apex (plate 10), which are not true pointed arches because they lack radiating voussoirs. In both mosques the arcades are compact blocks that fill the entire upper half of the space with their solid

FIGURE 2.9. Mnara (also named Tangana or Basheikh) mosque interior, showing the transverse arcade in the front half of the prayer hall (parallel to the mihrab). Photograph by the author, 2013.

mass. They compartmentalize the space into a series of small bays, in which one's view and bodily experience is always dominated by the solid mass of the stone. Between the five prayer times, the main hall is often divided into semi-private spaces for a series of activities: students and their teachers gather for small study groups in corners, while others use the spaces between the arches for quiet moments of contemplation, or even to take a restorative nap. In effect it is an intimate and nurturing space.

Despite these mosques' connection to the wider Indian Ocean world, the colonial-era assumption that they are somehow foreign or Arab is untrue. For example, although the pointed and ogee arch is an iconic Indo-Islamic form, the Swahili coast ogee arch is a unique regional variation. It curves upward gradually, complimenting the horizontality of the

FIGURE 2.10. Mnara mosque, showing external colonnade, photographed
before 1895. Courtesy of the Gladys Beecher and Hollis Collection,
National Museums of Kenya.

flat roof, rather than emphasizing vertical movement, like typical South
Asian arches,[38] although whether the arch was meant to look like a South
Asian arch or not is hard to know. We cannot assess the original intentions of its first architect or patron. Perhaps one can discern a dialogue
with South Asian architectural languages, translated into a local idiom.
One's experience of these mosques, however, is certainly radically different from those found across the sea. This is in part because coral—
the coast's main building material—creates an aesthetic particular to
the Swahili coast. It would be best, then, to describe these mosques as
stylistic and spatial entanglements, where diverse forms and histories
interlock and overlap to create densely layered structures that cannot
be broken down into distinct stylistic parts.

THE PILLAR FORM AS A SACRED ENTANGLEMENT

The minarets of the Mandhry and Mnara mosques exemplify this phenomenon of architectural entanglement. The Swahili pillar minaret, the
typology to which both belong but whose history and origins remain a
mystery, is distinct from other Indian Ocean minarets in that these are
not soaring or slender towers, emphasizing a skyward verticality. Rather,
they taper gradually into conical towers whose squat form only rises
about forty feet upward.[39] Their heavy proportions and chalky surfaces
stress the density and weight of stone, endowing the minarets with an
organic plasticity. Though they are hollow, their exteriors are experienced as solid sculptural masses. Only four examples of this pillar-type
minaret exist in all of east Africa, and the Mombasan examples are also
the only pre–nineteenth-century examples.[40] Mombasa's pillar minarets
also appear to be the prototypes for the other two, one of which stands in
the Malindi quarter of Zanzibar Stone Town (figure 2.11) and the other
(figure 2.12) in Shela, a small town on Lamu Island.[41] The Shela mosque
and its minaret were built in the 1820s.[42] Its Zanzibar cousin was built or
rebuilt in 1834.[43] The Zanzibar and Shela minarets are also slightly different from Mombasa's because they are topped with octagonal pointed
spires and feature geometric decorative patterns and moldings.[44] The
archeologist Mark Horton has hypothesized that the pillar form was
transferred by a Mombasan sheikh to Lamu and Zanzibar, where its form
was slightly modified to conform to local tastes.[45] In contrast to the later
examples, the Mombasan pillar minarets retain an unadorned simplic-
ity; their rounded pillars have not been modified by such additions as
pointed caps or geometric patterns. This austere purity links the Mombasan pillar form to a much older and local tradition of marking space.

Mombasa Island is in fact home to another mysterious pillar, known
as the Mbaraki Pillar (figure 2.13), whose form and size is strikingly similar to the minarets of the Mandhry and Mnara mosques. In fact, if one
were to search for the formal origins of the pillar minaret typology, the
Mbaraki Pillar presents itself as its clearest source. Like the pillar minarets, it is a hollow and tapering conical tower, just under fifty feet tall, built
of cut coral stone. Originally its smooth and unadorned lime-plastered
surface was also only interrupted by small slit windows, allowing light

FIGURE 2.11. Pillar minaret of Malindi mosque, Zanzibar Town.
Photograph courtesy of Raymond Silverman, 2005.

FIGURE 2.12. Pillar minaret of Mnara mosque, Shela Town, Lamu Island.
Photograph by the author, 2014.

FIGURE 2.13. Mbaraki Pillar with Mohamed Mchulla leaning against its base. Kilindini area of Mombasa Island. Photograph by the author, 2014.

into its interior. It is also capped by a short rounded finial, although the Mbaraki finial is part of a pyramidal superstructure that creates a roofed opening, presumably for the smoke of burning incense to escape heavenward. Its foundation date has not been clearly determined. One archeologist suggested it was constructed around 1700, based on ceramic shards found in the general vicinity during a preliminary excavation of the site.[46] Most likely it is much older since it is labeled an "ancient pyramid" on a Portuguese map from 1728.[47] Although the French explorer Charles Guillain, who visited Mombasa in the 1840s, called the Mbaraki Pillar a minaret, this description most likely is a misunderstanding of the world *mnara,* which is used interchangeably to describe a minaret, pillar, and a tower in the Swahili language.[48] Besides the fact that it is always represented as a freestanding pillar on Portuguese maps, certain structural features would also suggest that it never functioned as the minaret of a mosque. For example, it features an external arched doorway that is less than five feet high, necessitating that one crawl or hunch to gain entry into its interior.

The original meaning and function of the Mbaraki Pillar continues to puzzle scholars; even local residents have no clear explanation for its form. Like the pillar minarets of Old Town, it is a singular monument; its form is unknown in the Middle East or other Indian Ocean littoral locales. In fact, it is the only pre–nineteenth-century hollow freestanding tower in east Africa. Today it stands at the fringes of the industrial area of Kilindini Harbor, the largest and most modernized deep-sea port of east Africa. The site includes a small concrete mosque built in the 1980s and the ruins of another mosque and several undated medieval tombs. While little is known about its history, it is clear that Mbaraki Pillar was part of larger religious complex, and that before the modern facilities of the harbor were constructed its monumental form could be seen from the sea by ships approaching the west side of Mombasa Island. It once stood at the outer edge of an urban center known as Kilindini Town, which was founded in the fifteenth or sixteenth century by the Thelatha Taifa. The entire town was abandoned when it was burned in 1837 by the first Busaidi Sultan of Zanzibar.

Yet Mbaraki Pillar remained a popular religious site long after the town was abandoned. By the mid–nineteenth century it still functioned as a famous *panga*, a shrine for communicating with spirit beings, known as *majini*. Different *waganga* (pl., a title given to both Muslim and non-Muslim religious specialists) use the monument to communicate with and honor majini. In the mid–nineteenth century the pillar's *mganga* (sg.), Mwinyi Kasimba, gained great renown. Muslims from all across the region, including Ibadi Arabs and Hadhrami Sufis, consulted him.[49] Today Mbaraki Pillar is only nominally "active." No single mganga is recognized as the authority over the site, and because such practices are not as acceptable as in the past, it no longer has a prominent role in the religious activities of the Island's Muslim community.[50]

The fact that Mbaraki Pillar functions as a panga means it exists at the interstices of both mainland African and coastal strategies for engaging spiritual forces. Although such practices are often considered "pagan" or "African," majini are Islamic spirits, whose existence is discussed in the most orthodox texts of the faith, the Qur'an and Hadiths. However, whether the practice of consulting or being possessed by them is truly "religious" or simply "superstition" is always a matter of debate across the Muslim world. But on the Swahili coast, Islamic and non-Islamic spirit worlds overlap and intertwine. Most waganga in the coastal regions are Muslims, yet they must be experts in diverse religious cosmologies in order to engage both Muslim and non-Muslim spirit beings. The spirit world is conceptualized as a community that mirrors human society, and upcountry pagan and coastal Muslim spirit beings are seen to coexist. As in everyday life, this division is porous; non-Muslim spirits are often perceived to act like Muslims and therefore prefer "Islamic" offerings, such as rosewater and incense. The homes of the spirits in the human realm are clearly categorized as either Islamic or non-Islamic, and by this scheme panga are the purest Islamic dwellings. Some see Mbaraki Pillar as a panga connected to a very devout and high-ranking Muslim jinni (sg.), known as a *rohani*.[51] These spirits are believed to come from the Middle East, islands, or the sea, the main domain of powerful Muslim spirits.

The Mbaraki Pillar's role as a panga therefore sheds some light on its original use and on the historical significance of the Mombasan pillar form more generally. Although Hamo Sassoon, the only scholar to study the pillar in any detail, argued that it was originally built to function as a panga, this is highly unlikely; panga are not constructed by humans, at least not in Mombasa and its immediate surroundings.[52] Rather, an extant architectural structure is transformed into a panga when a rohani chooses it as a site of communication. Majini can choose elements in the natural environment, such as an ancient baobab tree or a deep cave or fissures, but many very devout majini prefer monuments associated with Islamic civilization—that is, structures that are built of stone. Also, unlike other structures chosen by less powerful Muslim spirits, a rohani prefers ancient religious structures as his or her panga. For example, the ruins of ancient mosques or stone tombs of Muslim holy men serve as panga for powerful rohani.[53] Stone tombs can serve as panga because tombs are also loci of Islamic devotion and prayer.[54]

Other evidence also suggests Mbaraki Pillar was part of an ancient center of Islamic religious practice. Archeological data indicates that Mbaraki Pillar stands next to the ruins of a fifteenth-century mosque and several ancient, but undated, stone tombs.[55] One strand of oral history, first recorded in the 1840s, states that Mbaraki Pillar was originally built as the mausoleum for a Muslim holy man who founded one of the lineages within the Thelatha Taifa.[56]

Mbaraki Pillar does indeed share some formal similarities with local tomb architecture, although it is hollow and most other tombs are solid pillars. Swahili coast tombs, like the stone-built towns to which they belonged, were first and foremost landmarks built by the patrician elite to give material form to their Islamic piety and ancient pedigree as the stewards of the coast's Islamic civilization. Stone tombs are found in all the urban settlements of the Swahili coast. Most are small structures, but one particular type, known as the pillar tomb, developed sometime in the thirteenth or fourteenth century to serve as mausolea of high-ranking leaders or famous religious figures. They all feature tall cylindrical, square, or polygonal pillars built of coral rag and covered with fine plasterwork (figures 2.14 and 2.15). Many were once decorated with inlaid porcelain bowls from China, the primary ornament of Swahili religious architecture for centuries (see chapter 4). These remarkable structures have no precedent elsewhere in the Muslim world. Their unique form has led one scholar to describe them a as the "most innovative and individual feature of the coastal architecture" of east Africa.[57] Pillar tombs were built until about the eighteenth century, when the form suddenly disappears from local practice, yet the ruins of many dozens still dot the coastal headlands. The pillars are usually part of a larger tomb structure that includes an open rectangular enclosure, whose wall features low relief panels, rows of both blind and real niches, and geometric patterns consisting of diamonds, squares and chevrons (figure 2.15). In many instances these decorations seem to simulate the structural components of domestic architecture.[58] The pillar usually is attached to the north wall of the structure, the wall closest to Mecca, forming the head of the tomb (Muslim are buried in such a manner that their heads are oriented in the direction of Mecca). Such structures also featured niches for offerings made in honor of the person buried within. Similar to the Mbaraki Pillar, the façades of pillar tombs often included doorways that were slightly miniaturized or smaller than life-size. For example, the façade of the pillar tomb at Gedi has two small blind arched doorways (figure 2.14) and the Malindi pillar tomb features a miniature central arched doorway (figure 2.15).

Because such pillar tombs have never been built by Muslim societies outside of east Africa, scholars have explored their connection to non-Islamic African monuments.[59] Indeed, the pillar tombs share some formal and symbolic similarities with the ancient building traditions of northeast Africa. The most often cited comparisons are the stelae of Aksum, in present-day Ethiopia. Like the Swahili pillar tombs, they are grave markers that commemorate high-ranking members of the local community. Furthermore, like the exterior walls of Swahili tombs, the Aksum monoliths mimic the exterior detailing of domestic architecture; their surfaces are covered with low-relief carvings of blind doorways, windows, and niches.

On the Swahili coast the stone pillar, as a minaret, tomb, and panga, occupies a heightened interstitial zone in the sense that its form and meaning are likely connected to and overlap with several African and Indian Ocean worldviews. It works as a palimpsest, and as such it can mean many things to many people, depending on their cultural background and the historical moment in which the pillar's meaning is accessed. Thus, while I am not suggesting that the pillar minarets of Mombasa Old Town should be read as originating in mainland African building

FIGURE 2.14. Pillar tomb at the Gedi archeological site, Kenya.
Photograph by the author, 2013.

FIGURE 2.15. Pillar tomb at Malindi, Kenya. Photograph by the author, 2013.

traditions, we can understand their multivalent meanings more fully if we view them in relationship to their connections to non-Islamic African building histories.

THE PILLAR MARKS INDIGENOUS POWER AND PROPERTY

Monumental stone architecture also animates claims to space, converting land into political territory. On Mombasa Island stone pillars—whether in the form of minarets or tombs—functioned in precisely such a way. During the colonial period the role of the Mbaraki Pillar and the Mnara and Basheikh mosques in the actuation of political claims was increasingly emphasized. But on Mombasa Island the pillar form was not just a Swahili marker; rather I believe it was specifically associated with the Thelatha section of the Thenashara Taifa of Mombasa Island. It visualized their authority as a distinct polity on Mombasa Island.

During the colonial period, after a series of ordinances instituted British property law in east Africa, the Mbaraki Pillar was presented as marker of landownership. In 1908 the Land Titles Ordinance was passed, leading to the expropriation of vast acreages of Taifa land on Mombasa Island. Any land deemed wasteland—that is, land not having a legitimate owner—became Crown Land, or government property. Mombasa's Taifa argued that Mombasa Island was not in fact wasteland but was held in communal trust by their lineages. For the first time the British administration began to compile ethnographic information on Taifa families, in the hope of finding evidence in their traditions that they did not have a concept of landownership before the arrival of Omani Arabs. They also feared that the Taifa would become involved in politics. One confidential report warned that even though "14 years of British rule had rendered their influence nugatory," the Thenashara Taifa was suddenly "coming forward in connection with land questions, and if they are properly organized and combined should succeed in wresting almost all the coast-land from the Government."[60] Indeed, both the Tisa and Thelatha (the two polities constituting the Thenashara) demanded the return of large tracts of land on Mombasa Island by filing several suits in the high court of Mombasa. The Mbaraki Pillar played a central role in the Thelatha case, where it was presented as physical evidence that

local land-use practices constituted a form of both private and communal property law. The latha elders argued that the pillar marked one of the
boundaries of their land.

Even more strikingly, the existence of another stone pillar was still
remembered at this time. The Mbaraki Pillar was called the *mnara mdogo*
(small tower) of a pair. The other, the *mnara mkubwa* (large tower), once
stood on the headlands of the northwest side of Mombasa Island, about
two miles outside Old Town.[61] Today faint outlines of several stone
foundations are still visible where this large pillar tower once stood.
These were significant enough for the presiding judge to acknowledge
in 1912 that ruins of a large tower could still be seen. The latha elders argued that the land between these two towers was their property, which
in their estimation was more than half of the entire island.[62] This claim
was still in general circulation as late as 1933, when a British publication
described Mbaraki Pillar as "the tower always mentioned by the present
elders of the three tribes as being one of two towers which marked the
land in their exclusive possession."[63] In all the cases brought before the
high court about local land-claims, the presiding judge always ruled in
favor of the colonial government. In their legal briefs the judges deemed
the evidence presented as "interesting," but not admissible as proof that
such "customs" ever carried "the force of law."[64] Viewing Taifa property
practices as lacking in judicial authority was one of the most effective
strategies of the colonial government to delegitimize the entire local
land-tenure system. This strategy was used by the colonial administration in many African colonies or protectorates. On the Swahili coast,
colonial lawyers and judges also argued that since coastal peoples claim
to be Muslims, only Islamic law, not "native" law or customs, should
be recognized. For example, one judge presiding over a Swahili land-
claims case argued that even if a Swahili custom could be interpreted
as evidence of communal landownership, "such a custom violated the
principles of the Sheriah [Islamic law]" and therefore "it would not be
binding in a Mohamedan Court."[65] As described previously, the implementation of Middle Eastern Islamic law by the British colonial government and the increased authority of Arab scholars who followed Middle
Eastern Islamic judicial texts meant that local interpretations of Islamic
law were increasingly under attack. Those practices deemed not properly

orthodox because they shared similarities with Mijikenda law were also no longer recognized as applicable in Mombasa. In response, Taifa elders and activists also began to deemphasize those aspects of their culture that could be seen as heterodox, or somehow as an African custom or tradition, as this would further erode their rights.

Precisely because the Mbaraki Pillar was a liminal space, existing at the edge of Islamic and non-Islamic practice, its prominence began to wane; today few people living in Old Town would readily admit visiting it for religious purposes. The site was increasingly marginalized as a monument of Swahili coast social and religious culture. Strikingly, most people no longer remember the oral histories associated with it, nor do they recall the significant role of the mnara mkubwa and mnara mdogo in the court cases of the 1910s. Old Town residents now see Mbaraki Pillar as a heterodox religious site, where Muslims who are not as sophisticated as townspeople go to engage in the spirit world, although, when pressed, they too acknowledge that Old Town residents—even "Arabs"—visit the Mbaraki Pillar from time to time. Its permanent iconicity has resisted an unencumbered erasure, and a family crisis or ill health will still draw people to visit the site.

From the 1860s onward those aspects of Swahili coast culture linked to other centers of power across the island slowly weakened. While in the past important urban settlements were dispersed across the island, once Mombasa was annexed into the Busaidi Sultanate of Zanzibar, the stone waterfront of what is now Old Town became the main center of religiosity as well. For example, because Kilindini Town was destroyed in 1837, its entire Thelatha Swahili population moved to Old Town. Their resettlement strengthened the Thelatha neighborhoods already established there, and as a result the community experienced a brief cultural efflorescence.[66] By this time Mnara mosque was already seen as belonging to the Tangana (a lineage within the Thelatha Federation); under the tutelage of their religious scholars many Omani Arabs converted from Ibadism to Sunni Shafi'ism.[67] Thus, in contrast to the general view that all things Arab became more valued during the Busaidi Sultanate years, evidence suggests that for about half a century Swahili coast cultural forms rose to prominence and became newly relevant in Mombasa Old Town.[68] Also, in the realms of popular culture—such as wedding celebrations, public festivals, devotional ceremonies, and dance competitions—not only did categories such as "Arab" and "Swahili" fuse, but local traditions often dominated.[69] According to Randall Pouwel, Omani practices only gradually influenced Swahili ideas about what constitutes civilization: "It was some time after the 1860s and 1870s then that 'civilization' was characterized less and less by *uungwana* and its implications concerning parochial concepts of Islam, and was replaced gradually by the word *ustaarabu*—that is, to be like an Arab."[70]

MOSQUES AS SITES OF INTERETHNIC RIVALRY

Mosques, and sacred architecture more generally, entered a new phase as an architecture of power with the rise of ustaarabu by the end of the nineteenth century, when questions of race and ethnicity increasingly mattered. Under the British administration, Arabs became the state-sponsored stewards of Islam. During this time Mnara and Mandhry mosques also played an increasingly important role in contestations over power and authority in Old Town.

By this time Arabs also wielded greater political power than the Taifa, and the British administration no longer directly dealt with "Swahilis," but instead saw the Arab Administration as the representatives of all Sunni Muslims. Sir Ali bin Salim, the *liwali* (Muslim governor) of Mombasa from 1921 to 1931, is blamed to this day by Taifa members for their marginalization during this time. He excluded them from participating in the first election for an "Arab" seat on Mombasa's legislative council, since according to Sir Ali, they were not "Arabs," but "natives."[71] This caused a serious rift in Old Town Mombasa. The leader of the Thelatha Taifa, Ahmed Matano, denounced the Arabs of Old Town during Friday prayers at the Basheikh (formerly Tangana) mosque in response. He accused them of betraying their Muslim brothers and sisters for political and financial gain and called upon all wamiji to boycott Friday prayers at the Mandhry mosque. As noted earlier, until then the Mandhry and Basheikh mosques shared the role of serving as the Friday mosques of Old Town.[72] Because it was in a sense still an unquestionably "Swahili" monument, Ahmed Matano used the Basheikh mosque as a platform of protest even though the Tangana no longer had the wealth to pay for its upkeep. Some elders also remember that the main aim of Ahmed Matano's protest was to reassert wamiji rights to pray in the mosques as the equals of Arabs. According to Mwalimu Mohammad Matano, some Mandhry and Mazrui Arabs had begun to demand that a section of the Mandhry mosque should be reserved for just them during Friday noon prayers, since as Arabs they were "superior" to other wamiji in the racial hierarchy of colonial Mombasa.[73] Wamiji refused to accept that communal prayer halls should be segregated according to ethnicity and no longer attended the Mandhry mosque. This meant that the Sunni community of Old Town was for a time divided into Africans versus Arabs. This shattered the ideal that all Muslims should be united during Friday noon prayers.

The ideal of being a single Muslim community was damaged by racialization of these spaces of communal prayer, affecting people's memories and actions to this day, although, since becoming part of the nation-state of Kenya, Mombasans no longer emphasize these divisions. Wamiji also like to point out that for centuries there were no "real" Arabs living in Old Town. As Mwalimu Matano explained:

> They [the Thelatha] told the Mazrui and Mandhry they are no longer pure Arabs, that they are Swahili too, that they were our guests in Mombasa and that they had forgotten that. My father used to tell me these feelings would come in and out and before independence and each group would really only go to its own mosque. They used to retaliate against each other; there was always a clash. It is not there now because what they fear of the government is what we fear. We are united now. But all this is the core life of Old Town. Young men don't understand this. Now they are joking, but it is still there, it is like a stigma. This is the big secret still.[74]

Today wamiji also prefer to see the architecture of both mosques as an undeniable testament of the non-Arab heritage of Mombasa. Matano argued that the Mandhry mosque was never really an Arab structure because its form mirrors the Tangana mosque and because it was "given" to the Mandhry by the local community. He observed that "the beginning of that mosque was the alliance between the Mandhry and Wakilindini [a Thelatha lineage]. The Tangana and Mandhry mosques have a great similarity. They have the same architecture."[75] Interestingly, today some locals see the pillar form as an ancient Persian structure, thereby validating their authority over these mosques since they also claim Shi-razi (Persian) ancestry.[76] The fact that pillar minarets are interpreted as Persian—a non-Arab architectural style—allows wamiji to create an alternate material geography for their Islamic heritage. As discussed in the previous chapter, Shirazi ancestry works to distance locals from Arab newcomers. Persians are not viewed as Arabs, and claiming connections to Persia allows the Taifa to establish a sense of closeness to ancient and famous centers of Islamic civilization that have had no recent political impact on the region. Taifa elders also emphasize that Shirazi merchants arrived "long, long ago" and that they intermarried with locals in the distant past. Seen within the context of the nativist politics of the nation-state of Kenya, this emphasis on Shirazi origins is also an attempt to create convincing indigenous narratives about Swahili heritage without divorcing it from the ideals of being a maritime-centered culture.

The pillar minarets of the Mandhry and Mnara mosques, like the Mbaraki Pillar, manifested wamiji strategies of place-making. While the conical pillar form might be dismissed as some peculiar or little under-stood fragment of the past, the three pillars still standing on Mombasa Island became pivotal sites for Taifa political struggles. As part of Mom-basa's sacred geography, the mnara form helped reshape people's notions of self and community during the revolutionary changes of the colonial period. Activated by a set of new demands and needs, it became a key site of collective agency.

THREE

Architecture Out of Place

The Politics of Style in Zanzibar

The third Busaidi sultan of Zanzibar, Seyyid Barghash (r. 1870–1888), created vistas and monuments of modern vision that radically transformed the way Zanzibar Stone Town's built environment was experienced. His reign was an era of unprecedented transcontinental competition, when would-be colonizers, financial speculators, adventurers, and merchants from all over the world converged on Zanzibar City. Zanzibar became a key node in the global market, selling cloves (produced by enslaved plantation workers) and ivory to the industrializing North and supplying African consumers with North American, South Asian, and European commodities. The Busaidi family and their business partners amassed huge fortunes as a result, and Barghash spent much of his considerable wealth building both public and private monuments; these defined the cityscape of Zanzibar from afar, eventually becoming the landmarks of the city and island.

While in many ways Barghash sought to present a fashionably "new" city to the world, his structures were a complex synthesis of old and new sign systems. This was especially the case with Beit al Ajaib, the House of Wonders (plate 11), his most ambitious architectural monument, and the focus of much of this chapter. As we shall see, the structure served not only to visualize his ambition to assert his control over the city in the face of European colonizing agendas, but also to subvert local histories and indigenous claims to the city. Further, what will become clear is that the House of Wonders was not only about geopolitical power; it was also an expression of Barghash's dream to make Zanzibar a center of artistic and technological innovation. The verandahs of the House of Wonders acted as a grand stage for new musical performances, and they framed his vision of Zanzibar as a perfect *picture* of modernity. The House of Wonders therefore represents a pivotal moment in the architectural history of the coast, when old and new systems of signification converged and overlapped to produce a spectacle of radical modernity.

OLD ALLIANCES AND NEW STATES: THE MAKING OF MODERN ZANZIBAR

Before Barghash came to power, Zanzibar was not the capital of a state or empire. Rather, it was a key node in a web of interconnected port cities. Political power was measured in terms of how many subordinate clients and partners one was able to amass, not in terms of territorial holdings. The relationship between the first two Busaidi sultans and Zanzibar's indigenous polities, the Tumbatu and Hadimu, was also not one of colonizer versus colonized.[1] In the first half of the nineteenth century locals saw the Busaidi sultans as powerful merchant princes whose patronage would benefit their island.[2] In fact, many locals today continue to emphasize that indigenous Zanzibaris had invited Seyyid Said, the first Busaidi sultan, to their island.[3] Cultivating a patron-client relationship with powerful families was a strategy used by many Swahili coast towns since at least the fifteenth century. It created a complex network of partnerships that connected a series of polities across the African continent and the Indian Ocean world.

In contrast, Barghash began to claim specific territories, delimiting the sultanate in spatial terms and forcing those living in his "state" to accept his authority in all matters. He began to think in terms of modern state-building and reduced the Hadimu and Tumbatu to his colonized subjects. Like the British in their territories, Barghash delegitimized local ways of managing land and people and set up new judicial and political institutions. Tumbatu and Hadimu institutions were increasingly presented as charming native customs, not as legitimate forms of governance.[4]

Barghash also deployed strategies of racial rule, transmuting western opinions that the Omani landowning elite represented the "ruling race" of the Swahili coast.[5] He justified his increasingly authoritarian policies by arguing that "blacks" were incapable of governing themselves. As Jonathon Glassman has recently argued, in Omani-ruled Zanzibar "race-making was connected to state-building"[6]—although when he deployed the racialized rhetoric of western colonialism Barghash was treading on dangerous ground: he himself was of "mixed race" in the eyes of Europeans, as his mother was a *suria* (high-ranking concubine) from present-day Ethiopia.[7]

Once he became sultan, many Zanzibaris not connected to Barghash's administration hated him. John Kirk, Britain's political agent and consul in Zanzibar, observed that "[Barghash's] unpardonable fault in the eyes of his subjects is his want of liberality to the people of the Coast and Town."[8] The sultan responded to his unpopularity by imprisoning many whom he saw as a threat to his authority. Especially prominent religious leaders with Sufi leanings were arrested and exiled from Zanzibar.[9] Because its doctrines fundamentally subverted established social hierarchies, Sufism was a threat to his sultanate. During his lifetime Zanzibaris also viewed Barghash as a mercurial man, whose unbridled ambition led him to transgress against accepted norms. For example, Zanzibaris suggested that Barghash used supernatural forces—the "black arts," in the words of a British report—to create his wealth.[10]

Barghash also isolated himself from his relatives ruling Oman and from other politically ambitious Omani Arabs living in Zanzibar. Although they helped him become sultan, by 1871 he wanted to suppress the Mutawa, a reform movement led by Omanis living in Muscat and Zanzibar who were openly hostile to the growing power of the British in the Indian Ocean and who wanted to reunite Oman and Zanzibar into a single Ibadi imamate.[11] Barghash even refused to pay the traditional annual subsidy to Muscat, which Zanzibar had always presented as a sign of allegiance. Instead he created a new network of advisors and business partners, drawing upon business and social connections developed in Bombay when he had been exiled there for several years after his father's death. In Bombay he had experienced a very different way of life than other Omani Arabs. Although his father had already begun to cultivate South Asian connections, Barghash cemented Zanzibar's dependence on the credit and monetary markets of Bombay. Much to the consternation of the British and other Omanis, Ismaili South Asians became Barghash's most trusted business managers and personal advisors. For example, his secretary was Pira Dewji (also spelled Dautji), and he leased the management of the customs house to Tharia Topan and Ijerman Sudji, two Ismaili financiers.[12] Also, South Asians managed the construction of the House of Wonders.[13]

But in terms of state policy, Barghash increasingly depended on the British.[14] Under British pressure, in 1873 Barghash abolished the slave trade, which was the basis of much Omani wealth since the mid-eighteenth century (the institution of slavery was abolished in 1897). The powerful merchants and landowners of Zanzibar (which included "Arabs" and "Swahilis") participated in the enslavement and sale of central Africans all along the Swahili coast and across the Indian Ocean in response to the growth of the plantation economy in the region. In fact, a few old Swahili patrician families, who had lost so much of their political independence, still managed to increase their wealth by organizing and leading slaving (and ivory) caravans during Barghash's reign. By abolishing the slave trade Barghash created a serious rift between himself and Zanzibar's wealthy. Friedrich Gerhard Rohlfs, the German consul general in Zanzibar, noted that by 1885 Barghash was seen as a "puppet of the English" by locals.[15] By 1890 Zanzibar was an official British protectorate.

Architecture as Empire

Barghash's desire to maintain some semblance of independence and authority led him to focus on the spatial and visual politics of place-making from 1873 onward. He increasingly devoted his energies to the spectacle of architecture, fashion, and public ceremony—that is, the material realm of sensory experience. The Zanzibar of Barghash's time also represents a city at the edge of a new age, the pivotal moment prior to the making of a colonial city, before the British actively sought to control all aspects of the urban and social fabric of the city. Although it often assumed that the city was always racially divided, scholars like

Abdul Sheriff and William Bissell have demonstrated that before the
establishment of the British Protectorate, Zanzibar Stone Town was a
truly heterogeneous city, one occupied not only by Arabs, Europeans,
and well-to-do South Asians, but by Swahilis and even recently arrived
mainland Africans. Neither was it a purely "stone" town. Rather, its built
environment was a mixed space, where humble wattle and daub structures far outnumbered the austere façades of stone merchant houses or
other monumental forms. Beyond key structures along the waterfront,
most of the urban landscape looked like any other Swahili coast city.[16]
Furthermore, in Barghash's Stone Town Europeans could not distance
themselves from the "natives," as was the practice during the high colonial period, because they did not control the land or its built environment. Barghash understood the spatial politics of colonial control,
blocking Europeans from obtaining private property or owning buildings in Zanzibar Stone Town, especially during the early years of his
reign.[17] With the exception of a few merchant firms, notably one from
Hamburg that had established an office on Zanzibar Island already in the
1850s, Europeans, especially if they lived in Zanzibar as representatives
of their governments, depended on the sultan for housing.[18]

Barghash was first and foremost invested in the palatial, building five
ostentatious mansions at various sites across the island. Four of these
new palaces functioned primarily as country retreats. Such structures
followed local precedent, since the landowning elite of the Swahili coast
and other port cultures in wider Indian Ocean maintained country mansions as symbols of their culturedness. Here families would retire to
recover from the demands and stress of urban life and to mark important
family celebrations. Maintaining country houses, even if they are much
humbler than in the past, is still seen as an important aspect of Swahili
heritage today. Yet Barghash's palaces represented an important innovation. He introduced the concept of "presentation" architecture, where
much if not all of the structure was dedicated to orchestrating a public
experience, especially for visitors from abroad. While the baraza of traditional merchant mansions was also a public and ceremonial space,
Barghash commissioned structures that primarily functioned as reception spaces.

FIGURE 3.1. Chukwani Palace, built in 1870s as a country retreat for the Sultan's family and for hosting foreign guests. Photograph courtesy of the Zanzibar National Archives.

His first presentation palace was Chukwani (figure 3.1), built in 1870 on a promontory overlooking the sea a few miles outside of town, which also functioned as a navigation marker for overseas ships arriving in Zanzibar from Bagamoyo, a port city to the south.[19] Chukwani was a two-story square building with balconies, large French doors, corbelled projections, piers, and columns on all four sides. These elements were directly imported from overseas; they created as much outward-oriented space as possible, accommodating European preferences for open ground plans and open spaces in warmer climes. It was not a house appropriate for Muslim women who observed purdah. Barghash's family did on occasion visit Chukwani, but he regularly invited Europeans and North Americans to use the palace as a vacation resort. Barghash himself was not present when Europeans resided at Chukwani, but Pira Dewji, his most trusted advisor, oversaw and managed these visits. He arranged day trips and orchestrated elaborate western-style dinners, lunches, and breakfasts on the balconies of the second floor. The presentation of these meals was an elaborate ceremony lasting several hours, during which an entire army of Goan servants presented visitors up to fifty different courses, according to one account. The interior of Chukwani was also decorated with European visitors in mind; here tables and chairs were arranged for utilitarian use, not simply displayed as symbolic objects, as was the local practice (described in the next chapter). Parisian chandeliers and Viennese mirrors filled both the first and second floor rooms. While such glasswork was in high demand for all domestic interiors on Zanzibar, the interior decorative program of Chukwani also mirrored European practices: it featured oleographs (chromolithographs printed on cloth) to create a space of Victorian domesticity. Much to the amazement of European visitors, the palace housed Russian-style carousels, complete with automatophones (self-playing musical instruments) powered by steam locomotives, which guests were free to use during their stay.[20]

Barghash's most ambitious presentation palace was the House of Wonders (figure 3.2). When completed in 1883, its structure was fantastically out of scale from the rest of the city. It still dominates the waterfront today and remains the largest structure on Zanzibar Island. It was part of Barghash's larger urban planning program for Stone Town, which included building roads, a railroad, and water systems and providing street lighting throughout the city.[21] The core of the building consists of a massive three-story square block. The exterior is encased by wide and high galleries supported by prefabricated cast-iron columns imported from Europe. Additionally, a corrugated pavilion, supported by another miniature colonnade, covered the flat roof of the building. This pavilion functioned as a secluded and covered space on top of the roof.

During the twentieth century, when it was used as a government building until 1963, the House of Wonders was increasingly associated with British colonialism.[22] Yet, one of the reasons Barghash built it was to counter British authority on the island, presenting his government as equally "global" as that of the Europeans. As historian Jeremy Prestholdt has noted, the House of Wonders clearly "domesticated new global objects in service of the state" and signified "a self-consciousness about Zanzibar's relation to the rest of the world."[23] These global ambitions

FIGURE 3.2. View of the House of Wonders from the sea. Completed in the 1880s, it was the largest building on Zanzibar Island. The free-standing clock tower at the left of the photograph was built by Seyyid Said in the 1830s. Photograph courtesy of the Zanzibar National Archives.

meant that Barghash's palace figured prominently international assessments of Zanzibar. Yet in western sources Barghash was repeatedly ridiculed for intermixing the visual culture of Europe, Africa, and Asia in his buildings.[24] He was especially derided for coveting European, South Asian, and American styles for the design of his private and public spaces; after accusations of not properly suppressing the slave trade, the most common charge leveled against Barghash was that he tastelessly mimicked European ways of living, with the House of Wonders held as the greatest transgression in this regard. Its sheer scale completely dwarfed the rest of the built environment of the city, and its ornamentation dramatically transformed the character of the city. Its façade was particularly, and repeatedly, ridiculed for showcasing the sultan's "execrable taste" through its pastiche of different "styles."[25] An American visitor at the turn of the twentieth century found it disappointing and inauthentic, writing that "the new palace is of somewhat too modern architecture and not nearly as dignified as the massive white walls of the native houses which surround it."[26] Other observations focused on its interior, describing it as being "furnished with all the bad taste that invariably prevails when the Oriental rejects his own treasures for the produce of the West."[27] Barghash's appropriation of international forms was disturbing to outside observers clearly because, in their view, European design elements did not belong to east Africa or "the Orient."

Through his building and infrastructure projects Barghash also attempted to negotiate the commercial and political rivalries between Germany and Britain to his own advantage. Before the Anglo-German Agreement of 1890, which effectively made Zanzibar a British territory, Zanzibar along with its coastal dominions was a contested site, and Germany was keen to thwart British suzerainty in the area. Germany supported rebellions against the British and claimed dominion over parts of the coast, such as the sultanate of Witu. While it was true that Barghash wholly depended on British military power to stabilize his regime, he also actively encouraged German interests in Zanzibar until at least 1886. He patronized German merchant houses and preferred working with Germans to modernize the infrastructure of his town. For example, although today Zanzibar's Department of Archives, Museums, and Antiquities (which manages the House of Wonders as a public museum) credits a British naval officer as being the architect of the House of Wonders, accounts from the period clearly document that Barghash had hired a "German adventurer" to design it (although South Asian masons planned and oversaw the construction).[28] When he acquired six steamships in 1883 to compete with the British India Navigation Company, he manned them with German captains and engineers.[29] His electricians were also German. During Barghash's reign German merchant houses also virtually monopolized the importation of European commodities to Zanzibar, much to the frustration of the British.[30] The perceived bias in favor of Germans immensely annoyed the British, who also mocked the House of Wonders as an example of Barghash's misguided reliance on "scoundrel" Germans. One British observer derisively noted that the German who built the House of Wonders "made a pretty penny out of it, notwithstanding that he had to make two tries before he could get the pile to stand up."[31]

LOCAL PRECEDENTS: ARCHITECTURES
OF INDIAN OCEAN MERCANTILISM

The House of Wonders was not only an expression of the politics of empire unfolding on the coast of east Africa; it was also closely related to
Barghash's family history on Zanzibar Island. One reason Barghash built
it was to fulfill an ambition his father had held: to transform the old
port of Zanzibar into a center of Indian Ocean mercantilism. In fact,
Seyyid Said's palaces and administrative buildings on Zanzibar's main
waterfront all looked like typical coastal merchant houses, not like the
traditional imperial palaces of Oman. Richard Burton, who visited Zanzibar in 1856, documented that Seyyid Said had begun construction on
an audience hall on the waterfront modeled on the Dutch factory, or
trading station, at Bandar Abbas, a Persian Gulf port city on the coast
of present-day Iran. This factory was a building on the waterfront that
likely featured a verandah. It was the main station of Dutch East India
Company (VOC) mercantile operations in the Indian Ocean until the
second half of the eighteenth century, when Oman took control of the
port.[32] By modeling his new palace on Zanzibar's waterfront on a VOC
administrative building and not on established Omani royal architecture, Said was reprising the material heritage of one of the most successful Indian Ocean maritime commercial institutions. At the height
of its power in the eighteenth century, the VOC virtually monopolized
the trade between Surat, the main port of the western Indian Ocean, the
Arabian Peninsula, and Indonesia. Oman itself had largely depended
on the VOC for its imports. Many of Said's efforts, including the establishment of a plantation economy driven by slavery on Zanzibar Island,
indicated that he was attempting to reproduce the commercial tactics
of European living in the Indian Ocean area.

However, Said never finished his "Dutch factory" palace in Zanzibar.
By the time Burton arrived, its remains stood as a dramatic "haunted"
ruin on the waterfront. It was at near completion and already in use when
it suffered a dramatic collapse, likely sometime in the 1840s. A huge chandelier and large structural walls crushed seventy masons. Zanzibaris
viewed the abandoned structure as evidence of a curse that troubled
the legacy and soul of Seyyid Said.[33] By building the House of Wonders

FIGURE 3.3. Troops of the Busaidi Sultante parading in front of Beit al Hukum, circa 1860s. It was built by Sultan Said in the 1840s and served as his official center of government. Photograph courtesy of the Humphrey Winterton Collection of East African Photographs at Northwestern University Library.

Barghash erased the material remains of Sultan Said's curse and failure. In fact, its exterior design likely paid homage to the original ornamentation of Said's failed palace. While we have no documentation of this structure, since its ruins were razed and likely incorporated into the structure of the present House of Wonders, we can surmise that it was similar in form to the one administrative palace Seyyid Said did complete on the waterfront of Zanzibar. Called the Beit al Hukum (figure 3.3), this three-story structure was completely destroyed in 1896, when the British Navy bombarded the waterfront; but photographs and written records indicate that it foreshadowed the form of the House of Wonders in significant ways. It too featured exterior balconies on all floors, albeit only on the main façade of the building, not on all four sides.

Seyyid Said, or a member of his court, first introduced the typology of the exterior colonnade to Zanzibar Island. Portico-like open spaces have long been part of the architectural vocabulary of east Africa, but before the arrival of Busaidi Arabs such exterior-oriented spaces were either diminutive alcoves (such as those seen in Lamu), or simple porches. For example, the more humble *nyumba ya makuti,* today called the Swahili house, often features a porch on the main façade (see figure 0.4). Yet the balconies of the Beit al Hukum, with their intricate balustrades and stained-glass ornamentation, were more akin to verandahs seen in other littoral regions of the Indian Ocean.

Barghash expanded upon his father's vision by elaborating on Seyyid Said's interest in the material culture of trading houses. In the process, Barghash created a regional variant of a merchant structure found throughout the Indian Ocean world. The long and thin colonnades of the House of Wonders may look like a strange British-Raj structure, but it represents a dialogue with much older architectural styles circulating in the Indian Ocean realm.

THE VERANDAH AS A SPECTACLE OF TRADE

In the House of Wonders the verandah form was transformed into a lavish decorative program that unified the façades of the entire structure. The sheer size of its cast-iron structural and ornamental elements had never been seen on the Swahili coast before. The high compression strength of cast iron allowed its builders to use thin and widely spaced columns, creating unusually wide and deep exterior verandahs. Regularly spaced electric light fixtures, green shuttered windows, floriate balustrades, and ornamental trim along the eaves created a staccato rhythm of vertical forms along the horizontal expanse of the encircling balconies. To western viewers the scale and proportions of the exterior ornament seemed out of sync with the solid mass of the building itself. The seemingly unbalanced relationship between surface and ornament prompted one nineteenth-century visitor to describe the House of Wonders as "a remarkably ugly edifice."[34] For European visitors, the House of Wonder's verandah was always somehow "off." In fact, when the British rebuilt the mansion after the 1896 bombardment of the waterfront, they added a clock tower to the main façade to give it a focal point, thereby deemphasizing the horizontal span and cavernous depth of the verandahs.

With the rise of North Atlantic imperial power all across the globe, verandah structures were increasingly seen as signs of western power, and most colonial buildings featured grand colonnades. Most significantly, by the late nineteenth century Europeans themselves viewed such structures as their heritage, providing a space of Victorian instrumentality and hygiene in the "troubling" tropics of the colonies. From a western perspective it functioned as a buffer zone between colonizer and colonized. Even today the verandah is viewed as the most iconic emblem of the spatial technologies of colonial governmentality.[35] It was the site where the will for panoptic control was transformed into a real platform of surveillance, a tableau that allowed one safe distance from the perceived disorder and chaos of the "native" city.

Yet the verandah was not originally a western architectural form; it was rather a spatial fragment of various precolonial maritime cultures. Its association with European colonial power in fact represents a kind of amnesia, an erasure of its non-European meanings and spatial practices. The form and icon of the verandahed trading post had existed for several hundred years in the western Indian Ocean, especially along the west coast of present-day India and the ports of the Red Sea. Portuguese merchants, and later the British and Dutch East India Companies, also used the Indian Ocean verandah form beginning in the seventeenth century. The original prototype for the verandah form is, in fact, impossible to trace to one place. It is more correct to think of it as a composite of forms, the result of the oceanic circulation of architectural typologies and intercultural contact between many littoral societies. The word *verandah* is said to derive from a Hindi word that in turn has its origins in Portuguese, and it originally described the deep porches and balconies of bungalows (a composite Luso-Asian type of building).[36] It was also a defining feature of the merchant architecture of present-day Gambia, where Portuguese and west African peoples lived together and founded a unique mercantile society in the sixteenth century.[37] Thus the verandah represents one of the most significant moments of oceanic reinvention, when Portuguese, South Asian, and African coastal residents created a composite littoral built environment.

In all of these diverse contexts the verandah functioned as a contact zone and site of commercial exchange for merchants who competed and depended on each other in the mercurial world of oceanic trading networks. The grand verandah of the House of Wonders is also part of this

FIGURE 3.4. British companies advertised their mass-produced cast-iron architectural ornaments in the *Zanzibar Gazette* from the 1870s onwards. Orders would be transmitted via telegrams, and steamships would deliver them to Zanzibar Island within one or two months.

long history of back and forth circulation between different littoral societies. Yet its materials and production derived from the increasingly planetary reach of the west's commodity culture. No matter the form's long presence in the Indian Ocean world, the structural and ornamental elements of the House of Wonder's verandah were all mass-produced and imported from Europe. Prefabricated for easy on-site assembly, such industrially manufactured elements were shipped across the globe from European industrial foundries throughout the late nineteenth century. Although no documentation has been found about which company fulfilled the order for the House of Wonders, a Scottish company called Saracen Foundry was especially successful in selling their products in the Middle East and Africa and the company's advertisements (figure 3.4) appeared regularly in the *Zanzibar Gazette* and *Mombasa Times.*[38]

The House of Wonders verandahs (figure 3.5) featured floriated trel-
lises on its railings and thin fluted Corinthian pillars, design elements
typical of the revival styles that became fashionable in Europe and the rest
of the world during this period. Like other modern structures meant to
embody the new aesthetic of global circulation and capitalist expansion,
the House of Wonders exhibited a kind of playful historicism, its style a
pastiche of various cultures and time periods. Patrons all over the globe
could simply order an assemblage of structural and decorative elements
in a range of styles, with names such as Greek Revival, Gothic Pharaonic,
Saracenic, and Neo-Mamluk. The pastiche-style of mass-produced ornament so favored by Barghash in his palaces was partly informed by the
emerging tastes of Victorian Europe, but his most extensive exposure
to this style was his two-year residency in Bombay before he came to
power and his visits to other port cities.[39] During his tour of Europe and
the Middle East in 1875, the facilities of various ports were the first vistas
Barghash would have gazed upon as he alighted at each new destination. For example, Khedive Ismail, with whom Barghash met, favored
"Neo-Mamluk" mass-produced ornamentation for his reconstruction
of the Mediterranean port city of Port Said. This imaginative style, ex-
emplified by the structure in figure 3.6, featured alternating horizontal
bands of light and dark stone and horseshoe arches as a kind of homage to grandeur of Egypt's imperial past. Like many of the commercial
structures of Port Said, the building was encased by a cast-iron verandah
on all four sides. The neo-Mamluk style was developed by German and
Austrian architects and marketed as the most historically appropriate
style for Egypt, since it was based on "local" Islamic forms. The exteriors
of Barghash's palace did not feature clearly identifiable "Neo-Mamluk"
ornamentation, but the House of Wonders' exterior colonnades were
strikingly similar to those of the commercial facilities of Port Said.

ARCHITECTURE AS MODERN THEATRE
AND PICTURE-MAKING

Barghash was also likely inspired by Khedive Ismail's ambitious transformation of Cairo into a center of the arts. The khedive had modeled
his lavish revitalization of Cairo on Haussmann's plan for Paris. He built

FIGURE 3.5. View of the verandah of the House of Wonders, featuring Greek Revival cast-iron columns and floriated railings. Such ornamental ironwork was mass-produced in England and shipped all over the British Empire. Photograph by the author, 2005.

FIGURE 3.6. Neo-Mamluk building on the waterfront of Port Said (Egypt),
circa 1890s. Photograph courtesy of the Humphrey Winterton Collection of
East African Photographs at Northwestern University Library.

European-style palaces (with neo-Mamluk ornament) and actively patronized the arts, building theatres, and an opera house. All of his public
buildings functioned as stages for the orchestration of elaborate state ceremonies and musical events. After his 1875 visit to Egypt, Barghash also
began to patronize the performing arts; to this day he is credited with
creating the musical genre known as *taraab*. Taraab is now celebrated as a
traditional Swahili musical form, but it is a "modern" composite in which
Swahili poetry and lyrics are accompanied by nineteenth-century Egyptian orchestral instrumentation.[40] Barghash's orchestras performed in
and in front of the House of Wonders as part of his lavish transformation
of Zanzibar's waterfront. The palace used taraab to reproduce "Arab"
modernity on the coast and to emphasize the difference between Omani
courtly culture and the performance cultures of the "African" colonized
population of the Swahili coast. Under Barghash's patronage Zanzibari

scholars and musicians also went to Cairo for further studies, and a Syrian merchant acted as his permanent representative and agent in Cairo. Barghash cultivated a cultural connection with Cairo to the extent that even Egyptian fashions became popular in Zanzibar during his reign.

The House of Wonders also functioned as a platform for staging elaborate state-sponsored parades and festivities, which fused local Swahili coast traditions of performance and public gifting with those of Egypt and other modernizing imperial centers.[41] Pira Dewji was in charge of organizing almost daily displays of military marches and musical concerts in front of the House of Wonders. Barghash had his own military band, staffed by Goan musicians and led by a German band director, which performed daily in the public square in front of the House of Wonders.[42] He also paid for overseas dance and circus troupes to travel to Zanzibar, leading to the infusion of new elements into the performance traditions of the Swahili coast. Because of his keen interest in all things Egyptian, Barghash spent considerable sums of his own money to arrange for Middle Eastern orchestras to perform in the evenings in front of the House of Wonders, its ornate façade and electric lights functioning as a scenic backdrop for such events. Foreign visitors often remarked on the fact that the façade itself was the highlight of these performances, the intense light of its many electric lamps creating a dramatic theatrical stage set, amazing both local and European audiences with its monumental size and the huge number of electric fixtures. Moreover, the plaza in front of the House of Wonders was paved in concrete to make it a more manageable space for staging state-managed splendor. During the high Muslim holidays the sultan provided mats for mass prayers and even served entire meals to those gathering in front of the House. Chairs filled the plaza when the sultan's band played operatic selections for European guests.[43]

The verandahs of House of Wonders also functioned as public and semipublic spaces for entirely new modes of representation, in which the body was presented as an image or vignette of vision. The richly ornamented body had always played a central role in Swahili coast culture, acting as a mobile armature for the presentation of exotic fashions and jewelry. Imported people and commodities were the most coveted symbols of mercantile wealth. It was a long-established practice on the

Swahili coast for patricians to dress and ornament dozens of young bonded women in identical or matching textiles so that they could dance and parade in the streets during festivals, their richly ornamented bodies and beautiful movements transforming the cityscape.[44] There even existed a category of bonded or servant women called *wapambe* (the ornamented ones); as their owner did not depend on them for labor, their primary role was "to signify the wealth and ability of their owners," and their ornamented and fashionably dressed bodies provided pleasing performances and assemblages of wealth. By the mid–nineteenth century exotic objects and people could be bought with increasing ease.[45] As a result, the difference between people and things became less clear; both were consumed in greater volume and made to stand for the power of capitalist consumption.

Barghash seemed to participate in this practice as well, but he also subtly transformed the aesthetic role of the wapambe by presenting their ornamented bodies as a tableau vivant, framed by the architecture of the House of Wonders. The photograph in figure 3.7 shows a row of wapambe posing on the exterior verandah of the Sultan's palace. Each is sheathed in a different *kanga*, their bodies creating a juxtaposition of contrasting patterns. Lined up against the mass-produced wrought iron balustrade, the bodies of the women are part of the Sultan's collection of worldliness and wealth. The photographic image and the verandah of the House of Wonders seem to produce very different modes of representation, yet they share compelling similarities. Just as the photograph transformed the women's bodies into an image-object, so too did their framing by the stage set of the verandah. When displayed on the exterior of the House of Wonders they became static ornaments. Their primary effect was visual, as objects that could be viewed and optically consumed.[46]

The photograph in figure 3.7 gives us just an anecdotal visual fragment of the way the body was turned into an image and object of ocular pleasure, but written accounts from this period also detail this phenomenon. For example, during such festivals as Maulidi, the annual carnival-like Swahili coast celebration of the birthday of the Prophet Mohamed, the wide galleries of the House of Wonders filled with hundreds of richly dressed men, women, and children, all belonging to the court of the

FIGURE 3.7. *Wapambe* (the decorated ones) arranged on the external balcony of the House of Wonders. Each is wearing a different factory-printed *kanga* cloth and Egyptian-style pants. Photograph courtesy of the Zanzibar National Archives.

sultan. The women of sultan's vast household filled the upper galleries, the gold and silver of their jewelry and embroidered dresses dazzling the mass of people gathered in the plaza below. As the sun set, the entire plaza was transformed into a theatrical stage, electric light and even fireworks illuminating the gilded bodies arranged along the ornate balustrades of the palace. The glinting mass of its façade, its upper reaches bedecked with bejeweled women, was the most "poetic image" of these evening spectacles, according to one observer.[47]

This emphasis on sumptuous pageantry was not new to the Swahili coast; it was traditional for Swahili coast patricians to sponsor parades of richly clad men and women to demonstrate that they had the power and connections to amass large households and followers. To dress hundreds of dependents in imported luxuries, such as jewels and silks, for such festivities meant one had control over the bodies and futures of others. Such performances temporarily transformed the city as their lush dress, singing, and dancing filled the narrow allies of the city. But Barghash transformed the cityscape itself, creating permanent spaces of public exhibition. His outward-oriented architecture allowed him to stage a new kind of mode of imperial self-representation, hinged on the idea of the static spectacle. Likewise, in many ways, the House of Wonders also represents the complete reversal of the Swahili city's architectural culture. The traditional merchant mansion was inward-oriented, its austere unadorned façade protecting the bodies of the household from the gaze of outsiders. Its solid and massive masonry walls symbolized the longevity and permanence of the family who owned the building. In contrast, the verandah, the dominant and unifying architectural feature of House of Wonders, creates an external and ocular-oriented architectural space. After all, the verandah is first and foremost a shaded place where people come to see and be seen. The verandah also extends the reach and watchful eye of the state across the port and the city. Nothing about the House of Wonders is geared toward the inner life of the domestic sphere; it exists only to impress the world and Zanzibaris with the public grandeur of the Sultanate.

Clearly, the idea of panoptic architecture, where all is visible to the modern and rational gaze, is embodied in the House of Wonders. In fact, Barghash not only presented the body of his sultanate to his people, but deployed the verandahs of the House of Wonders to heighten and sharpen his own gaze. Many contemporaneous observers noted that Barghash was an intensely public figure, conscious of how he and others represented themselves to the world. He was observed standing for hours on the verandahs of the House of Wonders, presiding over the many military marches and performances he had ordered to fill the public plaza below him.[48] Europeans were also keenly aware that Barghash was watching them, one noting that "he betrays an intense curiosity with regard to everything European . . . and his greatest pleasure seems to be watching the ways of foreigners from his palace."[49] He also "employ[ed] a powerful telescope" in order to assess European mores, customs and— most importantly—misconduct, much to the consternation of Europeans in Zanzibar. For example, he once interpreted the "eccentricities" of a missionary as evidence of public drunkenness, and reported it to the British consul John Kirk, inquiring why the missionary was not in jail for his behavior. Barghash was especially keen to observe things "not intended for his eye," and "he more than once revealed knowledge of a kind and extent which has rather unpleasantly taken some Europeans by surprise."[50]

In a sense, Barghash further sharpened the panoptic view engendered by the lofty height of his verandahs by deploying such modern technologies of sight as the telescope. The magnifying power of the telescope lens allowed him to observe people and things in a way not possible with the naked eye. Barghash was also the first Zanzibari leader who deployed another visual technology, photography. He distributed carte de visite portrait cards of himself to visitors and, as we shall see, large-scale paintings of him based on photographs filled the interiors of his palaces.

The House of Wonders' exterior form and ornament reproduces perspectival illusionism, where the world is sensed *as picture*. Its façade was itself a stage of ocular-centric experiences; its multitude of electric lamps aided in framing and making visible the bodies on display on its verandahs. Barghash created a decidedly "modern" experience on Zanzibar Island with his largest of presentation palaces, one that reproduced the increasingly global emphasis on vision as the dominant mode of perception. The monumental grandeur of the House of Wonders changed the way the visual and material field was mobilized in Zanzibar. Barghash and Dewji used architecture as a permanent stage set, transforming Zanzibar into a kind of modern state-managed ceremonial city.

THE HOUSE OF WONDERS AS SWAHILI ARCHITECTURE

Clearly, the House of Wonders' decorative program was part of Barghash's agenda to build a center of artistic modernity and imperial power on Zanzibar Island. Yet this international orientation is only a partial explanation of its significance; in building it Barghash was very much deploying local Swahili coast technologies and spatial strategies as well. The cast-iron verandas only formed an exterior shell, encasing a traditional nyumba ya mawe, a stone mansion of local mangrove timber, coral stone, and limestone. In fact, a European who visited Zanzibar in 1886— three years after the House of Wonders was completed—described it as a "wood and plaster" palace, never mentioning its imported ornament.[51] Although its builders likely used iron beams as structural elements in the original construction phase, the exterior and interior walls consist of local coral stone. Furthermore, the walls were whitewashed with local fine-grained lime plaster, endowing the House with the stark whiteness of classic Swahili coast edifices. The lime used to plaster the walls of the House of Wonders was likely imported from Pate, a Swahili city in the Lamu Archipelago. Pate was a center of traditional Swahili artistic creativity, where local craftsmen specialized in illuminated book production, leatherworking, and woodcarving. In the nineteenth century demand for its luxury goods had declined, but Pate's mason families still produced the finest lime plaster on the entire Swahili coast. By the second half of the nineteenth century it was mainly exported to Zanzibar, which had become the center of building activity on the Swahili coast.[52] The building materials of the House of Wonders changed significantly only after the British Protectorate government took charge of the building. For example, the clock tower that now dominates the central façade was added after 1896, and in 1911 and 1933 steel and poured concrete replaced much of the original wooden beams.[53]

Interestingly, the House of Wonders collapsed two times during its original construction phase, probably because of its accelerated building schedule.[54] Swahili coral-stone masonry techniques make it necessary for each floor's structural walls to set before another level is added. Also, masons could not work on structural elements during the monsoon season because coral limestone mortar only binds properly in drier weather conditions. As a result a traditional multistory building took several years to complete. Also, the grand scale of the House of Wonders far exceeded the size of stone structures built in the previous two centuries. The House of Wonders thus also represented the limits of Swahili coast masonry as it had been practiced in the 1800s. Combined with cast-iron ornament, it altered local practice in order to mirror the radical shift in scale that characterized the cityscapes of empire during this period.

The House of Wonders' interior layout is also wholly traditional in that it faithfully reproduces the floor plan of early-nineteenth-century merchant houses. Like the stone structures discussed in chapter 1, the

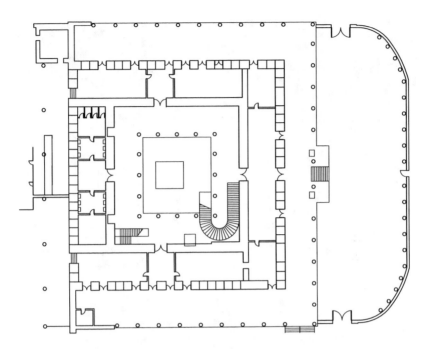

FIGURE 3.8. Ground plan of the House of Wonders (not to scale).
All the rooms are arranged around a central courtyard. Based on a
plan in the Zanzibar National Archives. Drawing by Tait Johnson.

interior was organized around a central courtyard and narrow rectangular rooms ran the length of the four sides the building (figure 3.8). But
the interior of House of Wonders (figure 3.9) was certainly experienced
in a radically different way compared to Swahili stone architecture. The
interior was dominated not by thick stone walls or load-bearing arcades,
but by thin iron columns that united the three levels of the interior, creating a spacious open floor plan.

A pyramidal pavilion constructed of modular prefabricated cast-iron
frames and mass-produced panes of glass also covered the central space
of the building. Thus, the open-air courtyard of a stone merchant mansion was transformed into a modern atrium that, instead of serving as
a transitional space for the movement of people and goods, functioned
as a cavernous ceremonial space. Only one historical photograph exists,
probably from the early 1900s, showing the central atrium of the House

FIGURE 3.9. The interior courtyard of the House of Wonders featuring a series of lofty cast-iron colonnades. Today the building is a public museum and the administrative center of the Zanzibar National Museum of History and Culture. A life-size *jahazi* boat is on display in the center. Photograph by the author, 2014.

FIGURE 3.10. Unidentified sultan sitting in state in the House of Wonders central courtyard, date unknown. Photography courtesy of the Zanzibar National Archives.

of Wonders when it was still used by the sultans for public functions (figure 3.10). The photograph was taken at hip-level, showing the sultan sitting in state underneath a brocaded canopy, surrounded by British Protectorate officials. The blurry and partial form of an attendant, floor tiles, and the garlanded base of a column dominate the foreground of the image, suggesting that the photograph was taken surreptitiously, as the photographer was entering the atrium. Nonetheless, the image documents how the Busaidi sultans presented themselves as modern monarchs during this period, wearing the trappings of European royalty, including Victorian-style insignias and sashes. While Barghash used the atrium in a similar fashion, he would have presented himself surrounded by Arab and South Asian advisors, not by representatives of the British government, and he never wore European fashions.

Another key difference between later uses of the House of Wonders
and its original meaning was that it was clearly connected to the sacral
geography and collective memory of the local populace. While it is often
assumed that Seyyid Said was the first to use the waterfront of Stone
Town as a center of power, in fact the site had been the focus of patrician authority and patronage since at least the seventeenth century. It is
still remembered by locals today that the House of Wonders was built
upon the now-invisible ruins of an indigenous royal structure, the stone
mansion of Mwana Mwema Fatuma. Fatuma was a queen of Shirazi Hadimu ancestry, who, according to oral history, had aligned herself with
Portuguese Goa in an attempt to protect Zanzibar against the growing
presence of Omani Arabs in east Africa beginning in the eighteenth
century.[55] Furthermore, until around 1840 the waterfront was used by
a Hadimu-Shirazi ruler, known as the Mwenye Mkuu.[56] Here he maintained a palace, the central Friday mosque of the city, and the Hadimu
dynasty's cemetery.[57] Although no detailed account of his complex exists, his authority over the area was even recognized by Seyyid Said when
he first visited Zanzibar Island in 1828. In fact, Said did not reside on the
waterfront of Stone Town when he first moved from Muscat to Zanzibar,
instead confiscating an Omani Arab's mansion at Mtoni, three miles
outside of Stone Town.[58] He spent most of his days at Mtoni, coming
to Stone Town only twice a week to conduct business.[59] Thus the waterfront was the focal point of religious and political life in local worldviews
long before Zanzibar became the center of Busaidi power.

But sometime in the 1830s Said began to claim Stone Town proper,
and the Mwenye Mkuu, Mohammed bin Ahmed, was forced to seek
refuge at Dunga, an ancient settlement in the interior of the island.[60] The
details of the power struggle between Said and the Mwenye Mkuu are no
longer known, but the Mwenye Mkuu built a new palace (completed in
1845) at Dunga, where he continued to rule over the indigenous population until his death in 1866.

A kind of dual monarchy existed on Zanzibar Island until the 1860s,
and in the early twentieth century Dunga palace was still remembered
as the last nyumba ya mawe endowed with the old *heshima,* or dignity,
of the Hadimu.[61] Furthermore, the legacy of the last Mwenye Mkuu figured prominently in the public imaginary of local peoples until at least

the late nineteenth century. While he was alive, his presence protected the island and maintained the honor of the local waungwana.[62] One strand of oral history recounts that when the last Mwenye Mkuu took refuge on the mainland after fighting with the sultan, a terrible drought befell Zanzibar, causing great hardship for all its residents. Prosperity was only restored after the sultan begged him to return to the Island.

The Mwenye Mkuu was also seen as someone who could transgress against the moral codes of average humans. He also harnessed great indigenous supernatural power. According to locals, Mohammed bin Ahmed, the last Mwenye Mkuu with any significant authority, interred dozens of enslaved Africans in the walls of his palace at Dunga to protect it from outsider aggressors.[63] Stories about powerful waungwana patricians sacrificing the enslaved in order to protect the stone walls of their mansions are part of Swahili coast lore more generally. As we have seen in chapter one, Mombasa's elders tell similar stories even now.

While Seyyid Said and his oldest son, Masjid, gradually subverted the political autonomy of the Mwenye Mkuu and Zanzibar's Hadimu and Tumbatu federations, Barghash aggressively coopted the material heritage of these indigenous polities. He confiscated the most important insignia of Hadimu power, including the ceremonial drums and ivory side-blown horns of the Mwenye Mkuu. During his reign the title of Mwenye Mkuu was terminated, and Dunga palace, the last remaining symbol of Hadimu independence, also passed into Omani hands. This came about when the Mwenye Mkuu's daughter, who had inherited the property, was married to Mohammed bin Seif, a member of Barghash's council of elders who also owned countless clove plantations on Pemba and Zanzibar Island.

The House of Wonders was part of this agenda of cooptation, since it was a metaphoric and physical reconstruction of a Hadimu site of power. The heightened theatricality that accompanied Barghash's remaking of the site also played an important role in naturalizing Busaidi claims to Zanzibar. The House of Wonders in various ways amplified indigenous strategies of ordering space: its whitewashed masonry form was recognizable as a patrician nyumba ya mawe, while the flamboyance of its exterior ornamentation emphasized Barghash's reinvention of the site. Clearly the House of Wonders is not simply a "new" space of global interconnectivity, but represents the remapping of a highly symbolic pre-Sultanic and precolonial built environment. It is startling that Barghash's will to reorder to waterfront as a space of Busaidi power was so effective, considering that, today, the site has been completely divorced from analyses of the politics of indigenous architecture.

ISLAMIC SPACE

While the exterior of the House of Wonders gave little indication that Zanzibar was a Muslim cultural space, Islamic religious imagery defined the interior decorative program. The eight massive carved wooden doorways, which today still dominate the interior of the palace, are each covered with sacred calligraphy (figure 3.11). While the tympanum and columns of the doorways feature the compact vegetal patterning typical of the British Raj style, their wings are filled with traditional texts from the Qur'an. Each door wing is divided into three registers of interlocking rectangle and diamond patterns, which act as a framing device for the Word. The individual words and phrases are wooden cutouts attached with tiny nails and glue as low-relief elements to the surface of the doors. The layout of the calligraphy is similar to the way Arabic texts are arranged on classic Middle Eastern tapestries or other textile arts. The legibility of the letters and words becomes secondary; instead they are transformed into arabesque flourishes and abstract designs that elegantly fill their designated geometric frames. Today the gilded letters and vegetal designs rest upon a black background, but originally it was dark green,[64] further heightening the religious ambiance of the space, as green is the color of paradise and evokes blessedness for Muslims. The texts consist of verses from some of the most popular *surahs* (or chapters) of the Qur'an. The Qur'an is recognized by all Muslims as the axis of their faith; its recitation creates a sense of belonging to the global community of faithful (the umma), and canonical interpretations present the Qur'an as the eternal and unchanging words of God. Dominating the design of the doors are the Yā Sīn, an-Naĥl, and al-Ĥijr surahs, sections of which are repeated over and over again. On the Swahili coast these surahs are often recited in the belief that through the act of recitation one embodies their sacred efficacy, their power to bless and protect

FIGURE 3.11. One of the gilt interior doorways of the House of Wonders. Each door's frame is carved in the British-Raj style popularized by Sultan Barghash. The door panels are covered with Qur'anic texts. Photograph by the author, 2014.

the speaker and the people in the vicinity of the spoken Word. In fact, the Yā Sīn surah is considered by some to be the heart of the Qu'ran, which when spoken creates an active space of blessed protection.

Local elders also remember stories from their grandfathers who described the Islamic character of the interior. They remember that calligraphic plaques covered the walls of most rooms in the House of Wonders. According to one account, a famous Sunni scholar selected the Qur'anic verses for each plaque.[65] Written accounts from the period also document that the interior was once filled with the sacred words of the Qur'an. A traveler in the 1880s wrote, "The best things in the palace were the verses from the Koran that covered the walls in raised white letters upon a superb blue background."[66]

Another source documents that the second-floor reception hall of the House of Wonders "shimmered in gold and silver because gilt Quranic verses ornamented the wall."[67] This hall was the most frequently used space of the palace. Here Sultan Barghash and subsequent sultans would hold their weekly Friday baraza assemblies, when freemen of means with connections to the Busaidi household met directly with the sultan and his councilmen. These audiences often lasted all morning. A single photograph of this reception room survives, taken right after the bombing of the waterfront by the British Navy in 1896 (figure 3.12). The photograph captures the destruction wrought by the attack, when the two palaces built by Barghash's father, the Beit el Hukum and Beit el Sahel, were completely destroyed. The House of Wonders sustained only partial damage, as can be seen in the photograph. The blast shattered mirrors and blew out most of the windows on the left side of the palace, and the force of the blasts scattered and destroyed the audience hall's furniture. The French chandeliers, so favored by Barghash and the entire population of Zanzibar during the 1880s, remained intact; they fill the picture-plane of the photograph. It is only upon closer viewing that one can discern the Arabic texts on the paneling of the walls. Likely made of fabric and gilt embroidery, these panels cover the upper reaches of the walls.

Thus, although only the doors survive today, in Barghash's time large-scale religious Arabic calligraphy was prominently displayed throughout the House of Wonders. This emphasis on scriptural calligraphy can

FIGURE 3.12. An 1896 photograph of the reception room in the House of Wonders
after it was partially destroyed by an attack by the British Navy. The space was filled
with imported chandeliers, and brocade with Arabic calligraphy covered the walls.
Photograph courtesy of the Zanzibar National Archives.

be understood as an extension of Barghash's vision of himself as the patron of classical Islam. Barghash was a staunch supporter of textual or canonical Islamic theology and practice. As mentioned previously, he was hostile to Sufism and local Swahili coast Islamic traditions, imprisoning scholars who belonged to Sufi orders and invalidating local judicial traditions. He financed Ibadi and Sunni scholars whose writings and teachings supported his own conservative views. He wanted to spearhead a renaissance of canonical Islam; after his visit to Cairo in 1875 he founded east Africa's first Arabic printing press, which published treatises by Islamic scholars he supported.[68] It seems particularly apt for Barghash, such a staunch supporter of conservative views, to fill the interior of his most public palace with the most universally revered chapters of the Qur'an, creating a sense of unity. In reality Zanzibari Muslims were actively engaged in various religious reform movements that directly threatened Barghash's authority on religious grounds.

SPACES OF MIMETIC DOUBLING

Ironically, because he used western cultural codes and modes of self-presentation, many Zanzibaris questioned Barghash's religiosity. Arthur Hardinge, the first consul general of Zanzibar, recounted that Barghash scandalized locals after a photograph of him with unveiled European women circulated locally.[69] Barghash did indeed orchestrate the circulation of photographs and mass-produced images of himself across Zanzibar's various publics. For example, he proudly reprinted engravings published in the *Illustrated London News* of his public appearances during his tour of Europe in 1875 and kept a scrapbook of the images.[70] During his London visit he also commissioned several cartes de visite of himself and his councilors from the most fashionable photography studio of London, Maull and Company (figure 3.13). This studio specialized in serving the social and political elite of England, including members of the British Parliament. Once Barghash returned to Zanzibar he would present a copy of his London carte de visite as a gift to various people. The one illustrated in figure 3.13 was part of the memorabilia album of Sir John Kirk, the British Resident of Zanzibar. Barghash's embrace of photography was also a local trend. Although some old Zanzibaris felt reservations

FIGURE 3.13. *Carte de visite* of Sultan Barghash and his council. The photograph was taken during his visit to London in 1875. Photograph courtesy of the Trustees of the National Library of Scotland.

about photography's ability to reproduce physiognomic likeness, many avidly collected cartes de visite photographs.[71] Having one's portrait taken in a local studio was also immensely popular all along the coast from the 1860s onward.

Barghash did not introduce photography or mimetic modes of seeing and self-representation to Zanzibar. These were already popular before he came to power. But he did recombine them in new and creative ways to construct intensively visual and vision-oriented experiences. As discussed previously, much of the exterior of the House of Wonders framed various spectacles of sight, and Barghash also crafted the interior of his main reception hall as a grandiose exhibition space of vision and duplication. This hall functioned as an imaginarium, overflowing with reflected images, machinic objects of vision, and modern instruments of measurement. Rows of grand gilt mirrors and deep wall niches occupied the entire length of the long rectangular space. The mirrors hung opposite each other and reflected the likeness of individuals occupying the room *ad infinitum,* while the niches bristled with modern instruments of measurement and visualization. As one visitor noted, "The niches had as many clocks and telescopes" as the room itself had mirror images of "persons on every side."[72] Other visitors also commented on the "medley assemblages of kitchen clocks, ormolu timepieces, aneroid barometers, thermometers, anemometers, telescopes, opera-glasses . . . photographic albums, photographs glazed and framed and faded" occupying the shelves on either side of the mirrors.[73]

On one level such collections express what Jeremy Prestholdt aptly describes as a "new global consciousness." According to Prestholdt, an exotic object such as a chandelier or a clock "became a poetic metaphor for material luxury" during this period of heightened commodity consumption.[74] Yet, as we shall see in the next chapter, the desire for imported things has significant historic precursors on the Swahili coast and in many ways represents the reification of a very old Swahili coast sign and object system.[75] The coastal "culture of things" was part of the ancient mercantile history of region. It celebrated oceanic mobility and the ability to master near and far cultural logics. Furthermore, Barghash's palaces were filled with a specific type of import: instruments and images of vision and optic observation. These objects are not only about his global consciousness; they also reflect his specific fascination with technologies of seeing and reproduction.

This is especially evident in Barghash's main reception hall, whose true focal point was the reproduced likeness of the sultan himself. The upper end of the room featured a gilt mirror at its center, on either side of which hung identical full-length oil paintings of Barghash, likely similar to the painted portrait still hanging in the House of Wonders (plate 12) today, which has an Arabic inscription that reads "picture taken by the mortal hand of Baihly, in 1397 (1880)." When Barghash himself was present, he sat in state in front of the central mirror, flanked by his life-size doubles. A British explorer, Harry Johnston, who had an audience with Sultan Barghash in 1884, described how the reproducibility of the photograph also facilitated the creation of these perfectly identical paintings. According to Johnston, the works were painted in Paris, but instead of sitting for his portraits in person, Barghash simply sent his carte de visite to the painter. To fulfill Barghash's wishes for a full-length portrait, the artist first created a photographic collage, fusing Barghash's image with that of another. According to Johnston, "The Parisian artist, in no way at a loss, cut off the head the sitting Sultan and stuck it on the de-capitated portrait of some Algerian Arab photographed erect. The combination was enlarged, and in due time gave rise two oil paintings in the palace at Zanzibar."[76] Once hung in the mirror-filled reception hall, they further imbued the room with an aesthetic of repetition and doubling.

All, including the working poor, favored the ornament- and object-culture so prominently displayed in the House of Wonders and Barghash's other palaces. The emphasis on mimetic reproducibility was part of a larger attraction all along the coast to perspectival visions and images during Barghash's reign. In fact, although Barghash had the means to create a tableau of vision and reproduction unlike any seen in Zanzibar in the past, mirrors, paintings, photographs, and lithographs were already popular on the Swahili coast in the 1860s. Glass and porcelain objects and other exotic ornaments could also be found in the homes of many. Europeans of course dismissed these collecting strategies and regularly cataloged instances of the "incorrect" use and display of European material culture by Zanzibaris. For example, Karl Schmidt, who wrote one of the most detailed descriptions of local life during the last quarter of the nineteenth century, mocked such practices as a form of wasteful consumption, since utilitarian things were not put to their intended use but just displayed. He noted that even chairs and tables were avidly collected "only [as] curiosities with which their owners show off in front of indigenous and foreign guests."[77] According to Schmidt, the entire population had succumbed to an almost baroque affectation for things that did not belong to the coast. Yet, as we shall see in the next chapter, they did "belong," given that locals have long avidly collected exotic imports. In a sense, multiple histories of consumption, circulation, and self-representation rapidly congealed in the spaces and image worlds of coastal life during Barghash's reign.

The House of Wonders' seeming visual and material dislocation and dissonance from the local landscape does speak to Barghash's desire to command and claim Zanzibar city as a global imperial center. But in its original inception it was not a project of the colonized periphery, where the "global" was localized. Rather it was meant to enact a vision of Zanzibar's profound centrality in the world. Its symbolic and material fabric sits at the intersection of multiple ways of marking territory and claiming place.

PLATE 1. The whitewashed façades of new and old stone buildings on the waterfront of Lamu Town. Photograph by the author, 2014.

PLATE 2. Stone houses rented by the Hamburg-based trading firm of
William O'Swald and Co. on the waterfront of Zanzibar Town, 1847–1890s.
This is a page of a memorabilia album featuring a watercolor painting and
small photograph of the two houses occupied by William O'Swald when
he lived on Zanzibar Island. Image courtesy of the Melville J. Herskovits
Library of African Studies Winterton Collection, Northwestern University.

PLATE 3. Mandhry mosque in Old Town Mombasa.
Photograph courtesy of Raymond Silverman, 2005.

PLATE 4. View of the skyline of Old Town Mombasa
at dawn. Photograph by the author, 2013.

PLATE 5. Members of the Thela Wakilindini at one of their favorite baraza spots (with a family friend on the far left). Left to right, beginning with the man second on the left: Mohamed Ahmad Nassir, Mohamed Abdallah Mohamed Matano, Ustadh Ahmad Nassir Juma Bhalo, Ali Omar, Mohamed Matano. Photograph by the author, 2013.

PLATE 6. *Facing:* Alleyway in Old Town Mombasa. Photograph by the author, 2013.

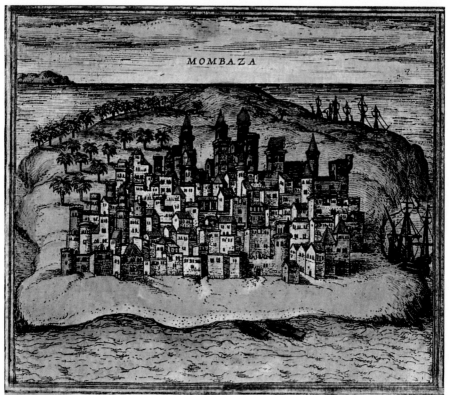

MOMBAZA

PLATE 7. Illustration of Mombasa City in the *Civitates Orbis Terrarum*, 1572. Courtesy of the National Library of Israel and the Hebrew University Historical Cities Project.

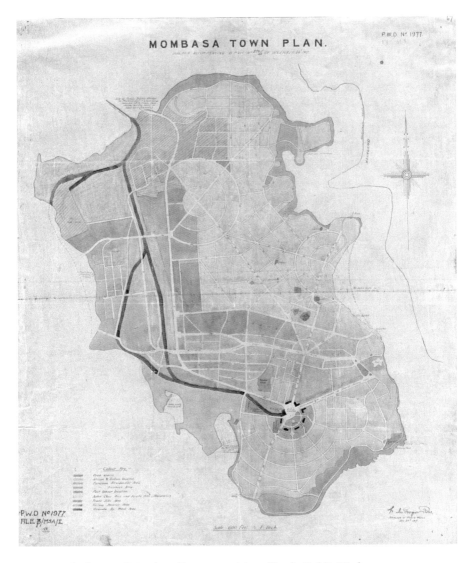

PLATE 8. The future of Mombasa Town as envisioned by the Public Works Department of Mombasa in 1917. The different colored areas represent the proposal that different racial and ethnic groups should be cordoned off from each other in distinct neighborhoods. Image courtesy of the National Archives of the United Kingdom.

PLATE 9. The Basheikh mosque, also known as the Tangana or Mnara mosque, founded circa fourteenth century. Photograph by the author, 2013.

PLATE 10. View of Malik Feisal framed by the ogee arches inside the Mnara mosque. Photograph by the author, 2013.

PLATE 11. The Beit al Ajaib (House of Wonders) today. The British
Protectorate added a clock tower to the central façade after bombing
it in 1896. From then until 1964, the House of Wonders functioned
as a center of colonial power. Photograph by the author, 2014.

PLATE 12. *Facing:* Portrait of Sultan Barghash, oil on canvas. The Arabic
text in the lower right-hand corner reads, "Picture taken by the mortal
hand of Baihly, in 1397 (1880)." Hanging in the House of Wonders today.
Photograph by the author, 2014.

PLATE 13. *Facing:* The ground-floor living room space in the Swahili House Museum of Lamu features a classic kiti cha enzi (left). Photograph by the author, 2014.

PLATE 14. *Above:* Abdulwahid Hinawy surrounded by an important collection of locally collected antiques in his family's stone mansion on the waterfront of Old Town, Mombasa. The most prized pieces are two viti vya enzi. Photograph by the author, 2013.

PLATE 15. Chinaware on display in home of Rukiya Abdulreham and Mohamed Mchulla. Photograph by the author, 2014.

PLATE 16. Chinaware fastened to the walls of the dining room of Layla Khamis Rashid Sood Shikely. Photograph by the author, 2014.

FOUR

ᴗᵻᴗ ᴗᵻᴗ ᴗᵻᴗ

At Home in the World

Living with Transoceanic Things

Swahili coast interior design and ornament invites an extended exploration of the meaning of objects when their "life" is shaped by transoceanic
circulation. As we have seen in the case of Zanzibar, its modern palaces existed at the intersection of new and old building cultures. Sultan
Barghash deployed a multiplicity of forms and technologies to manufac-
ture architectural theaters of triumph and pleasure. His project was part
of a larger nineteenth century phenomenon: the desire to transform east
Africa's port cities into strategic sites of imperial power and capitalist
modernization. This chapter presents a more intimate analysis of the
social lives enacted within the architectural spaces of the Swahili city.
I explore the reasons why imported ornament and objects captured the
imagination of Swahili coast residents for centuries and how the impact
of industrial modernity intensified the local desire to collect things from
overseas.

THINGS IN MOTION

People give meaning to objects by arranging them in relationship to
other things. The production of meaning therefore has a physical effect
on the material environment, since such arrangements change how we
experience a particular room or material landscape. When an object
comes to rest in a new place it also expresses a new idea or concept.

139

Through its arrangement in real space it will become commodity, artifact, art, souvenir, or relic. How objects take on different values and
meanings as they move through time and space is now often called
the "social life of things," after Arjun Appadurai's seminal edited book
of the same title, published in 1988. But it is people who set this life in
motion through various actions upon things, including trading them,
buying them, or placing them on altars or graves. In a sense the agency
of things is always constituted by someone's actions. Scholars such as
Patricia Spyer and Nicholas Thomas, among others, have complicated
our understanding of human–object relationships by foregrounding
how the act of appropriating things from a foreign society simultaneously consolidates *and* displaces existing systems of signification.[1] The
moment of displacement from one context to another brings the thing
into sharp focus: it presents the object laid bare, before it is assimilated
and before it transforms and is transformed by its new context. When
objects are displaced, we become particularly aware of their physical
presence and materiality. They stand out. This is especially the case with
trade objects that circulate across physical borders and move into vastly
different cultural settings. Because they are exotic or foreign they tend
to retain something uncanny and untranslatable about their form, even
long after they have come to rest in their new homes. We can apprehend
them as a thing, or we see their pure presence, outside of the cultural
meaning projected onto them, more easily. This thing-ness is exactly
what was cultivated as an aesthetic in the interior spaces of the Swahili
coast. The Swahili culture of things celebrates the ability to displace
objects and values across great distances.

I have already addressed the interior design of the House of Wonders
and Barghash's other palaces, but it is important to emphasize now that
his collections reflected the tastes and desires of the larger coastal population. While his palaces featured the most ostentatious and flamboyant
assemblages of exotic imports and objets d'art, he was in fact following
local precedent. The display of objects connected to the Indian Ocean
trading networks has long been a central design element of Swahili domestic architecture.

This emphasis on exotic imports was not simply a result of capitalist
globalization. Already by the fifteenth or sixteenth century the heredi-

tary leaders of Swahili port cities and towns had created a visual culture of mercantile plentitude. Patrician members of coastal society visualized their sophistication, Islamic identity, social mobility, and privileged connection to other Indian Ocean rim cultures by constructing complex display tableaux of imported objets d'art in their homes. Specifically, those who wanted to present themselves as sophisticated city residents cultivated a multilayered aesthetic, fusing objects, forms, and material performances from many sites connected to east Africa via oceanic trade routes. Objects linked to mercantile exchange and long-distance travel also signaled success in the mercurial and highly competitive context of life in a port city. Great distances separated the ports of east Africa from the cities of the Middle East and South Asia, but having direct access to the artifacts of those faraway places endowed the port with an aura of worldly sophistication. In a sense, one was able to surmount distance by dressing in and living with things from faraway places.

Swahili coast visual culture emphasizes overseas connections, not those with inland Africa—although they are equally important from the perspective of daily practice. Peoples' homes are filled with images, textiles, and even sounds that seem typically "Middle Eastern" or "Asian." Thus, one of the most startling and perhaps even disconcerting characteristics of the Swahili city is that it is not typically "African." The Swahili coast aesthetic eschews place-based authenticity, much to the discomfort of scholars trained as Africanists. Foreign objects, especially mass-produced forms that conform to a recognizable type, are most cherished and valued. Even when a local artisan has made an artwork, ornament, or textile, it is likely to evoke or at least pay homage to an object-type or design element originating in a faraway place, although it is important to emphasize that creative originality was (and continues to be) very much valued and celebrated. The deftness and elegance by which a carver translated an overseas form was key to his success. But an object could be "translated" without altering it physically. The graceful and sophisticated display of imported objects was equally important, since it signaled one's means and expertise to cultivate the beauty of distant places.

This aesthetic also celebrates reinvention. For example, when British Raj interior design became popular in the nineteenth century, Zanzi-

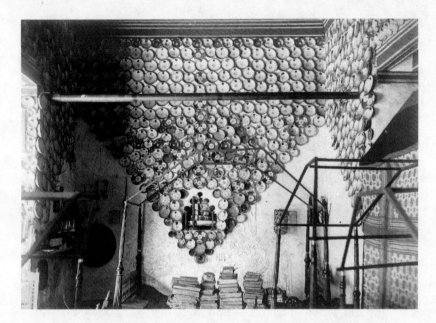

FIGURE 4.1. An 1884 photograph of the interior of an eighteenth-century merchant mansion in Lamu, Kenya. The walls are covered with hundreds of Chinese (specifically Kangxi) export-style enameled porcelain dishes. Photograph courtesy of the Trustees of the National Library of Scotland.

baris had no interest in using imported chairs, sofas, or tables to recreate Victorian domesticity or household productivity. People continued to receive guests and eat seated on carpets, mats, and cushions. Chairs, tables, and even entire tea and coffee sets were collected only as *things*, to intensify the material spectacle of static display. As we shall see, to master the faraway meant one had the means to *not* use imported objects in any recognizably practical way.

MODERNITY'S TRANSFORMATIONS

Sometime in the eighteenth century the Swahili coast culture of things was gradually inflected by the aesthetics of mass production and modern consumption (figures 4.1 and 4.2). Patricians staged increasingly baroque displays of exotic objets d'art in their public spaces.[2] In fact, because local merchant and landowning families regained the means to

FIGURE 4.2. Photograph of patricians, 1884, sitting in state on *viti vya enzi* (chairs of power) inside a merchant house in Lamu Town, Kenya. Imported porcelain, English clocks, French mirrors, photographs, and chromolithographs cover the walls. Photograph courtesy of the Trustees of the National Library of Scotland.

patronize the arts again after years of Portuguese oppression, the eighteenth century has been described as a Swahili renaissance.[3]

There are several interconnected factors that facilitated the ability to amass exotic things in unprecedented numbers. In the sixteenth century the Portuguese had colonized many of the key port cities of the Swahili coast, including Mombasa and Pate, wresting control over the local economy out of local hands. They monopolized the export of ivory, for example. During this period many patrician stone houses and settlements were abandoned, and locals built few monumental tombs or mosques. But by the second half of the seventeenth century the Portuguese increasingly lost control over their Indian Ocean empire. Mombasa, with help from the merchant princes of Oman, permanently defeated their former oppressors in 1698. Omani Arab presence and

power in east Africa increased from then onward, but the Swahili elite
and local merchants had more opportunities to participate in the transcontinental trade than they did under Portuguese rule. They revived
their connections with their former ivory trading partners in central
and mainland east Africa. By the second half of the eighteenth century
they also led slaving caravans, exporting people from deep inside the
African continent to French plantation owners on the Indian Ocean islands of Reunion and Mauritius. The French imported thousands of enslaved Africans each year to labor under extremely harsh conditions on
Caribbean-style sugar plantations. The enslaved were also forced to
work on Omani plantations, and were even sold as far away as Brazil
once the British blocked slaving ships from west Africa.[4] This marks
the beginnings of the unmatched objectification of human beings in
this region of the world. In the plantation system the enslaved became
objects and agents of labor, without a social life or place in the society
of those who enslaved them.

   During the second half of the eighteenth century locals built luxurious mansions and created new forms of genteel living. The home was
reinvented as a modern spectacle of plentitude. For example, fine lime
plaster was used to cover entire walls with low-relief patterns and abstracted images, which shared great similarities with textile and jewelry
designs. Sometimes large rectangular panels of interlocking triangles,
which mirrored the intricate geometry of Islamic mosaics or woodwork, filled entire walls.[5] Other designs included organic forms that
resembled animals, such as turtles, or suggested the curvilinear arcs
of Arabic calligraphy (figure 4.3). Some rooms also featured long rows
of miniature wall niches. These niches were filled with porcelain dishes
and vases, further adding sculptural mass and volume to the interior
spaces of mansions (figure 4.4). Long and high grid-like banks of niches
covering entire walls became especially prevalent along the northern
coast of what is now Kenya.[6]

   In 2007 I discovered the photographs illustrated in figures 4.1 and 4.2
in the National Library of Scotland. They are the first visual evidence
we have of the interior design programs of Swahili coast stone houses
before the twentieth century. John Kirk, the British consul general at
Zanzibar, took the photos when he spent several weeks in 1884 in Lamu

FIGURE 4.3. Finely carved lime stuccowork on one of the main entrance walls of the Lamu Museum, part of the National Museums of Kenya. This composition, which dates to the eighteenth century, is in the form of a turtle. Photograph by the author, 2014.

FIGURE 4.4. Long banks of niches once covered the walls of eighteenth-century patrician stone houses. A porcelain dish would have been displayed in each niche. This house is now the Swahili House Museum of Lamu. The staff of the National Museums of Kenya recently renovated the niches and stuccowork. Photograph by the author, 2014.

and Mombasa, where he inspected his government's vice-consular offices and settled property disputes.[7] But judging from the many photos he took on his trip, he was also keen to document the unique culture of Lamu and Mombasa, which was quite different from what he was familiar with in Zanzibar. His photos document interior spaces that are dramatically different from the way "classic" Swahili architecture is presented today. Instead of the sparse elegance of unadorned white-washed walls and dramatically-placed singular objects, these images show that furniture, wood ornaments, clocks, mirrors, and porcelain dishes filled every inch of patrician domestic space. The layering of hundreds of mass-produced porcelain dishes created a decidedly modern *horror vacui* aesthetic in these spaces.

The 1884 photographs document a key transformation in the presentation of porcelain during this so-called Swahili renaissance period.

FIGURE 4.5. Porcelain dish collected in Lamu in the late nineteenth century. Courtesy of the Ethnologisches Museum, Staatliche Museen zu Berlin—Preußischer Kulturbesitz.

Dozens—sometimes hundreds—of porcelains dishes were now directly attached to the walls of domestic spaces, instead of being displayed in niches or on shelves. Significantly, the porcelain featured in these rooms does not date from the time the photograph was taken. Instead, it is Chinese export-style Kangxi ware from the seventeenth and early eighteenth centuries. At some point, although it is difficult to know when, it became fashionable to cover entire walls of living rooms with porcelain dishes, either by plastering them onto the walls directly or by hanging them with nails. In fact, the practice of drilling holes into the rim of dishes to hang them seemed to be the most common display manner by the late eighteenth century. A porcelain dish with a tiny hole on the edge of its rim, collected in Lamu and now at the Ethnological Museum of Berlin, was clearly displayed in this manner (figure 4.5).[8] One British collector also

observed "that nine-tenths of [china] was bored for hanging purposes."
This frustrated him greatly, because it reduced its resale value in Europe.
He also described a room that must have been even more ostentatious
than the interiors featured in Kirk's photographs. He wrote, "One room
in particular I remember well; it was a good thirty feet or more long, by
about sixteen in width, and there was not a six-inch square of wall showing" because it was "filled with a vast collection . . . [of] many beautiful
bowls."⁹

There was such an intense desire for chinaware in the eighteenth
century that the dishes spilled out of their niches, so to speak, to cover
even the upper reaches of entire walls. The delicate low-relief stucco ornament was obscured by the mass and volume of porcelain. The very
density of this ceramic "skin" emphasize the sheer mass of porcelain.
The display of so many plates also made the interiors more ostentatious:
they almost bristled with the contrasting patterns and different sizes
of the many plates. The plates were hung in such a manner as to create new patterns and designs that obscured but also incorporated the
older stuccowork. In figure 4.1 the dishes crept from the top of the wall
downward, forming an inverted triangle, which enveloped the upward-
pointing triangular form of the central stucco poly-lobed niche. In effect, the stucco niche nested within the ceramic triangle. The placement
of the plates within the triangle was also not haphazard. Identical plates
were placed on either side of the vertical axis of the triangle to create a
subtly bilateral design. Identical plates also encircled the niche, creating
a radial design within the form of the triangle. More colorful dishes were
concentrated in the bottom half of the composition, further emphasizing the tapering point of the inverted triangle. This manner of displaying
the plates also undermined the three-dimensionality and circular form
of the individual plates; their individual forms were absorbed into the
larger triangular composition.

THE HISTORY OF PORCELAIN ON THE SWAHILI COAST

The porcelain hanging on the walls in figures 4.1 and 4.2 was mass-produced for centuries, first in China and later Europe and North America,
expressly for east Africa consumers.¹⁰ John Kirk and other high-ranking

colonial officials stationed on the coast, such as George Mackenzie, the IBEAC's Administrator at Mombasa, amassed huge porcelain collections on the Swahili coast. Buying and even stealing old china from graves was a major European pastime during the early colonial period. It was a very widespread practice, and even temporary visitors to coastal east Africa made a point of purchasing it. For example, Lord Kitchener focused on "old china" during his visit to Zanzibar in 1885, to such an extent that he disappointed British officers living in east Africa: when he came to Zanzibar, Kitchener, a British national hero at that time, wanted to only talk of "old china." Collecting it was in fact a kind of competitive game among Europeans living in east Africa. In Lamu the greatest collector of the most priced porcelain pieces was a German doctor, who took it from locals as payment for his services.[11] Valuable old Chinese and Middle Eastern porcelain was also readily available for purchase by the 1880s. Swahili patricians, having been reduced to ceremonial figureheads by the Omanis and British and no longer holding any political or economic power, had to sell their family collections.[12] Being reduced to selling their family's most important material possessions, including their stone houses, indicated their desperation. Some British Protectorate administrators realized that a key aspect of local heritage was being carried off, but their calls for legislation to stop this "curio craze" did not produce laws to that effect.[13] By the 1920s old porcelain had all but disappeared from the Swahili coast, and Europeans who came to collect it could only reminisce wistfully that just a decade ago "Mombasa and Lamu were the most happy hunting ground for those interested in collecting old china."[14] Most pre–nineteenth century Swahili coast porcelain was carried off to Europe, but it was one of the most valued icons of Swahili coast heritage for centuries.

Glazed ceramics were traded for hundreds of years along the commercial trade routes that connected the Indian Ocean and coastal and mainland Africa. Archaeological research at Kilwa Kisawani has revealed that glazed ware from the Persian Gulf was already an important import commodity in coastal east Africa in the tenth century, which also meant it reached further into central and south Africa. For example, sixteenth-century Ming blue and white porcelain was found as far inland as Great Zimbabwe, which was once one of many African empires in contact with the merchants and polities of the Swahili coast during the early modern period. Chinese enameled wares first began to arrive in the thirteenth century in east Africa, and by the fourteenth century they exceeded the quantity of Middle Eastern glazed wares being imported.[15] Indeed, the Swahili coast was a central node in the early modern "world system" of porcelain, whose fulcrum was China, although Persian pottery also remained desirable.[16] But China dominated the production of export ware, providing porcelain for much of the globe for over five hundred years. In fact, Robert Finlay has argued that the "globalization of material culture initially came to pass under Chinese auspices" because of the global preference for ceramics from China.[17]

The reason this ware was so avidly imported on the Swahili coast was that it registered primarily as an Islamic cultural artifact, visualizing belonging to the Muslim maritime networks of the western Indian Ocean. Rarely used for utilitarian purposes, it was collected for its beauty and symbolic significance.[18] From at least the thirteenth century onward it was the most visible form of ornamentation on public architectural monuments. As discussed in chapter 1, a defining feature of all Swahili stone architecture is its emphasis on the expansive solidity and the gleaming purity of lime plastered walls. The exterior featured little or no ornamental forms or decorative treatments. The one striking exception is the use of porcelain dishes to decorate the exterior of tombs (figure 4.6). Imported porcelain was pressed into the wet plaster of the ornamental areas of stone memorials and burial structures, becoming part of the permanent surface articulation of these monuments. Great numbers of such tombs dot the coastal landscape of Tanzania and Kenya, although all their porcelain has long since been removed. Besides the exterior of graves, imported plates and bowls also ornamented the spandrels and pilasters of the mihrab area of mosques. Especially blue-painted Chinese and southwest Asian ceramics were part of the permanent decoration of religious architecture for centuries during the golden age of Swahili maritime trade. These were probably also displayed inside secular structures, since fifteenth and sixteenth century sites sometimes feature shelves and niches in public areas of still-standing palace walls. In fact, the presence of large amounts of imported glazed ceramics is

FIGURE 4.6. Domed tombs of Siyu, Pate Island, Kenya. The exterior walls
once featured rows of hundreds of porcelain dishes. Individual plates were
also pressed into the surface of the domes. Photograph by the author, 2014.

one of the primary means by which archeologists have dated coastal
archeological sites.

Until at least the seventeenth century porcelain remained a priced rarity; it never displaced the production of indigenous terra-cotta pottery,
and only 5 percent of the pottery shards excavated on the Swahili coast
derived from trade imports.[19] A significant change in the consumption
of porcelain occurred in the late seventeenth century, when Chinese
manufacturing centers developed new systems of mass producing export ware and northern European stock-companies, primarily the Dutch
and British East India Companies, supplied much of the Indian Ocean
world with much more porcelain. Both companies had permanent offices in Canton, which allowed them to respond to changing demands
efficiently and quickly.[20] Northern Europeans soon dominated the trade

in luxury goods between Africa, the islands of the Indian Ocean, South Asia, and the Arabian Peninsula. European glazed ceramic ware was also shipped to east Africa by the 1820s, mostly through the port of Bombay. By the last quarter of the nineteenth century, after the opening of the Suez Canal in 1869 made the export of even cheap North Atlantic commodities extremely profitable, European factories became the main suppliers of china to coastal east Africa. Private trading houses, such as Smith Mackenzie and Co. Ltd., shipped factory-produced china from England, the Netherlands, and German Saarland to Mombasa, Lamu, and Zanzibar until the 1930s. South Asian merchants, who continued to import cheap wares from Bombay, also participated in the trade. The Swahili coast demand for imported pottery lasted until around World War II.

The design and quality of European pottery differed significantly from Chinese export porcelain. European glazed stoneware was much cheaper and thus available to larger segments of the population than porcelain; it also broke easily. It often featured simple multicolored flowers and vegetal motifs. A crescent moon and star design often dominated the center of plates destined for east Africa, a motif reserved for plates created for Muslim consumers. At the turn of the twentieth century even recently manumitted enslaved peoples inserted these visual markers of refinement into their homes.[21]

THE SYMBOLIC WORLD OF ORNAMENT

The ornamental displays in figures 4.1 and 4.2 clearly represent the intensification of the ability to accumulate power and wealth, but they also expressed complex cultural and philosophical concepts. Ludwig Krapf, a German missionary stationed in Mombasa in the 1840s and '50s, documented specific Swahili-language words and concepts used to describe architectural ornament. These registered a subtle distinction between porcelain and stuccowork as forms of interior decoration. The art of lime stuccowork was called the *uwezo wa niumba,* the talent or ability of the house, while porcelain was part of the *mapambo ya niumba,* the decoration of the house. Both clearly coexisted in homes, but they represented two different periods in the history of house decoration.

Decorative stuccowork was an older fashion that was already disappearing by the early nineteenth century. The uwezo wa niumba stuccowork, like building a stone mansion, took serious artistic and financial investment. It also represented the apex of a mason's knowledge and craft, since creating these delicate low-relief compositions in lime plaster was extremely complicated. The preparation of the coral and shell lime alone took sometimes years and had to be planned in advance. The uwezo wa niumba was also symbolically significant, embodying the beginning of a new generation. According to nineteenth-century sources, soon after a female patrician child was born, a new lime pit was prepared for her wedding ceremony two decades later, when she would sit in state in front of a new stucco composition that was completed to coincide with her wedding. An important component of her wedding celebration would be the *fola la kuwaza*, the feast of the stucco, in which the masons revealed their completed designs to the family of the bride.[22]

Most significantly, the uwezo of the stuccowork was directly linked to the uwezo of house owners. *Uwezo*, which can be translated as dignity, ability, honor, or power, is a multivalent concept, signifying the capacity to make something happen, to enact causality. Uwezo is primarily an attribute of humans, suggesting consciousness and will. Only inanimate things that amplify human actions also have uwezo. When things, like stuccowork, are also categorized as uwezo, they matter; they are understood to have a direct effect on people. This is one of the reasons coral stone architecture is so symbolically significant on the Swahili coast. Stone architecture reflects, encapsulates, and heightens the uwezo of the owner. Cultivating the material aspects of uwezo took time and the wealth and stamina to plan for the long term, which was a privilege only the waungwana enjoyed until the nineteenth century.

Significantly, from the eighteenth century onward the stuccowork that signified the uwezo of the house and the owner was increasingly displaced by the accumulation of *mapambo,* decorative things like massproduced porcelain dishes. *Mapambo* simply means decoration or finery, and it describes any form of embellishment added to spaces or things of daily use, from embroidery on clothes to tassels on curtains to framed photographs—objects one has the means to buy.

However, the very density of porcelain display on view in the rooms in figures 4.1 and 4.2 signals more than simply one's power to consume. Rather, each porcelain dish also guards the house and its inhabitants and speaks to a long tradition of deploying imported porcelain in spaces and places in need of talismanic protection.[23] Glazed plates deflected the envious gaze—often described as the evil eye in western accounts. According to popular belief, shared by many Muslims in other parts of the world, one can protect oneself against the harmful desires of others through two primary means: first, through discretion, by avoiding the public display of one's finery and by not calling attention to one's blessings or good fortune (only if a person's beauty or material wealth is made visible to the eye can it become the focus of another's desires); second, by distracting the gaze with a compelling object, ornament, or image. Creating a pleasing visual experience can be a protective act because jealousy is linked to the sense of sight. The decorative beauty of porcelain therefore could shield the more fragile treasures in the house, the well-being and good life of the family, since it acted as an ocular diversion. The layering of identical plates across the surface of the walls in a sense amplified the protective power of their beauty.

Although today porcelain's protective significance is no longer emphasized, an early twentieth-century description of the Jaffer, Sheriff, and Co. store in Mombasa notes that a local collection of porcelain could not be sold publicly "owing to rites of religion."[24] Also, to this day people in Mombasa and Lamu remember their grandmothers believing that every time a displayed plate cracked, it had "caught" and neutralized someone's envious gaze. When the plate broke it was, in effect "working," since it had absorbed feelings of jealousy that might have hurt the owner of the house and his or her family.

Like the real mirror in the room, visible on the left in figure 4.2, such displays aimed at endless multiplicity, which is the opposite of a synecdochic collecting strategy found in modern museums, where singular objects *represent* something or someone. In contrast, in the late eighteenth century on the Swahili coast, one object was never enough; what was desired was the amassing of the physical materiality of things. The order of display created in these spaces also disregards the original context of each object. For example, dishes were not placed on tables or used in the preparation or consumption of food. The very erasure of the use-value of a china dish makes it such an effective thing, allowing it to manifest talismanic protection and plentitude. This strategy of multiplying and gathering imports so that independence from a specific place or single region is achieved is characteristic of Swahili coast aesthetic practice.

THE UWEZO OF CHAIRS

Perhaps the most complex objects of interior decoration present in the room in figure 4.2 are the six chairs, called *viti vya enzi* (pl.) in Swahili, four of which are occupied by patricians. *Kiti cha enzi* (sg.), which is usually translated as "chair of power," is an emblem of uwezo, like the stuccowork. *Enzi* is an adjectival version of the noun *uwezo*, which means power, ability or agency. The kiti cha enzi (plate 13) is a high-backed chair that is unique to the Swahili coast, although its form is a fusion of many overseas styles. It design is defined by an overall angular rigidity; its body comprises flat pieces of plainsawn hardwood, pegged together at right angles, which allows each chair to be easily disassembled. All extant examples feature a raised footrest and rectangular and square string panels. The artistry of older chairs lies in the mother of pearl, bone, and ivory inlay designs covering their backs and cresting rails. The inclusion of ivory, a token of mercantile power on the Swahili coast, was especially significant. Ivory was east Africa's most important commodity for centuries; the wealth and prestige of any Swahili port depended on participating in its export.[25] In the late nineteenth and early twentieth centuries, Swahili coast craftsmen used the flat plane of the chair's cresting rail to create imaginative compositions of abstracted trees and flowers. Some inlay designs begin to resemble peaceful and fecund landscapes, the flora and fauna arranged in perfect symmetry.

The kiti cha enzi is one of the most celebrated icons of Swahili heritage; even today old and new versions are coveted for display in peoples' homes in Lamu, Mombasa, and Zanzibar (plate 14 and figure 4.7). As early as the nineteenth century it was a romanticized object, one that was seen to be an "ancient" symbol of authentic Swahili coast culture. As is often the case in moments of colonization, it became widely popular precisely because it represented a waning tradition. Europeans avidly

FIGURE 4.7. Noor Sood Mohammad Shikely sitting in state on one of her family's viti vya enzi, which were carved in the early twenty-first century. Mombasans prefer to collect and commission viti vya enzi in pairs. Photograph by the author, 2014.

collected viti vya enzi because, unlike so many other forms of Swahili ornament, it was made locally. Its decorative schema also ignited the European imagination, which interpreted it as the last material remains of the impact of sixteenth-century Portuguese culture on Swahili coast life. The white inlay on the pediment of the kiti often featured medallions with four V-shaped arms, which Europeans believed to be representations of the Maltese cross. John Haggard, the British vice consul who lived in Lamu and Zanzibar from 1883 to 1908, sent two viti vya enzi to his brother in England and explained that "the Mohammedan workers probably don't know it's a cross at all but simply perpetuate the old pattern and fashion which was originally Christian."[26] This iconographic reading is doubtful, but the British continued to focus on Portuguese origins of the kiti cha enzi throughout the colonial period.

The kiti cha enzi also encapsulates the fact that Swahili visual culture and ornament cannot be reduced to a single place of origin, much to the frustration of art historians, who seek to create a typology of discrete forms and influences. Previous scholarship traced its origin to such vastly different places and time periods as Mamluk Egypt (thirteenth century), late Mudéjar Portugal (sixteenth century) and British Raj South Asia (nineteenth century).[27] Such attempts to find the stylistic origins of form or ornament are particularly pointless in such borderland cultures as the Swahili coast, where material models imported from elsewhere are always physically reconstituted and symbolically refabulized. Its form does indeed share compelling similarities with a bewildering range of foreign chairs, and this "foreign-ness" of course is intentionally cultivated. Most probably, the kiti cha enzi as it exists in its present form was a nineteenth century invention based on an older form. In fact, all extant viti vya enzi—even when they are celebrated as ancient icons of power—date from the nineteenth century. During the Zanzibari and British colonial periods this "ancient" chair was produced in great numbers in workshops all along the Swahili coast, and it was available for purchase in souvenir shops (figure 4.8). Used for all kinds of ceremonies sanctioned and officiated by the colonial government, they acquired their great popularity because they signaled the administration's appreciation of local tradition. For example, when the Sultan of Zanzibar visited Mombasa in 1906 he sat in state in a kiti cha enzi on a dais in the Jubilee Hall, an architectural space constructed specifically by the British for meetings with the "customary elders" of the city.[28] The Queen Mother was also enthroned on one during her visit to Mombasa in 1959.

During the colonial period imported chairs functioned as prestige chairs; they were assembled by well-to-do women to fill the central spaces of living and reception rooms. In the nineteenth century it was a matter of honor to collect as many imported chairs—or locally made chairs based on imported models—as possible. Embellished chairs, especially those with heraldic ornaments, were imported from North America, Europe, and South Asia in large numbers. Although chairs became more readily available during this period, they were connected to waungwana power in the local imaginary. To sit on a high-backed wooden chair meant one's body took on the posture of a high-ranking member of coastal city life (figures 4.2 and 4.9). Its form molded

FIGURE 4.8. Jaffer, Sheriff, and Company's sale room in Old Town Mombasa in 1906. The shop sold diverse imported objets d'art and also Swahili coast heirlooms, including old porcelain and viti vya enzi. One kiti cha enzi is visible against the left far wall of the shop. Illustrated in Playne and Gale, *East Africa (British): Its History, People, Commerce, Industries, and Resources* 1908, page 114.

the body both physically and socially to embody the still dignity so celebrated as a key characteristic of *uungwana*-ness, the Swahili way of being civilized. It also encapsulated the very essence of Swahili autonomous personhood because it signaled freedom over one's own body and also authority over the body of others. To sit upright was the posture of a nonlaboring body, a body that was engaged in governance and in control of others.

Yet the kiti cha enzi is slightly different from other chairs. It is the material trace of a time on the Swahili coast when sovereign kings and queens ruled local towns. Its form evoked a type of sacred throne that symbolized indigenous royal authority, which had been largely destroyed with the establishment of the Busaidi Sultanate in the 1830s. The many viti vya enzi in circulation during the early twentieth century in fact were copies of ancient emblems of independence. Ludwig Krapf observed

FIGURE 4.9. Unidentified Zanzibari woman sitting in state on an imported high-backed chair. Photograph courtesy of the Zanzibar National Archives.

that a kiti cha enzi was the "chair of state of a chief or king" and was no longer in use when he was living in Mombasa, in the 1840s. He explained, "Formerly all the independent chiefs of the Swahili coast had a 'kiti cha enzi' until the power of the Iman of Muscat [Sultan Said of Zanzibar] swept them away."[29]

Before Sultan Said annexed the Swahili coast into his mercantile empire, only patrician families could use a kiti cha enzi. Such thrones belonged to a group of objects that functioned as sacred relics, which also included magnificent ivory side-blown trumpets and monumental barrel drums. Locals revered these objects because they manifested a sacrosanct environment, a place where the ancestors became present in the space of the living. The physical presence of these insignia transformed ceremonies and festivals into sacred moments. No important funeral or wedding would be considered complete without their public display and use. Most importantly, no new ruler could be installed without them since they were the physical manifestation of his sacred connections to the land and his ancestors. Krapf's observations and other fleeting commentaries from the nineteenth century suggest that the first three Omani sultans of Zanzibar were keenly aware of the political and religious power of these objects. They perceived them as a real threat to their authority, believing their presence in the local community could inspire rebellion.[30] Sultan Barghash in fact finally confiscated the most "dangerous" insignia, placing them in the hands of British colonial officials, who attempted to deactivate their power by putting them on public display as items of Swahili heritage—that is, as objects of the past that had no political or sacred authority in the present (figure 4.10).

THE IMPACT OF ZANZIBARI MODERNITY

In the nineteenth century, new forms of ornamentation and arts of adornment became popular even in seemingly remote areas such as the Lamu Archipelago, creating a palimpsest of the old and new. For example, in the room in figure 4.2 we can clearly discern the impact of British Raj and Arabian Peninsula (especially Omani) material culture. The seated men, all Lamu patricians, wear turbans and *joho* robes, a style of high-status menswear made popular by Omani Arabs in the

FIGURE 4.10. A museum-like public space in the British Residency in Zanzibar Town with three viti vya enzi on prominent display. Photograph taken by Sir John Kirk in the 1880s. Photograph courtesy of the Trustees of the National Library of Scotland.

1830s. Mechanical British wall clocks, gas lamps, French gilt mirrors, chromolithographs, and photographs fill the rest of the room. All these objects were associated with Zanzibar and its mercurial consumption habits, where the focus was on the latest import from among the mass-produced commodities of the North Atlantic world and Asia that now flooded the local market.[31] The local dhow trade continued to expand the long-established triangular exchange among east Africa, southern Arabia, and western India, while European steamships dominated the trade with European and North American markets.

Colorful chromolithographs of Qur'anic calligraphy also hang in the dimly-lit upper regions of the walls of figure 4.2. The growing importance of mass-produced lithographic materials was closely intertwined with the rise of Sufism in east Africa during the colonial period. A 1911 report on the nature of Islam in east Africa documents the flooding of the coast with printed materials from Cairo and Bombay. This modern print culture consisted of "lithographs or printed stories, which contain single episodes from the 1001 Nights . . . popular handbooks, devotional books . . . and little books which are employed in huge quantities as amulets."[32] In established centers of Islamic scholarship, such as Mombasa and Lamu, Sufism, especially Qadiriyyah teachings and practices promulgated by Hadhrami immigrants, challenged locally established tenets and the social norms they endorsed. Sufi orders became key vehicles for marginalized peoples, such as women and formerly enslaved peoples, who sought alternative paths of religious expressions. The doctrinally conservative Islamic teaching of scholars endorsed by the colonial government was increasingly questioned by all levels of society during the social revolutions of the late nineteenth and early twentieth centuries.[33]

Especially during the reign of Sultan Barghash, the contemporary cultures of the British Raj influenced east African fashion and tastes. Rich Arabs and South Asians and European residents juxtaposed the latest technological innovations, such as electric lighting, with the latest neo-Hispano-Baroque and Anglo-Indian furniture designs. The interior space documented in figure 4.11 was a domestic private space in a large mansion stone mansion in Stone Town Zanzibar. During this period the Omani and South Asian elite owned the majority of such stone mansions, although Europeans rented them too. Their interior display logics were an amalgamation of diverse cultural strands. Large arched niches typically dominated the walls of reception and private living spaces, and as can be seen in the photograph, they were divided into shelves for the display of the same porcelain collections so prized in Lamu and Mombasa. A member of the Sultanic court, Princess Salme Said, who later immigrated to Germany and took the name Emily Reute, described Zanzibari display logics in her memoir in this manner:

> Rich and distinguished people generally furnish their houses in the following style: Persian carpets or very fine soft matting cover the floors; the thick, whitewashed walls are divided from floor to ceiling into several partitions by deep recesses; these recesses are again subdivided by shelves of wood,

FIGURE 4.11. Interior view of a large mansion in Zanzibar. Such mansions were associated with the Omani Arab elite during the sultanate years. The room is filled with European glass chandeliers, British Raj furniture, mass-produced porcelain, and portrait photographs. This photograph was taken by Souza and Paul, a photo studio located in Zanzibar Stone Town. Photograph courtesy of the Historisches Fotoarchiv im Rautenstrauch-Joest-Museum – Kulturen der Welt, Cologne.

and painted green, forming a kind of open cabinet. Upon these shelves are symmetrically ranged the choicest and most expensive objects of glass and china. To an Arab nothing can be too costly to decorate these shelves; a handsome cut glass, a plate beautifully painted, or an elegant and tasteful jug, may cost any price.[34]

This photograph was also published in a British newspaper, where the byline for the image noted, "The conflict between Oriental and Western civilization is clearly discernable in the decorations of the chamber."[35] Yet, from a local perspective, this layering of diverse cultural strands in the space of daily life consolidated, rather than displaced, Swahili coast cultural values. The young man sitting in the center of the room, his name no longer known, was clearly affiliated with the Sultan's court. He is dressed in official Omani ceremonial garb, which included a multicolored turban, and a long black overcoat with gold embroidery. His body language is relaxed as he leans against the curve of the chair's back, extending his legs slightly before him. He causally holds a walking-stick between his legs and gazes with calm certainty across his right shoulder. His posture and presence declare his confidence and authority.

The carefully arranged collection of prized furnishings and objets d'art reflects the young man's good taste and aesthetic sensibility. His porcelain collection is ordered and classified according to formal features only. That is, each shelf is reserved for one particular object type—vase, bowl, lidded vessel, or cup. Similar to the interior space of Lamu houses, this taxonomic logic suggests the desire to duplicate a singular form multiple times. It is a collection of volume, where material mass is celebrated, rather than singularity.

The circumstances of this photographic encounter are unclear: did the newspaper, a European traveler, or the young sitter himself commission the image? All we know for sure is that the photograph was taken by Souza and Paul, which was one of many photography studios operating in Zanzibar and Mombasa during this period. In fact, studio portraits are an important element of the room's design program; two framed portraits are displayed on the Indo-Portuguese cabinet in the right foreground of the image, and another occupies the small night-stand next to the bed. Photography became immensely popular during this period as well. Sultans and other members of the court actively collected cartes de visite of British aristocrats and government officials and in turn commissioned such images of themselves for distribution, redeploying European performances of power and novelty to indicate their own imperial ambitions.

Thus the materiality of the photograph, its objectness, engendered the display of selfhood for diverse audiences, who inserted such objects into an array of visual and symbolic systems, endowing them with overlapping but also divergent meanings. Locally, portrait photography became extremely popular; because it allowed the sitter to capture a tableau of his or her public self in exacting detail. For example, the photograph of Sultan Ali (figure 4.12) is obviously in dialogue with official portraits from various imperial centers, including Egypt, most likely the source of the lavishly inscribed fabric backdrop, and undoubtedly it is

FIGURE 4.12. Portrait of Sultan Ali bin Said (r. 1890–93). In this photograph he presents himself enthroned on a golden Victorian armchair with lion's heads, against an Egyptian tapestry featuring Qur'anic texts in its upper registers and central roundel. His turban, robes, and ceremonial weaponry are the insignia of the Omani elite. Photograph courtesy of the Zanzibar National Archives.

FIGURE 4.13. Carte de visite featuring the sitting room of the British Residency in Zanzibar, circa 1880s. European architectural interiors in Zanzibar were an amalgamation of Victorian, British Raj, and coastal east African display logics. Porcelain collected in East Africa was especially prized by European residents. Photograph courtesy of the Trustees of the National Library of Scotland.

meant to signal his religiosity and connection to other centers of Islam. It is also an artifact of European empire; like members of the British government, sultanate officials began commissioning public portrait photographs to bestow upon visiting dignitaries from abroad. As a circulating sign, a portrait photo was an image intelligible to the diverse communities and visitors to Zanzibar.[36] On one level it was the staging of a cross-cultural performance, expressing a desire by the sitter or commissioner to develop new reciprocities between older forms of self-expressions and recently arrived North Atlantic technologies of transacting meaning.

Europeans also appropriated and inserted Swahili oceanic design and display aesthetics in their official administrative and leisure spaces to evoke an authenticity of place. Images of the interior spaces of the British Residency in Zanzibar became important to the visual economy of empire during this period. Postcards featuring the drawing room of the residency were produced for public circulation back to the imperial metropole (figure 4.13), and the official photo albums of protectorate staff members are replete with countless images featuring the changing interior design programs of the residency (figure 4.14). These interiors are also typical of Victorian tastes, with every surface and open space bristling with ornate furniture, objects, framed pastoral scenes, and photographs. The densely carved and pierced blackwood tables and side-tables on display were exported all over the globe from Bombay in the 1870s and 1880s. Typical of this style, their dark massive forms are based on Victorian prototypes that have been transformed into teeming shapes of intertwining serpents and flowers and foliate ornaments inspired by Gujarati wood carving to evoke the imaginary opulence of the Raj in India.

Locally collected porcelain plates and vessels were also prominently displayed in the residency (figure 4.15). The arrangement of the dishes in this photograph evokes the interior of the Lamu houses featured in figures 4.1 and 4.2. Sir John Kirk, the British consul of Zanzibar who lived in the residency during the 1880s, was the photographer for figures 4.14 and 4.15. He was also the most ambitious collector of ancient porcelain on the Swahili coast, amassing thousands of pieces. His entire collection was lost at sea when the ship carrying it to England caught fire.[37] Of course, the display of porcelain was in a sense also typically European. Porcelain was fashionable in homes of aristocrats and the bourgeoisie from at least the seventeenth century, and by the nineteenth century chinoiserie and exotic bric-a-brac were essential for the Victorian staging of English-ness across the vast territory of the British Empire.[38] Yet the display in the residency was also specific to the maritime world of the western Indian Ocean. Here Swahili, Arab, South Asian, and Victorian consumer tastes and aesthetic practices intermingled in new ways.

HERITAGE AT THE EDGE OF THE NATION-STATE

Today objects of interior ornament associated with nyumba za mawe exist at the intersection of the two different geographies, that of the postcolonial nation-state and the mobile world of the Indian Ocean. With independence, when the coast became part of Kenya and Tanzania, it

FIGURE 4.14. Hallway in the British Residency decorated with furniture imported from Bombay, chinoiserie, photographs, spears, and a mounted rhino skull. Photograph courtesy of the Trustees of the National Library of Scotland.

FIGURE 4.15. Middle Eastern, Chinese, and European glaze ware on view in the British Residency. The glaze ware was mostly collected in Lamu by Sir John Kirk in the 1880s. Photograph courtesy of the Trustees of the National Library of Scotland.

became imperative for coastal residents to present themselves as citizens of independent African nations. Locals had to consider what it meant being called a "Swahili" in relationship to a new web of opportunities and restrictions.

How an object is transformed into national heritage says much about the mobility of objects that empowers them to present and represent multiple meanings. On the Swahili coast objects anchor contrary spectacles and practices. In Mombasa, for example, the semipublic and private spaces of the home share striking visual and material commonalities with nineteenth-century Zanzibari interiors. Women in particular stage their appropriation of nineteenth-century material legacies by designing layered assemblages of heirlooms, commodities, and art objects that are in dialogue with the past. These domestic interiors are enactments of the past that reconfigure and even ignore officially conceived "national" heritage.

For many locals there is a focus on recouping the "lost" time of the Sultanate period through including "things of the past" in their homes. Mombasa's Old Town citizens' understanding of local culture is very much influenced by their memories and idealization of the Sultanate of Zanzibar, which is celebrated as the last time Mombasa belonged to a unified Islamic cultural space. Today architectural settings articulate seemingly nostalgic desires to create a cultural space beyond the framework of the nation-state of Kenya. Porcelain, luxury commodities from the Arabian Gulf and Mumbai, and locally created "Swahili" arts are all central to this practice. Many women cherish these objects, for they prove the adage, "We do as our ancestors do, we don't live like those outside."[39] In these discussions, "outside" means mainland Kenya.

Even such seemingly mundane things such as brass-embossed wooden sandals (*mitawanda*) are vitally important to contemporary displays (stacked on top of the two miniature chests in figure 4.16 and in the center of figure 4.17). Such sandals, today on sale all over Old Town, are copies of the nineteenth-century versions that only mwungwana women were allowed to wear (the patrician woman in figure 4.9 is wearing them). As ornamental items in contemporary domestic interiors, they celebrate "Swahili" heritage, but they also evoke precolonial sumptuary

FIGURE 4.16. Bi Rahima Ali, a leader of the Kilifi mtaa of Mombasa, in her reception room. She is presenting one of her Zanzibari-style chinaware heirlooms. Photograph by the author, 2005.

FIGURE 4.17. Bi Rahima Ali in her reception room, surrounded by her favorite brass and copperware ornamental objects, including a large *upatu* (platter), two miniature *kasha* (chests), and *mitawanda* (platform sandals). Photograph by the author, 2005.

FIGURE 4.18. Zanzibari-style ceramic platter in Rahima Ali's collection.
Photograph by the author, 2005.

laws meant to patrol the lines between enslaved and freeborn peoples.
Slavery and local systems of bondage were abolished in the late nineteenth century, but the politics of birthright still inflect local social life
today.[40] The display of patrician material culture in contemporary domestic spaces thus represents a significant claim about one's own identity
in relationship to the social hierarchies of the past.

Many women, such as Rahima Ali, a respected member of the Thenashara Taifa, cherish their family's porcelain collection (figure 4.18)
for similar reasons. Porcelain dishes are now anchored to romanticized
memories of the glories of the Zanzibari Sultanate. Rahima Ali described her collection as "just like those things of the Sultan of Zanzibar. They came from far-away China. These are Chinese, very hard to
get these days." Others, like Mohamed Mchulla Mohamed, who lives in
Mombasa but is originally from the Lamu Archipelago, collects porcelain dishes (plate 15 and figure 4.19) because they are part of his family's

FIGURE 4.19. Mohamed Mchulla's chinaware collection.
Photograph by the author, 2013.

heritage. He works as an archeologist for the National Museums of Kenya and therefore also has a scholarly appreciation for his collection. Some of his most cherished pieces are inherited heirlooms, but he has added new ones to his collection since living in Mombasa, where traders and collectors sell colonial-period crockery to locals and tourists as antiques. He displays them at home, but many are packed away for most of the year. In rare instances he loans them out to friends and family for wedding feasts, because it has become fashionable again in recent years to serve wedding meals on "ancient" dishes. Layla Khamis Rashid Sood Shikelly also collects antique chinaware; for her it embodies the refinement of a bygone era (plate 16). Strikingly, her porcelain display evokes the way porcelain was hung on walls in the nineteenth century in Lamu merchant houses (cf. figures 4.1 and 4.2).

"ARAB" THINGS

Locals now also like to commission craftsmen to make furniture in the "old Arab style."[41] Another woman, Bi Aisha Abdul Raisul, believes these objects are "more elegant and respectable," and when she ordered her furniture she thought it fashionable to return to *mapambo ya zamani* (decoration styles of times past). Objects from Zanzibar, such as copper plates and chests, are also important. Especially Arabian Peninsula coffee pots (*dele*) and their accompanying cups and rosewater sprinklers (*mrashi*) are icons of sophistication, Muslim domesticity, and codes of refinement. They were popularized during the nineteenth century and continue to be avidly bought and collected by women for their homes. They play important roles in public celebrations, such as the holy days of Ramadan and weddings.[42]

In Bi Zeineb Mohammad's display (figure 4.20), the mrashi standing on a miniature ornamental shelf anchors a symmetrical tripartite display of contemporary icons of sophisticated living. A set of the latest chromolithographs, featuring romantic renderings of Mecca's religious architecture, are hung on the wall across from the main entrance to her reception and sleeping room. Directly below each image three copper plates (*upatu*) enforce the tripartite arrangement of the layout. Two miniature ornamental side-blown musical horns (*masiwa*) hang on either

FIGURE 4.20. Main reception and sleeping room in Bi Zeineb Mohammad's house. Photograph by the author, 2005.

side of the mrashi, below which hangs another upatu. These contemporary masiwa are hand-carved out of wood or horn and are miniature versions of the grand ivory masiwa of the past. Like the kiti cha enzi discussed previously, they were part of the regalia owned by patrician lineages.[43] Such decorative stagings are today often described by locals as being typically Arab.

What *Arab* means is a contested and vitally important issue on the Swahili coast. People often talk about "living like an Arab." Yet in these conversations Arab-ness is often meant to evoke a *local* cultural world, one that is defined by oceanic refinement. It is not necessarily a racial claim, although many people do say that they are ethnically Arab. But for local Thenashara Taifa activists, such as Sheikh Abdullahi Nassir, Ahmad Nassir Juma Bhalo, and Stambuli Abdullahi Nassir, this is simply a conflation of Arab and Islamic. When people say they are living like an Arab they mean they are devout Muslims. These three men are also

very much committed to disengaging their heritage from the appellation *Arab*, as they consider the Arabization of their heritage part of the
injustices experienced by the Taifa community of Mombasa during the
colonial period. Yet at the same time they also remember the sultanate years with a wistful nostalgia; to them it was the last time Kenya's
coast belonged to a wholly Islamic cultural world. "One was never at
a loss when going to Zanzibar, Mombasa or Lamu," explained Sheikh
Abdillahi Nasser when describing his youth in colonial Mombasa. "We
all had one culture, same dress, same food," he recalled. Most important in these accounts of the Sultanate period was the common practice
of Islam, which in Mombasa is understood as being interterritorial but
specific to the east African coast.

This evocative remembrance of Lamu, Mombasa, and Zanzibar as
intertwined cities sharing a familiar physical and cultural geography is
key to understanding people's memories of Arab-ness. But many Mombasans are in fact distressed by the growing power of Muslims from the
Arab world in recent years. Educators from Saudi Arabia, Egypt, and
Syria are now the teachers and imams at mosques and therefore command the respect of the community. Sheikh Abdillahi Nasser explained
that "those new sheikhs are introducing *hanbali* jurisprudence [from
Saudi Arabia]. Our people don't even know it, but those new sheikhs are
too oriented toward Mecca and Medina. Tragically our people do not
recognize that they come with something alien."[44]

People living outside of Old Town also critique the celebration of the
elite culture popularized during the sultanate years. Wachangamwe
members (one of the moieties in the Thenashara Taifa), who live on the
mainland directly across from Mombasa Island, are derisive of their relations in Old Town for emulating Arab manners and customs. Important
leaders of this mainland community, such as Fatuma Mbwana Amiri and
Hadija Mmwana Amiri, are of the opinion that Old Town people are
simply putting on Arab (or waungwana) airs. Both women suggested that
people go to live in Old Town to forget and ignore their connections to
Mijikenda peoples. Fatuma Mbwana Amiri was more specific in regard
to performance cultures, noting that people of Old Town prefer taraab
now, when really "they are people of *chakacha*." Taraab is a musical genre
that is sung in Swahili but uses much Arabic instrumentation. It was the

product of the late nineteenth century, when under the patronage of Sultan Barghash Egyptian orchestras were brought to Zanzibar. Their music and instruments spearheaded a new local musical movement, which today also features a range of mainland influences. In contrast, chakacha is considered typically mainland African, although it is popular in coastal port cities too. Fatuma Mbwana Amiri noted with sardonic humor that "over there in Kibokoni [a section of Old Town] it's Arab time now."[45]

The many meanings and object-cultures on display in homes on the Swahili coast illuminate the complicated reciprocities enacted in fluid border zone societies. As we have seen, on the Swahili coast locals collect objects and "curate" spaces in their homes that produce a sense of living in multiple places all at once. The layering of diverse cultural vignettes and forms creates a montage of diverse temporal and cultural sites. They all signal a sense of transregional and global connectedness, yet the details of the staging are deeply embedded in local hierarchies and systems of signification. Coastal object entanglements are also highly fractured and even create contradictory narratives about locality and belonging.

❧ ❧ ❧

Conclusion

Trading Places

Today ornate doorways such as the one in figure 5.1 are often celebrated in the west as emblems of local authenticity and Swahili identity. Yet from a local perspective, and much to the discomfort of Africanist art historians, they give material form to the circulatory networks of the Indian Ocean. Their design program was originally meant to evoke a faraway place. Carvers were constantly changing their compositions by incorporating the latest styles and patterns of ornament from objects being imported from overseas. Yet, they did not simply produce copies, but masterfully transformed exotic forms to create works that exist at the edge of stylistic categories, such as African, Asian, and European. For example, the design of this door is typical of nineteenth-century innovations and fashions. This was a time when the tradition of carving doors reached new heights of intricacy and delicacy. As can be seen, carvers cultivated an Indian-inflected style, often preferring the lush ornamentation of British Raj woodwork. The pediment and central post feature minimalist rosettes and abstracted pineapples, their repeating forms creating a rhythmic movement along the horizontal and vertical planes of the massive doorway. Especially the restrained linearity of the floral motifs exemplifies the way local carvers created strikingly innovative works.[1]

Although by the late nineteenth century even entire doorways were mass-produced in Bombay for export to Zanzibar and Mombasa.

FIGURE 5.1. Nineteenth-century carved wooden door. Located in the courtyard area of Fort Jesus in Mombasa, but originally it was the main doorway of a stone house in Old Town. Photograph by the author, 2014.

This meant that larger segments of the population could decorate their porches with fashionable ornament. Of course, just having some freedom to decorate your home with imported things did not imply the ability to overcome exploitation or degradation at the hands of the more powerful; still, it was an act—however small—that they did not control. Such acts expressed a desire to make daily life more livable and to create a new experience for oneself and for others.

Similarly, each time Zanzibar's Sultan Barghash received visitors in the House of Wonders, he structured his and other people's corporeal experiences through the aesthetics of his style and way of living. Bodies rested on neo-baroque chairs from Bombay, fingertips brushed across the surfaces of delicate chinaware ordered from Germany, and the glittering lights of French chandeliers allowed all to gaze upon his collection of British telescopes and automated wall clocks. He lived like this not only to produce tactile pleasure or to perform his identity as an "Arab" monarch, but to convince others—especially his British overlords—that his desires and dreams were real. He wanted to shape a concrete experience of his persona as a worldly sophisticate who was in control over the making of empire on Zanzibar Island.

BEYOND "ETHNIC" CULTURE

In this book I have not set out to prove that this material culture is uniquely African or Swahili, although many readers will of course assert that it is both. I would very much agree with them, especially if my project centered on rejecting the racist scholarship of the colonial past, which always presented the stone cities of the coast as Arab and not African. The important work of scholars who came of age during the independence period has already shown us that if we must choose between these two categories, then the culture of the east African littoral is unquestionably African. Yet instead of affirming the notion that it always makes sense to use racialized geopolitical and ethnic labels to think about the history of cultural production, I have considered the specific moment when such categories became operative for managing people and culture. In doing so I have argued for the centrality of history to understanding ideas that now seem ubiquitous and true.

During the colonial period, assigning the materiality of daily life (including artifacts and architecture) to a specific racial or ethnic category became an increasingly important strategy to police the imagined difference between peoples.[2] The notion that an architectural style can be linked to a single place, or a single people, is an extension of European desire to see a constitutive link between culture, race, and place. It was exactly during this time that questions about what is foreign and what is indigenous about Swahili coast culture became increasingly important. To this day, questions about whether Swahili coast cities—and by extension their peoples—are "African" and "native" or somehow "foreign" shape discussions about Swahili coast heritage. Even Kenyans and Tanzanians are concerned with the essential ethnic identity of stone architecture, posing questions like "Is this architecture really Kenyan?" or "Are the Swahili Africans?"

Yet, contrary to popular notions, this singular focus on ethnic and territorial belonging is a relatively recent phenomenon on the Swahili coast. Local history throws the constructed nature of land-based nativism into sharp relief.[3] Coastal peoples' insistence on in-between-ness, on presenting their society as local and supralocal simultaneously, was incommensurate with assuming a natural link between social identity and the geography of a piece of land. Because they did not want to be chained to the physical boundaries of the African continent, nor did they "look" distinctly African, Arab, or Asian, coastal peoples came to be viewed with ever-greater suspicion from the colonial period onward. And today, as the anthropologist Jemima Pierre has recently pointed out, "Africa could not represent a more racialized location" in the contemporary imaginary.[4] Indeed, as we have seen, colonial-era processes of racialization continue to shape the contours of contemporary identity politics in postcolonial east Africa. To be recognized as a full citizen of Kenya and Tanzania means one must claim an autochthonous ethnicity, one that is "of the soil" and recognizably African.

Presenting the cultural history of Africa in ethnic terms remains popular in academia as well. Art historians and curators still write about Dogon, Yoruba, Kongo, or Senufo arts. One could point out that these are practical shorthand labels, similar to calling artworks made on the European continent German, Italian, or Polish. In many instances this is indeed the case. Yet, by my reckoning, the discipline of Africanist art history continues to overemphasize group belonging. In contrast, scholars of the history of art in Europe do not concentrate on understanding how artistic practice produces nationality or ethnicity. The work of Europeanists might in fact benefit from considering such topics, but the study of material culture as a form of identity negotiation can easily become a straightjacket, reproducing the same answers to the same questions and ultimately limiting our understanding of the plurality and ambiguity of aesthetic experience. After all, as the anthropologist Michael Jackson reminds us, peoples' creativity, their imagination, and the life of the senses are not simply representations of collectivities, social processes, or communal beliefs.[5] They might, in part, speak to such social science themes, but they do much more. They also show us, for example, how people seek to make life interesting, they reveal flights of fancy, and they might even express an individual's unique vision of what it means to feel good on a drab day.

It is important, however, to remember that this focus on social function and ethnic identity in Africanist art history has to do with its formation as a discipline. The study of African visual culture was shaped by the major intellectual and political revolutions of the 1960s, when Africanist art history was first established as a new subject of study in North American universities. The first generation of academically trained Africanists completely transformed how African and African diaspora visual culture was understood in the west. They rejected the then-dominant idea that the arts of Africa express an innate and primeval "tribal" character, and that "tribes," such as Dogon, Yoruba, Senufo, and Swahili, each have a style of art that is biologically determined.[6] Instead they focused on the constructed nature of ethnic identities. One lasting effect of this vibrant era of scholarly revolution is that now the arts are presented as cultural expressions of Yoruba, Dogon, or Swahili communities. Ethnicity has replaced tribe, and culture is understood as performed and not biological.

This shift is of course laudatory, since it rejects the racist essentialism of colonial-era scholarship. Yet it also perpetuates a certain problematic notion—namely that Africans are eternally concerned with producing categorical commonalities, such as ethnic identities. As Frederick

Cooper put it, "The language of identity disposes us to think in terms of bounded groupness. It does so because even constructivist thinking on identity takes the existence of identity as axiomatic. Identity is always already 'there,' as something individuals and groups 'have,' even if the content of particular identities, and the boundaries that mark them off from one another, are conceptualized as always in flux."[7] Indeed, Africanist conceptions of culture are often still undergirded by the assumption that each ethnicity produced singular cultural traditions that can be traced back to a specific place on the African continent, where the ethnic group originated. Even important studies of encounters between different societies inadvertently present material artifacts, such as architecture, in racialized terms such as "hybridity," which, as Robert Young has shown, is a biological concept describing organic processes that was grafted onto the study of culture during the colonial encounter.[8] In critical theory hybridity has also gained valence, but it is largely used to describe symbolic acts of subversion and improvisation and is not linked to groupness. In the study of the arts of Africa, however, its ethnic roots constitute the term because here "hybrid cultural patterns" are framed as encounters between different ethnicities, or "peoples."

My study has purposely resisted identitarian interpretations of local culture because they limit our understanding of the coast—and of other regions of Africa, for that matter.[9] I have attempted to make a simple point that has significant implications for how we study the visual arts of Africa: Africans are not always negotiating their ethnicity (or other social identities) when they make things attractive to the eye or pleasing to the touch.[10] As noted earlier, poor Swahili coast families added exotic elements to their verandahs, carved seemingly foreign patterns on doorways, and displayed imported commodities in their humble homes to create aesthetic experiences of the elsewhere in much the same way as landowners, merchants, and the colonial elite did. Such acts were not simply about claiming a particular identity. Of course, to beautify and ornament the house was and continues to be a political action as well. To live and dress in Zanzibari fashions meant one insisted on being seen as someone who possessed the good taste and sophistication of the powerful. Many deployed such aesthetic performances for strategic reasons: it was a way to gain recognition in the eyes of others; one became visible in the city through such material acts.

Using architecture and ornament to make others see you in new ways was by no means easy or uncontested. In the competitive world of nineteenth-century Zanzibar, for example, the adornment of homes and bodies was intensely scrutinized, because so many newcomers arrived daily to make claims of belonging to the culture of the port. Being able to build and fashion spaces of mercantile plentitude was always central to Swahili coast aesthetic practice, but it was increasingly accompanied by the risk that it could be devalued as an act of audacious self-invention, or worse still, as an act of tasteless pretension. Yet this was a risk many were willing to take.

MOBILITY IN STONE

By focusing on the sensory world of architecture this book has revealed the way diverse actors, including people often categorized as Swahilis, Africans, Arabs, and Europeans, worked together to make the Swahili port city exist "elsewhere" in time and place for a variety of reasons. By "working together" I do not mean that the powerful and urban poor lived together in a multicultural utopian world. Rather, I have suggested that people shaped each other's experiences on a much more intimate level than the archival remains of the past can ever suggest. The material fabric of architecture structured their feelings of attraction and aversion, superiority and subjugation; it is where they acted out their sense of personhood. By emphasizing that it is often hard to delineate where the African experience ended and the European or colonizers' experience began, I have problematized the taxonomy of native versus foreign that often accompanies our accounts of the visual culture of Africa. In this study I have done this by making what might initially seem like a curious temporal move: I repeatedly delved into precolonial histories to make sense of the colonial period and even the present. In fact, many of the houses, mosques, and built landscapes I have written about have long precolonial histories; but I have focused on their inscription into colonial ways of seeing Africa. This focus supports my argument that we need a more layered understanding of African cultural practice, one that is not demarcated only by the temporal division of before and after colonization. The duration of Swahili coast built form reveals the unique way the past can be recast to make sense of the present and to imagine a future of possibilities.

Swahili coast homes were, and continue to be, filled with exotic things imported from far away, but I would argue that this should not be interpreted as the "localization" of "global" forms. People in east Africa are not interested in "localizing" things; being authentically local is not one of their concerns. In fact, few things on the Swahili coast can be categorized as either authentically local or truly foreign. Such a binary suggests that a parallel and self-contained space was produced, whereas in reality their overlapping interaction resists attempts to tease out what is local and what is global. And residents of such port cities as Zanzibar and Mombasa actively cultivated a cultural tactic that emphasized a sense of the nonterritorial and nondiscrete. In fact, people have avoided being anchored to one place or one culture. In that sense, then, the stone house perfectly encapsulated life on the edge between land and sea, where gazes and objects are constantly being traded, shifted, and of course also commodified. Ultimately I want to suggest that the stone house functions as a place of social and symbolic mobility.

Swahili coast people struggle to reconcile precolonial ways of articulating cultural distinctiveness with colonial and postcolonial strategies for managing subjecthood and citizenship, which present culture, including architecture, as an expression of distinct ethnicities bound to a specific territory. Residents of Old Town who position themselves as the descendants of the precolonial patrician elite (the waungwana) now articulate a sense of household and home that is a complex interpolation of precolonial, colonial, and postcolonial systems of signification. Few waungwana descendants live in merchant houses of the waterfront since they lost ownership over them, but it is still important to see oneself connected to the *culture* of living in stone architecture. Objects and ornaments, such as a kiti cha enzi or a porcelain dish, evoke the classic Swahili coast culture of stone. Also, seemingly paradoxically, while contemporary Swahilis are aware that it is pivotal to claim indigenousness or else risk marginalization within the nation-state, many still proudly declare, "Our houses are like those in Arabia."[11] Such a declaration resurrects precolonial idealizations of the port city as a space connected to the wider Muslim world, but because "Arabia" now demarcates a refusal to be Kenyan or Tanzanian, the speaker also knowingly engages colonial and contemporary politics of identity and belonging.

One of the tragic effects of colonization and postcolonial nation-building is that the Swahili coast desire for in-between-ness has been under attack. This indeterminacy appears incommensurate with modern autochthony, which is based on the assumption that one's essential self is constituted by some ancestral relationship to a piece of land. The local desire to emphasize connections across the Indian Ocean is difficult to reconcile with the territorial rootedness required of contemporary citizenship, creating a double bind for coastal residents. This means that the Swahili port city now exists as an over-determined and fraught symbol, its evocation of the "elsewhere" now haunted by the modern specter of foreignness. Even more tragically, this specter is now associated with acts of violence in the imaginary of people not familiar with the coast's historic connections across the sea. For example, the tensions between the central governments of Kenya and Tanzania and their coastal citizens have been heightened in recent years as the "war on terror" has made the Swahili coast one of the main battlegrounds against supra-state Islamism. Moving easily outside state-sanctioned networks of affiliation and community-building, Swahili coast Muslims are now even more suspect in the eyes of others. Yet locals continue to hope that their towns and cities will be recognized as reciprocal places, where foreignness is superseded and solidarity emerges.

APPENDIX

Aziz Ahmed, November 2005
Rahima Ali, May 2005
Bi Shuali Amran, May 2005
Sheikh Msellem Amin, January 2005
Fatuma Mbwana Amiri, March 2005
Hadija Mmwana Amiri, March 2005
Mzee Hamid Mohammad al Baloushi, 2004–2005, 2014
Ustadh Ahmad Nassir Juma Bhalo, February 2004 and July 2013
Mama Hubwa, 2004–2015
Abdul Rasul Hussein, April 2005
Zaiten Hussain, February, May 2005
Mohammad Jaffer, April 2005
Ma'allim Ali Jemadari, August 2003
Sheib Khamis, June 2005
Nawas Khan, September 2004–July 2005
Waffyahmed Kotaria, March 2005
Ustadh Khamis Al Kumri, April 2005
Mwalimu Mohammad Matano, July–August 2003, 2004–2005
Mohamed Abdallah Mohamed Matano, July 2013 and July 2014
Mohammad Miran, February 2005
Mohamed Mchulla, 2004, 2005, 2014, 2015
Sheikh Abdullahi Nasser, January, February, April 2006

Stambuli Abdullahi Nasser, February 2004, August 2005
Aisha Mohammad Nassir, 2005
Mama Hadija Abdul Rahman, March 2005
Mzee Mohammad Shalli, October 2004–August 2005, July 2014
Abdulkarim Ali Mohammad Yunus, January 2005

ARCHIVES CONSULTED

Germany

Ethnologisches Museum Staatliche Museen zu Berlin, Berlin
Political Archives of the Federal Foreign Office of Germany, Berlin
Rautenstrauch-Joest Museum, Kulturen der Welt, Cologne

Kenya

Friends of Fort Jesus Collection, National Museums of Kenya, Mombasa
National Museums of Kenya, Nairobi
Kenya National Archives, Nairobi
Kenya National Archives, Coast Section, Mombasa
Mombasa Old Town Conservation Office Archives, Mombasa
Wakf Commission of Mombasa Collection, Mombasa

Tanzania

Zanzibar National Archives, Zanzibar

United Kingdom

India Office Library, British Library, London
National Archives of Scotland, Edinburgh
National Archives of the United Kingdom, Surrey
MacKinnon Collection, School of Oriental and African Studies Library,
    University of London, London

NOTES

INTRODUCTION

1. I draw on studies that consider how mobile objects instantiate multiple experiences across different societies. See especially Appadurai, *Social Life of Things*; Clifford, *Predicament of Culture*; Flood, *Objects of Translation*; Myers, ed., *Empire of Things*; Spyer, *Border Fetishisms*; Thomas, *Entangled Objects*. I am also inspired by Ikem Okoye's analysis of the interpenetration of European and local building technologies in nineteenth-century southern Nigeria. Okoye, "'Hideous Architecture.'"

2. For an excellent overview of the varied positions taken up by scholars often identified as new materialists see Coole and Frost, *New Materialisms*.

3. A perfect example of this trend in art history is Hunter and Lucchini, "Clever Object."

4. Blier, *Anatomy of Architecture*.

5. Dean, *Culture of Stone*.

6. Doris, *Vigilant Things*.

7. Pietz, "Problem of the Fetish"; Pels, "Spirit of the Matter."

8. Pietz, "Problem of the Fetish," 7.

9. Today only the denigration of this transcultural materiality remains. The fetish was reduced to an "African" thing of primitive superstition in the racist imaginary of Europe from the eighteenth century onward.

10. This book is very much informed by Walter Mignolo's concept of "border thinking," which allows us to move beyond the local-versus-global binary in our understanding of the cultural dimensions of globalization. Mignolo, *Local Histories/Global Designs*.

11. Social, political, and ideological differences do divide the diverse Muslims living around the Indian Ocean. For example, contestations between different schools and sects of Islam are very much part of the Muslim experience on the Swahili coast. Yet, the universalism of Islam remains a powerful unifying ideal.

12. Important works on the Indian Ocean as a site of African experience are Alpers, *East Africa and the Indian Ocean* and "Recollecting Africa"; Campbell, *Structure of Slavery;* Hofmeyr, Kaarsholm, and Frederiksen, "Introduction."

13. For excellent overviews of Indian Ocean historiography see, Hofmeyr, "Universalizing the Indian Ocean"; Rappaport, "Sea Tracks and Trails."

14. Beaujard, "Indian Ocean"; Bose, *Hundred Horizons;* Chaudhuri, *Trade and Civilisation;* Pearson, *Indian Ocean.*

15. Many cultural anthropologists and scholars of religion, such as Engseng Ho and Anne Bang, have focused on the impact of Hadhrami Sufis and sharifs on Islamic practice in the Indian Ocean. Bang, *Sufis and Scholars of the Sea;* Ho, *Graves of Tarim.* See also Risso, *Merchants and Faith.*

16. See for example Desai, *Commerce with the Universe;* Hofmeyr, *Gandhi's Printing Press;* Larson, *Ocean of Letters.*

17. Swahili coast scholars have begun to focus on how the consumption of commodities shapes personhood. Paola Ivanov's chapter on the relationship between consumption and aesthetic practice in contemporary Zanzibar is especially innovative. Ivanov, "Cosmpolitanism or Exclusion?" Also, Jeremy Prestholdt has considered the symbolic significance of imported objects in precolonial Mombasa. Prestholdt, *Domesticating the World,* 35–57.

18. For understanding the "Africanity" of Swahili coast expressive culture, see especially Askew, *Performing the Nation.*

19. My focus on the transactional role of coastal architecture is very much informed by Nancy Um's study of the port city of Mocha, in present-day Yemen. From her perspective Mocha's merchant houses "functioned as spatial tools of transition from one realm to another, allowing those who traveled to make sense of their long-distance journeys and to alleviate the alienation inherently involved in the interactions of cross-cultural trade." Um, *Merchant Houses of Mocha,* 12.

20. Scholars have embraced the concept of cosmopolitanism to describe a range of phenomena, including patterns of migration, histories of commerce, and the social effects of mobile technologies. The term is especially popular in Swahili coast and Indian Ocean studies. Drawing on the work of Mamadou Diouf, Kelly Askew deployed the term in 2003 to analyze the transcultural nature of coastal east African expressive culture. She called on scholars to "consider how Swahili cosmopolitanism constitutes a means of 'domesticating the foreign and the global.'" Askew, "As Plato Duly Warned," 632. Works that answered her call include LaViolette, "Swahili Cosmopolitanism," Prestholdt, *Domesticating the World;* Sheriff, *Dhow Culture of the Indian Ocean;* Simpson and Kresse, *Struggling with History.* For a critique of the use of cosmpolitanism to analyze the social dimensions of globalization, see Cheah, *Inhuman Conditions;* Gikandi, "Between Roots and Routes."

21. In Kenya the material culture of the coast is often neglected because it is seen as not being properly African. For discussion of this issue see Kusimba, "Kenya's Destruction."

22. The people of the coast were increasingly seen as "Arab" foreigners by mainlanders during the struggle for independence in the 1960s. The sultanate of Zanzibar (which included the coastal regions of present-day Tanzania and Kenya) was indeed ruled by Arabs from Oman, but the majority of Muslims living in east Africa were not part of this ruling elite, although much intermarriage took place between these newcomers and local

Muslim families. It is often impossible to categorize who is "foreign" or "indigenous" on the Swahili coast.

23. Wealthy Omani landowners and their financiers established a slave plantation economy on the Swahili coast in the 1830s. For analyses of the history of slavery in east Africa, see Alpers, *Ivory and Slaves*; Cooper, *Plantation Slavery*.

24. White, *Speaking with Vampires*.

25. Those elite families who owned large plantations during the sultanate years often presented slavery as a benign form of paternalism. For a full analysis of how and why they sought to justify slavery, see Glassman, *War of Words*, 92–94.

26. See especially Cooper, *On the African Waterfront*; Fair, *Pastimes and Politics*; Glassman, *Feasts and Riot*; Willis, *Mombasa*.

27. The British, who also choreographed the separation between Oman and Zanzibar in the 1850s, supported the annexation of Zanzibar by the Busaidi dynasty of Oman. Another branch of the Busaidi family ruled Muscat and its Arabian Peninsula dominions and the sultan of Zanzibar paid an annual subsidy to the sultan of Oman until the 1870s. A clear independence of the two empires was not recognized until the establishment of the British Protectorate in 1890.

28. Jonathon Glassman's *Feast and Riot* has inspired many Africanists to focus on the history of commodification and globalization on the Swahili coast. For example, Jeremy Prestholdt's work considers how local consumer desire shaped the making of a new global world order. Prestholdt, *Domesticating the World*.

29. The recent work of Allen F. Roberts challenges prevailing thinking about the effects these networks had on the lives of Europeans and Africans during the early days of the colonial period. Roberts, *Dance of Assassins*.

30. On how colonial ideology made Zanzibar into an "Arab" stone town, see Bissell, *Urban Design*, 61.

31. Horton, "East Africa," 199.

32. Allen, "Swahili Culture"; Donley-Reid, "Structuring Structure"; Ghaidan, *Lamu*.

33. Cooper, *On the African Waterfront*; Fair, *Pastimes and Politics*; Glassman, *War of Words*; Prestholdt, *Domesticating the World*. See also Brennan, *Taifa*.

34. Bissell, *Urban Design*; G. Myers, *Verandahs of Power*.

35. Bissell, *Urban Design*, 334.

36. Fleisher and LaViolette, "Changing Power of Swahili Houses"; Juma, *Unguja Ukuu on Zanzibar*; Wynne-Jones, "It's What You Do with It That Counts."

37. Key publications that focus on the mainland origins of Swahili coast architecture include Chami, "A Review of Swahili Archaeology"; Horton, Brown, and Mudida, *Shanga*; Kusimba, *Rise and Fall*.

38. For an excellent overview of how archeological interpretations of Africa have changed since the colonial period see Connah, *African Civilizations*.

1. DIFFERENCE SET IN STONE

1. Until the 1870s Mombasa mainly exported agricultural goods, such as grain and coconuts, grown on estates on the immediate mainland across from Mombasa Island. The caravan economy, bringing interior commodities (especially ivory) for trade across the Indian Ocean, was also important. Especially after 1895, an upsurge in the western

demand for ivory ushered in a decade of prosperity in Mombasa. Mombasans, especially Thenashara Taifa members and Baluchis, worked as caravan overseers during this period. Berg, "Mombasa under the Busaidi Sultanate," 230–236. Many Swahili Federation elders link their family's past prosperity to their great-grandfathers' generation and their grand adventures as great caravaners. Mwalimu Mohammad Matano and Aziz Ahmed, author interview, 25 November 2004.

2. Alpers, *Ivory and Slaves,* 44–45.

3. For example, in the sixteenth century Mombasa ratified an ultimately unsuccessful allegiance with a Mocha-based representative of the Ottoman Empire, in the hope of repelling Portuguese attempts to colonize their city. The Portuguese sacked the city and occupied Mombasa Island for over a hundred years. Casale, "Ottoman Age of Exploration," 249–275.

4. The two exceptions are the Wakilindini and Wamvita, which are named after places on Mombasa Island.

5. The Thenashara Taifa is divided into two groups, the Thelatha (Three Nations) and Tisa (Nine Nations). For a history of the Taifa, see Berg, "Swahili Community of Mombasa."

6. For a detailed discussion of this phenomenon in colonial Mombasa, see Willis, *Mombasa.*

7. "Waungwana" even became a category of personhood in nineteenth-century central Africa. Roberts, *Dance of Assassins,* 15–49. Glassman, *Feasts and Riot,* 60-61.

8. A few Hindu families who made their homes in Old Town during the colonial period still reside there.

9. For an analysis of these issues, see Kresse, *Philosophising in Mombasa.*

10. Although scholars usually emphasize that mitaa are clan territories or that they reflect the spatial boundaries of groups, in Mombasa they encapsulate important historical migrations or population shifts.

11. Mzee Hamid Mohammad, Mzee Mohammad Matano, and Aziz Ahmed, author interview, 26 November 2005.

12. Mwalimu Mohammad Matano, author interview, 25 January 2005.

13. The association between majini and maritime trade has also been noted by Linda Giles in her comprehensive study of Mombasa's many spirit associations. She was able to detect a hierarchy of spirit beings. The "sea majini" are considered most powerful because they are associated with "Arab-Swahili" privilege. Giles, "Spirit Possession," 64–65.

14. Mwalimu Matano often returned to stories of his grandfather, Mzee Matano, a caravan leader who often traveled to Ethiopia. He also "worked" with majini and was an adept of *uganga* (magico-religious medicine). In Matano's view, such practices were necessary precisely because overland trading was "tricky," since so many men sought to gain advantage over other traders by the use of uganga.

15. Written accounts from the nineteenth century also make this point. See Krapf, *Dictionary,* 240.

16. Mohammad Dalloky Matano, conversation with author, 12 August 2014.

17. Abdulaziz and Hajj, *Muyaka,* 20–21. The poetry of Muyaka bin Hajj (c. 1776–1840) was groundbreaking because it focuses on social justice issues and the abuse of power, themes rarely considered in precolonial poetry. Today politically engaged poets often pay

homage to him in their work. For example, Ahmad Nassir Juma Bhalo, Mombasa's most
important contemporary poet, often makes reference to Muyaka's verses in his poems.

18. This emphasis on the non-Arab origins of Mombasa was especially important to
counter Seyyid Said's claim that Mombasa belonged to him. But in 1837 Mombasa did
become part of Said's empire. Initially, the federation shared power with an Arab governor
installed by Said, who mainly concerned himself with economic affairs, while local elders
presided over local issues. This power-sharing system was still in place in the 1857, when
Richard Burton noted, "The city is now governed by three Shaykhs—of the Arabs, of the
Wamvita, and of the Wakilindi-ni." Wakilindini and Wamvita were the most powerful
moieties in Taifa. Burton, *Zanzibar,* 76.

19. For analyses of the complex connections between the Swahili of Mombasa and
their Mijikenda neighbors see Willis, *Mombasa;* McIntosh, *Edge of Islam.*

20. Spear, "Shirazi in Swahili Traditions," 300.

21. For a critique of constructivist studies of identity see Cooper, *Colonialism in Question.*

22. Hardt and Negri, *Empire.*

23. For a general overview of the use and meaning of Swahili stone architecture, see
Middleton, *World of the Swahili,* 59–68. For a provocative reassessment of the early history
of Swahili stone architecture, see Fleisher and LaViolette, "Changing Power of Swahili
Houses."

24. Her argument that "the coral house and its internal divisions provided the structuring framework for creating and maintaining power relations" has come to be the
classic interpretation of Swahili coast architecture. Donley-Reid, "Structuring Structure," 119.

25. James de Vere Allen was the first Swahili coast scholar to discuss the meaning
of permanence in local understandings of stone architecture. See Allen, "Swahili House."

26. Nancy Um has discerned a similar but slightly different logic defining the layout
of the port city of Mocha, on the coast of present-day Yemen. She has emphasized the
psychological impact of its built environment on newcomers, arguing that it helped them
to move between the hinterland and maritime foreland. The overall urban layout of Mocha can be understood "as a built tool of spatial translation for those . . . who struggled to
cope with the dislocation that accompanies long-distance travel." Um, *Merchant Houses
of Mocha,* 124.

27. Ma'allim Ali Jemadari, author interview, 1 August 2003; Abdulkarim Ali Mohammad Yunus, author interview, 26 January 2005; Mwalimu Mohammad Matano, author
interview, 20 December 2004 and 25 January 2005; Mama Hadija Abdul Rahman, author
interview, 10 May 2005.

28. Mwalimu Mohammad Matano, author interview, 25 January 2005.

29. Krapf, *Dictionary,* 264.

30. Mwalimu Mohammad Matano, author interview, 24 February 2005.

31. At the beginning of the nineteenth century, the urban space of the city was in fact
dominated by a dense concentration of domestic earthen wattle and daub architectural
forms. To present Mombasa as a stone town was a symbolic claim-making strategy. Most
stone towns had more earthen structures than stone ones. Also see Sheriff, "Spatial Dichotomy of Swahili Towns."

32. Strandes and Kirkman, *Portuguese Period*, 151.

33. Barbosa's trip to coastal east Africa took place in 1518, but his book was originally published in 1528. It was translated into English in 1918. Barbosa, Magalhães, and Dames, *Book of Duarte Barbosa*. Barbosa's descriptions of Mombasa are quoted in Elliot, "Visit to the Bajun Islands," 20. Also quoted in a slightly different version in de Silva, "Indian Ocean but Not African Sea," 686.

34. Strandes and Kirkman, *Portuguese Period*, 79–80.

35. National Archives of Rhodesia and Nyasaland and Ultramarinos, *Documents on the Portuguese*, 531–533.

36. Burton, *Zanzibar*, 2, 39.

37. Freeman-Grenville, *East African Coast*, 85–86.

38. The "Utenzi wa Al-Akida" of Abdallah bin Mas'ud bin Salim al-Mazrui, for example, memorialized the struggle for control of the citadel in the 1870s. Cf. Hinawy and al-Mazrui, *Al-Akida*.

39. New, *Life, Wanderings and Labours*, 52.

40. "The Slave Coast of East Africa," *Illustrated London News*, 6 March 1875.

41. Peter Mark's pioneering study of the "Luso-African" architecture of the Senegambia has also shown that stone architecture was not simply a foreign building technology appropriated by "Africans." Rather, it was a mixed and overlapping form that was increasingly seen to be purely Portuguese as the racial politics of colonialism impacted the area in the nineteenth century. Mark, *'Portuguese' Style*.

42. Jeremy Prestholdt's analysis of how western observers attempted to categorize coastal peoples based on the clothes they wore very much informs my understanding of the relationship between the colonial project and architecture as typology. Prestholdt, *Domesticating the World*, 155–161.

43. Bennett, "Exhibitionary Complex."

44. Mombasa was a major trading center for African ivory since at least the sixteenth century. From Mombasa, ivory circulated along Indian Ocean routes but also to Europe and China. From the mid-nineteenth century onward the east African ivory trade was controlled by US and European merchants and almost exclusively shipped to North Atlantic markets. Alpers, *Ivory and Slaves*, 44–45.

45. The missionaries also declared the expectations of home societies that female converts must be dressed in "European fashions" as "utterly preposterous." Sheldon, *Sultan to Sultan*, 67–68, 70.

46. This adds a gendered dimension to Peter Pels' observation regarding the relationship between missionaries and locals: "Plunged into a foreign society without resources, missionaries often had no choice but to create a niche in a local polity by adapting local customs. It is hardly surprising that missionaries were often practicing something resembling modern day ethnographic fieldwork." Pels and Salemink, *Colonial Subjects*, 16.

47. *East African Standard and Mombasa Times*, 2 July 1904.

48. Frankl, "Old German Consulate," 137–138.

49. Topan, originally from the Kutch, became one of the most powerful men of the Swahili coast when he was appointed chief of customs in Zanzibar by Sultan Barghash in 1876.

50. Report by Walter Rössler to Grafen von Lützow, Mombasa, 28 May 1903. Political Archives of the German Foreign Office, Berlin. File R 136998.

51. A member of von der Decken's expedition described the inner courtyard as the "holy inner sanctum" of the home. He also confessed his desire to somehow gain access to such a courtyard, in the hope of seeing and locking gazes with a patrician woman. Decken and Kersten, *Reisen in Ost-Afrika*, 225.

52. The house already had its distinctive exterior columns in 1893 when it was noted as being owned by Tharia Topan and having a verandah "supported by large stone pillars." *Gazette for Zanzibar and East Africa*, 9 August 1893.

53. Ibid.

54. The British established a two-year unofficial "protectorate" over Mombasa. This mainly took the form of a garrison and small settlement of British sailors and soldiers under the command of Captain Owen and later Lieutenant J. B. Emery. They were encouraged to "protect" Mombasa by the Mazrui rulers of Mombasa, whose suzerainty at the time was threatened by the growing presence of Busaidi Arabs in east Africa.

55. Gray, *British in Mombasa*, 160–161; Jackson, "Ghost of Leven House."

56. Hoyle, "Urban Renewal," 195.

57. Letter from Mackenzie to Secretary of IBEAC, London, 23 October 1888. Mackinnon Papers, SOAS.

58. Mombasa's leaders formed various alliances and counteralliances with diverse outsiders throughout their history in an attempt to negotiate a degree of autonomy and self-rule. The Mazrui clan from Oman was invited by the Thenashara Taifa to serve as governors of the city in the eighteenth century.

59. Jackson, "Ghost of Leven House," 163. Papers of Sir John Kirk, diary entry, 16 August 1884. Acc. 9942/36. National Library of Scotland. Once ousted from Mombasa by the Sultan of Zanzibar, Mazrui families regrouped and established their own semi-independent enclaves at Takaungu and Gazi. But the British colonial administration of Mombasa soon employed Mazrui members in the Arab Administration. Many Arabs used their positions to claim large tracts of land on Mombasa Island and its immediate hinterland during the colonial period.

60. Huebner and Sieberg, *Zeitenumbruch in Ostafrika*, 93–94.

61. The British constantly complained that locals did not want to work for them. They blamed this not on poor pay or harsh labor conditions, but on "the laziness of the Swahilis (coast people)." They also did not want to employ "poor whites" coming from Bombay because it would be "unseemly" in the context of the racial hierarchy of colonial Africa for Europeans to perform menial labor. *The Gazette of Zanzibar and East Africa*, May 1896.

62. *East African Standard and Mombasa Times*, 22 December 1906.

63. Report by Dr. Brode to Dr. von Bethman Hollweg, Mombasa, 27 October 1909. Political Archives of the German Foreign Office, Berlin. File R 141624.

64. The name *mtaa ya mzungu* is not remembered by residents today. The term is recorded in a 1903 *Mombasa Times* article and in nineteenth-century municipal records now located in the Kenya National Archives (KNA DC/Msa/8/2).

65. *East African Standard and Mombasa Time*, 9 February 1907.

66. Yet Omani Arabs who worked as government officials reported to the British Government of Kenya, not the Sultan of Zanzibar.

67. Mzee Mohammad Matano, author interview, 9 March 2005.

68. Today the structure is still the property of relatives of Sir Mbarak Hinawy.

69. Great Britain Admiralty, *Handbook of Kenya Colony*, 275.

70. Bellingham, *Mombasa*.

71. Zeynep Çelik was the first scholar to reveal the temporal ideology undergirding colonial urban planning policies. During the colonial period, the "traditional" casbah came to be seen as a place of the past, while the "modern" city of the colonizer was a place where one could experience the present and future. Çelik, *Urban Forms*. See also, Wright, *Politics of Design*.

72. No. 11/2/27a Health Office, Msa, KNA, Coast Section, Mombasa, CY 4/1 (23 June 1919).

73. *Gazette for Zanzibar and East Africa*, 4 and 8 March 1905.

74. Bissell, *Urban Design*, 121.

75. For an in-depth analysis of colonial urban planning polices that created the stone versus earthen architecture binary in Zanzibar, see Myers, "Sticks and Stones"; Bissell, "Conservation and the Colonial Past."

76. "The Mombasa Building Amendment Rules," 1917. KNA, Coast Section, Mombasa, CY 4/1.

77. Ibid.

78. "Town Planning: Mombasa," report by Medical Officer of Health to Principal Sanitation Officer, Nairobi. KNA, Coast Section, Mombasa, CY 4/1 (7 July 1919).

79. Such preservation efforts are part of an attempt to implement a 1991 United Nations– and UNESCO-funded conservation plan for Old Town, which eventually led to the ratification of several national and municipal bylaws.

80. Old Town was gazetted as a "national heritage monument" in 1990 under the Antiquities and Monuments Act of 1983.

2. A "CURIOUS" MINARET

1. Histories collected in the 1830s in Zanzibar also mark the beginning of a new epoch with the arrival of "three brothers" from overseas. The one brother who settled in Zanzibar married the daughter of a Hadimu patrician and united all the leading houses of Zanzibar under his authority. All Swahili versions emphasize that these outsiders were only settled on the Swahili coast because locals allowed them to do so. For example, the Zanzibari version states that "Zanzibar was not conquered by the people from Shiraz . . . but was given up to them in consequence of their munificence." Kirkman, "Zanzibar Diary," 290.

2. Ludwig Krapf's account, collected in the 1830s, is the first written documentation of this story. Krapf, *Dictionary*, 170.

3. This chapter focuses on Thelata Taifa accounts. It is important to point out that other local families have different interpretations of the history and meaning of the Mandhry and Mnara mosques. For example, Mandhry and Basheikh elders sometimes disagree with Taifa interpretations of the past, although they are all related to each other and so share intertwined histories.

4. Parkin and Headley, *Islamic Prayer*, 3. Pearson, *Indian Ocean*, 76–77.

5. Flood, *Objects of Translation*, 1.

6. Abdul Sheriff has analyzed the history and significance of the dhow in shaping a cosmopolitan Muslim identity among the littoral societies of the Indian Ocean. Sheriff, *Dhow Culture*.

7. The Omani Busaidi dynasty of Zanzibar was able to gain control over Mombasa because several families within the Taifa no longer wanted the Mazrui to lead their city. They aligned with the Busaidi because they wanted to regain more autonomy, an autonomy that was recognized by the first Busaidi sultan of Zanzibar. Berg, "Mombasa," 53 and 98.

8. Mombasa's hate of Barghash is mentioned in British administrative letters as early as 1874. "Report from Holmwood to Prideaux, November 17, 1874," British Library, IOR/L /PS/9/51.

9. While his troops never reached Mombasa because the British halted them at Brava (present-day Somalia), rumors of the impending invasion inspired Mombasans to commit this act of symbolic rebellion. Salim, *Swahili-Speaking Peoples*, 45.

10. For example, Hardinge was told that "more devout Arabs" ceased to call Barghash Imam, but chose the "less sacred" title of Sultan after he went to England and allowed his photo to be taken with unveiled European women. Hardinge, *Diplomatist in the East*, 85–86.

11. Pouwels, *Horn and Crescent*, 116–19.

12. George S. Mackenzie noted, in a letter to the home office of the IBEAC in London, that he saw the giving of such gifts as essential, because it is in keeping with local custom and signifies the official acceptance of a new ruler: "All negotiations regarding the establishment of the Company being now satisfactorily closed I propose making presents to the principal Sheiks and people in the neighborhood. This has always been the custom here on a new Sultan coming to the throne, and I am pleased to find that the natives are quite willing to accept similar gifts at my hand, which I hope, will have a beneficial effect." He later requests gold watches and inlaid rifles from the home office for this purpose. *Mackinnon Papers* (microfilm reel 23, SOAS), 23 and 24 October 1888.

13. In an attempt to assert his control and to punish Pangani for its intransience, the leader of the German East Africa Company marched into the town's main mosque during Friday prayers wearing shoes and accompanied by a dog. Whether he knew his actions would be considered offensive is unclear, but shoes can never be worn in the prayer hall of a mosque and dogs are considered particularly unclean and would not even be allowed into domestic spaces in many Muslim societies. Because Pangani was still officially part of the Sultanate of Zanzibar, locals felt that Zanzibar had sanctioned this action. For a full analysis of the event at Pangani, see Glassman, *Feasts and Riot*.

14. Mackenzie's account of this rebellion still exists: "On the night of the 20th the town was thrown into a condition approaching panic, as it was said a body of several hundred of the disaffected were under arms and intended on making an attack on the quarter of town where I am living." George S. Mackenzie to the Secretary of the IBEA Co., London. *Mackinnon Papers* (microfilm reel 23, SOAS), 23 October 1888.

15. Hardinge, *Diplomatist in the East*, 176. The strength and span of Islamic networks along the Swahili coast was a source of great anxiety for the British administration. The Swahili coast was part of the British concept of Islamdom, which was imagined as an undifferentiated and monolithic opponent to western civilization.

16. "Mwenye Jaka, the Mombasa Mzee of the Wadigo, accompanied the Mweli expedition [the British force sent from Zanzibar to capture Sheikh Mbarak bin Rashid]. At Mdole, the place where the punitive expedition was attacked, he ran away ... [and] joined the rebels." *Zanzibar Gazette*, 6 November 1896. Mwenye Jaka was a Mijikenda elder.

17. *Zanzibar Gazette,* 6 November 1895.

18. Hardinge, *Diplomatist in the East,* 167.

19. Salim, *Swahili-Speaking Peoples,* 82 and 86.

20. Pouwels, *Horn and Crescent,* 73.

21. Kenya National Archives, PC/Coast/1/3/110.

22. "Complaints about Wakf Property in Mombasa Township," Kenya National Archives PC/Coast/1/12/61; "Mazrui Cemetery," Kenya National Archives, PC/Coast/1/1/186.

23. "Wakf Properties," Kenya National Archives, PC/Coast/2/3/1.

24. "Scrap book from the palace." Zanzibar National Archives, AQ 2/1.

25. Many mosques were patronized by relative newcomers, such as the Alawis from the Hadramaut in present-day Yemen, reflecting the rise of Sufi Islam all along the coast beginning in the eighteenth century. Sufi Islam was especially important to the formerly enslaved. The Islamic reform movements of Egypt also became popular with Mombasa's religious leaders and public intellectuals during the early twentieth century. Pouwels, "Sh. Al-Amin B. Ali Mazrui."

26. Siravo, *Zanzibar,* 40–41.

27. Berg and Walter, "Mosques," 63.

28. Mandhry Arabs have been the accepted stewards of this waterfront mosque for at least two hundred years. According to oral history, they had immigrated to Mombasa from Oman even before the arrival of the Portuguese in the fifteenth century. Their role was different from Arab newcomers in colonial Mombasa; their first language was Swahili, and they belonged to the Thelatha Federation of Mombasa, although during the colonial period they began to reemphasize their ancient origins in Oman. The indigenous Taifa held onto the Mnara mosque much longer. The Tangana lineage claimed and patronized the Mnara mosque well into the twentieth century. But sometime during the colonial period, members of the Basheikh lineage from present-day Yemen took control. Abdulkarim Ali Mohammad Yunus, author interview, 26 January 2005; Mwalimu Mohammad Matano, author interview, 25 March 2005.

29. Ma'allim Ali Jemadari, author interview, 1 August 2003. See also Topan, "Swahili and Isma'ili Perceptions," 105–106.

30. Berg and Walter, "Mosques," 68.

31. Ahmad Nassir Juma Bhalo, conversation with author, 9 July 2013.

32. At this point the Mandhry distanced themselves from their Taifa connections because "Swahilis" were increasingly reduced to "tribal natives" in the colonial system, which meant they had access to fewer educational and economic opportunities.

33. Bellingham, *Mombasa,* 69.

34. As a reporter for the Zanzibar newspaper enviously put it when visiting Mombasa, "Telephones and the small railway are signs of civilization which are at present entirely wanting in Zanzibar," *Gazette for Zanzibar and East Africa,* 9 August 1894.

35. Mark Horton has suggested that the basic plan for such mosques was originally derived from a type developed in the Persian Gulf region between the ninth and tenth centuries. Horton, "East Africa," 200.

36. Peter Garlake believed that arched colonnades were rarely used on the Swahili coast prior to the eighteenth century and that they became prevalent only in the early nineteenth century. Garlake, *Early Islamic Architecture,* 25.

37. In the second half of the twentieth century the Mandhry mosque was expanded to include a madrasa and a second-floor gallery for female congregants. More recently its prayer hall was also enlarged.

38. For a discussion of the influence of South Asian building technologies on the Swahili coast, see Lewcock, "Architectural Connections."

39. The Mnara minaret also features a wooden cornice encircling the very upper section. It serves no functional role, but rather acts as a framing ledge for the small arched opening, which today houses a loudspeaker for the call to prayer.

40. Until the late nineteenth century, Swahili coast mosques usually did not feature minarets; instead the call to prayer was executed from the flat rooftop of the mosque. Garlake, *Early Islamic Architecture*, 84.

41. The congregational mosque of Chake town on Pemba Island has a minaret that shares some formal similarities with the others, but it is polygonal rather than round.

42. Horton, "East Africa," 202.

43. Abdul Sheriff suggests its minaret dates to the seventeenth century. Sheriff, "Mosques," 49.

44. Francesco Siravo has suggested that the Zanzibar pillar minaret is similar to one found in southwestern Oman. Siravo, *Zanzibar*, 41.

45. Mark Horton, personal communication, 19 July 2006.

46. Sassoon, "Mosque and Pillar at Mbaraki," 95.

47. The Portuguese were very familiar with Mombasa Island and its landmarks, having occupied it for extended periods of time since the end of the fifteenth century. Ibid., 80.

48. Guillain, *Documents sur l'histoire*, 219.

49. Mwalimu Mohammed Matano, author interview, 2 April 2005. Berg, "Mombasa," 160.

50. For an overview of contemporary spirit practices associated with the Mbaraki Pillar, see Giles, "Mbaraki Pillar and Its Spirits."

51. Ibid., 46. However, this is disputed by local elders today. Ustadh Ahmed Bhalo, conversation with author, 10 July 2013.

52. At Pujini on Pemba Island there is a subterranean shrine that is a panga constructed by humans. Jeffrey Fleisher, personal communication, 19 August 2014.

53. Horton, "Islam, Archeology, " 86–87.

54. Middleton, *World of the Swahili*, 61.

55. Sassoon, "Mosque and Pillar," 83.

56. Kirkman, *Men and Monuments*, 129.

57. Garlake, *Early Art and Architecture*, 185. See also, Wilson, "Swahili Funerary Architecture," 33–34.

58. Fleisher and LaViolette, "Changing Power," 186–187.

59. See Wilson, "Swahili Funerary Architecture."

60. "Memorandum on Coast Federations," by O. F. Watkins, 31 December 1909, Kenya National Archives, DC/MSA 3/1.

61. Today the ruins abut a popular seashore promenade. The entire area belongs to the municipal government, which, because local politicians regularly attempt to privatize the land to sell to developers, is often embroiled in various scandals.

62. Judge Bonham-Carter wrote a long report in which he documents all the evidence presented to him by the Thelatha Taifa (or "Three Tribes," in his words). The report is

over twenty pages long, although it is missing pages and is damaged. In the end he comes to the conclusion that the federations never had a tradition of property ownership and on that ground denies their claim to the land. Kenya National Archives files DC/MSA 3/1. In 1918 the high court also refused to recognize Tisa Taifa land claims. The final blow to all Taifa claims came when Mombasa's Arab *liwali* (governor), Ali bin Salim (from the Busaidi clan) endorsed the British government's ruling. Salim, *Swahili-Speaking Peoples,* 123–130.

63. A guidebook to Mombasa from 1933 also recorded this claim. See Bellingham, *Mombasa,* 60.

64. "Appellate Civil Case: Joao Baptist Coutinho vs. Land Officer," *East Africa Protectorate Law Reports* vol. VII, part I, 1917, 181.

65. Ibid., 182.

66. The Thelatha experienced "unprecedented wealth" during this period, which they used to build and renovate several mosques in Old Town. Berg, "Mombasa," 165.

67. Pouwels, *Horn and Crescent,* 111.

68. Many scholars assume that Omanis came to dominate local culture because they were powerful Muslims and that locals would simply respect them because of this. For example, August Nimtz argued that "since Islam was the sine qua non of Swahili culture, this meant that Arabs were destined to have, if not the leading role, then certainly a major role in molding the culture." Nimtz, *Islam and Politics,* 33.

69. Margaret Strobel has emphasized the role of Swahili coast women in the transformation of local culture after the abolition of slavery. Strobel, *Muslim Women in Mombasa.*

70. Pouwels, *Horn and Crescent,* 72.

71. Until then the Thanashara Taifa belonged to the Coast Arab Association, which was founded in 1921 to represent the interests of leading Arab and Taifa landowners on the coast. In response to the events of 1926, Taifa leaders founded the Afro-Asian Association in 1927. For more information on the ensuing community split, see Salim, *Swahili-Speaking Peoples,* 180–187.

72. The most famous written account of this event is in the autobiography of Hyder Kindy, a wamiji activist and politician in 1950s Mombasa, who was a member of the Thelatha Taifa. He never mentions any mosques by name, however. Kindy, *Life and Politics in Mombasa,* 27–32. Farouk Topan recounts Hyder's version but goes into further detail, explicitly naming the Mandhry and Mnara mosques. Topan, "Swahili and Isma'ili Perceptions of Salat," 104–105.

73. Mwalimu Matano, who recounted the event as told to him by his father, argued that the issue of voting rights was only secondary in causing the "war" over the mosques. Mwalimu Mohammad Matano, interview with author, 19 May 2005.

74. Matano interview, 19 May 2005. It should be made clear that Mwalimu Matano spoke of this only after several months of weekly and biweekly meetings. Discussing such tensions is a very delicate matter, as many locals are very aware of the fact that this goes against the ideal of unity in Islam.

75. Matano interview, 19 May 2005.

76. Ma'allim Ali Jemadari, interview with author, 1 August 2003; Abdulkarim Ali Mohammad Yunus, interview with author, 26 January 2005.

3. ARCHITECTURE OUT OF PLACE

1. The Busaidi sultans were only "first among equals" before Barghash came to power. Reichard, *Deutsch-Ostafrika*, 98. See also, Müller, *Deutschland, Zanzibar, Ostafrika*, 88.

2. An American missionary recorded that the only reason the Omanis were on Zanzibar was because the "natives became impatient [with the Portuguese], and sent to Muscat, entreating the sultan to come." "Descriptive," *Boston Recorder*, 3 January 1840.

3. Swahili oral histories and Portuguese chronicles document how Zanzibari leaders sought alliances and counteralliances with Portugal or Oman whenever the other's presence became too oppressive in the eyes of local leaders. Most notably, Portuguese documents mention how Zanzibar's ruler, Queen Fatima, sent emissaries to Portuguese Goa, requesting intervention against Omani incursions in her sphere of influence during the eighteenth century. Pearce, *Zanzibar*, 91–92.

4. Barghash imported Ottoman imperial laws to invalidate local systems of jurisprudence. Farsy and Pouwels, *Shafi'i Ulama*, xvii.

5. Bissell, *Urban Design*, 336 n10.

6. Glassman, *War of Words*, 31.

7. Johnston, *Kilima-Njaro Expedition*, 35.

8. Letter from John Kirk the Political Agent and HM's Consul to Zanzibar, to Wedderburn, acting Secretary to Government, Bombay. 4 March 1871. Secret Letters Received from areas outside India, vol. 49: Zanzibar. IOR/L/PS/9/49. India Office Library, British Library, London.

9. Sheikh Abdulaziz, a Sunni *qadi* who practiced and taught Qadiriyya Sufism, was imprisoned by Barghash and was barred from attending or leading Friday prayers. This prompted armed confrontations between Sheikh Abdulaziz's followers and government troops. Pouwels, *Horn and Crescent*, 118–120.

10. Cameron, "Zanzibar," 425.

11. When Barghash first returned from exile to Zanzibar, the British Agent was hostile toward him. In his weekly missives to Bombay he reported on Barghash's "increasing fanaticism" and believed that Barghash was organizing a "secret party" with the aim of expelling the British. Letter from Henry Churchill the Political Agent and HM's Consul to Zanzibar, to Wedderburn, acting Secretary to Government, Bombay. September 30, 1870. Secret Letters Received from areas outside India, vol. 49: Zanzibar. IOR/L/PS/9/49. India Office Library, British Library, London.

12. Dewji easily moved in European and Arab circles, providing Barghash with updates on their plans. Barghash briefly attempted to manage the customs house himself in 1887, with disastrous results. He lost money during that year. Bennett, *History of the Arab State*, 91–105. Schmidt, *Sansibar*, 30.

13. Meinecke, *Aus Dem Lande Der Suaheli*, 100.

14. John Kirk reported that Barghash quickly ceased his "impish acts" after initially trying to distance himself from the British during the first year of his rule. Letter from John Kirk the Political Agent and HM's Consul to Zanzibar, to Wedderburn, acting Secretary to Government, Bombay. 24 December 1870. Secret Letters Received from areas outside India, vol. 49: Zanzibar. IOR/L/PS/9/49. India Office Library, British Library, London.

15. Müller, *Deutschland, Zanzibar, Ostafrika,* 74.

16. Sheriff, "Spatial Dichotomy of Swahili Towns."

17. Schmidt, *Sansibar,* 10.

18. Crofton, *Old Consulate at Zanzibar,* 6.

19. Schmidt, *Sansibar,* 104.

20. Ibid. Also Willoughby, *East Africa,* 12.

21. Barghash's projects and palaces are surveyed in Sheriff, "Outline History," in Sheriff, *Zanzibar Stone Town.*

22. Myers, *Verandahs of Power,* 2. After the 1964 revolution, the house became the headquarters for various national political parties (including the ASP and CCM). Today it houses the Museum of History and Culture of Zanzibar and the Swahili Coast.

23. Prestholdt, *Domesticating the World,* 109.

24. In this point I am indebted to Prestholdt's analysis of Barghash's palaces. Prestholdt, *Domesticating the World,* 160–165.

25. Johnston, *Kilima-Njaro Expedition,* 31.

26. Davis, *Congo and Coasts of Africa,* 217.

27. Vizetelly, *From Cyprus to Zanzibar,* 399.

28. Ibid., 392. Meinecke, *Aus Dem Lande Der Suaheli,* 100.

29. He employed eleven Germans to operate the ships. Ropes, *Zanzibar Letters,* 34. His steamships gave free passage to Zanzibaris going on the hajj, and his original reason for acquiring the steamships was to reduce the price of food staples, since at this point rice was imported from overseas. Norman Bennett also notes that this allowed local merchants, who traded in smaller lots and did not have their own ships, to cut into the import and export business, which until then was dominated by American, European, and Indian merchants. Bennett, *History of the Arab State,* 106.

30. "On the Track of the Germans in East Africa." Barghash quickly disengaged from German merchants and officials after 1886, when Germany began to aggressively claim authority over his coastal and central African territories. Zanzibar was forced to "lease" Pangani and Dar es Salaam to Germany.

31. Vizetelly, *Cyprus to Zanzibar,* 392.

32. Burton, *Zanzibar,* 2, 256.

33. Ibid.

34. Willoughby, *East Africa,* 10.

35. Myers, *Verandahs of Power,* 2.

36. For an analysis of the global circulation and constant reinvention of the South Asian architectural form now called the "bungalow" see, King, *Bungalow.*

37. Mark, *"Portuguese" Style,* 46–49.

38. During the 1920s British architects built Saracenic-style administrative buildings on Zanzibar Island, such as the Peace Memorial Museum and the Law Courts. During the colonial period "Saracenic" was used to describe objets d'art and monuments that were supposed to evoke Islam.

39. Cf. Crinson, *Empire Building,* and Mitchell, *Colonizing Egypt.*

40. Kelly Askew, the leading ethnomusicologist of the Swahili coast, emphasizes that while historically taraab is connected to Egypt, Swahilis Africanized it, especially from

the 1920s onward. She points out that "the predominance of *ngoma* rhythms such as *kumb-waya, chakacha, vugo, goma,* and *mudurenge* in taraab performance throughout the region grounds it firmly within its local African setting." Askew, *Performing the Nation,* 107.

41. It was also a local tradition for Swahili coast leaders, such as the Mwenye Mkuu, to orchestrate elaborate dance and music performance in front of their palaces. Each dynasty had a set of *ngoma kuu,* or great drums and *siwa,* side-blown horns, whose presence and activation were central at these festivities. These musical instruments were also the important insigia of waungwana authority. Glassman, *Feasts and Riot,* 153; Allen, "Siwas of Pate and Lamu."

42. Ropes, *Zanzibar Letters of Edward D. Ropes,* 15.

43. Thomson et al., *To the Central African Lakes and Back,* 26.

44. Glassman, *Feasts and Riot,*130.

45. Prestholdt, *Domesticating the World,* 118–122.

46. In my analysis of the House of Wonders as a spectacular image I am very much indebted to Tony Bennett's work on the Crystal Palace as a space of new forms of spectacle and vision. Bennett, "The Exhibitionary Complex."

47. Schmidt, *Sansibar,* 102.

48. Ibid.

49. Thomson et al., *To the Central African Lakes and Back,* 28.

50. Ibid.

51. Vizetelly, *From Cyprus to Zanzibar,* 392.

52. Fitzgerald, *Travels in the Coastlands,* 388.

53. Annual Report of the Public Works Department, 1914 and 1933, BA 18/6 and BA 9/2. National Archives of Zanzibar.

54. The collapse was documented by two different visitors to Zanzibar during Barghash's reign. Vizetelly, *From Cyprus to Zanzibar,* 392; Schmidt, *Sansibar,* 8.

55. The Hadimu, like the Taifa of Mombasa, claimed ancient connections to Shiraz, to distinguish themselves from Muslim newcomers, like Omanis.

56. By the 1830s the Mwenye Mkuu bore the patronym "al Alawi," signaling the fact that the Hadimu elite had intermarried with Alawis from Hadhraumat (Yemen). Gray, *History of Zanzibar,* 161. But this did not mean Hadimu elites claimed an Arab identity.

57. Some accounts credit the Shatri family from the Haudramaut for the building of the Juma mosque on the waterfront. Said Abdulwahab Alawy, author interview, 6 June 2005.

58. Ruete and Donzel, *An Arabian Princess,* 145; Kirkman, "Zanzibar Diary."

59. When comparing western accounts of Zanzibar it becomes clear that sometime between the 1840s and 1850s Seyyid Said attempted to have a greater presence in Zanzibar Town by building an official ceremonial structure for his assemblies, likely the Beit al Hukum.

60. The Mwenye Mkuu took refuge at Dunga because it was the ancestral center of an important indigenous lineage, the Wachangamwe. Ingrams, *Zanzibar, Its History and Its People,* 150. The Wachangamwe belong to the Thenashara Taifa of Mombasa. They claim their ancestors immigrated to Mombasa and Zanzibar from Shiraz in the distant past.

61. Gray, *History of Zanzibar,* 164.

62. Middleton, *World of the Swahili,* 42.

63. British chroniclers of local lore focused on stories of the Mwenye Mkuu inter-
ring the bodies of countless enslaved Africans to "consecrate" the foundations of his new
palace; Ingrams, *Zanzibar*, 152. Robert Lyne also documented the reports of interment
of humans in the walls of Dunga palace. But he asserted such stories were simply not true,
although he believed it to be haunted. Lyne, *Zanzibar*, 239–240.

64. Pearce, *Zanzibar*, 203.

65. Mwalimu Idris, author interview, 17 July 2005.

66. Vizetelly, *From Cyprus to Zanzibar*, 399.

67. Meinecke, *Aus Dem Lande Der Suaheli*, 101.

68. Reese, *Transmission of Learning*, 189.

69. Hardinge, *A Diplomatist in the East*, 85–86.

70. Pearce, *Zanzibar*, 265.

71. Prestholdt, *Domesticating the World*, 95.

72. Thomson et al., *To the Central African Lakes*, 22–23. See also: Prestholdt, *Domesticating the World*, 105.

73. Johnston, *Kilima-Njaro Expedition*, 32.

74. Prestholdt, *Domesticating the World*, 96–97.

75. Bissell has also noted that the "ostentatious lifestyle of urban Arabs" can be seen
"an extension of older Swahili patterns." Bissell, *Urban Design*, 31.

76. Johnston, *Kilima-Njaro Expedition*, 32.

77. Schmidt, *Sansibar*, 18.

4. AT HOME IN THE WORLD

1. Spyer, ed., *Border Fetishisms;* Thomas, *Entangled Objects*.

2. The work of the archeologists Jeffrey Fleisher and Adria La Violette has shed new
light on the transformation of religious and domestic architectural ornament between
the fourteenth and nineteenth centuries. They suggest that patricians created highly ornamented private spaces after the expulsion of the Portuguese for psychological reasons,
to come to terms with the intense socioeconomic changes shaping daily life. According to
them, "It was here, in the inner spaces of the Swahili stone house, in the *ndani* and later in
the mihrab-style toilet . . . that members of the house would have found powerful places for
soul searching, where they 'speculate[d] on the order of the universe' . . . and reinforced to
themselves the appropriateness of their world." Fleisher and LaViolette, "Changing Power
of Swahili Houses," 194.

3. Allen, "Swahili Culture Reconsidered," 120.

4. Pearson, *Port Cities and Ontruders*, 161–162. Stanziani, *Sailors, Slaves, and Immigrants*, 69–79.

5. James de Vere Allen argued that the walls featuring the most ornate plasterwork
functioned as the dramatic backdrop against which a bride would sit in state during grand
patrician weddings. Allen, "Swahili House," 16–21.

6. Fleisher and LaViolette, "Changing Power of Swahili Houses," 186–189; Allen,
"Swahili Ornament."

7. Item 36 (Notebook, 17 October 1883–1 September 1884), Item 37 (Notebook, 29 January 1883–16 July 1884), and Item 38 (Notebook, 31 August–20 November 1884). Sir John
Kirk's Papers (Acc.9942), National Library of Scotland.

8. Dr. Paola Ivanov, the curator of the Africa collection at the Ethnological Museum of Berlin, has provided me extensive access to the museum's Swahili coast holdings and their collection history. I am grateful for her guidance, advice, and insights.

9. Jackson, *Early Days in East Africa*, 17.

10. Europeans first observed and documented "great quantities" of such ceramics on the Swahili coast during the first half of the nineteenth century. Guillain, *Documents sur l'histoire*, 347.

11. Jackson, *Early Days in East Africa*, 17–19.

12. Stigand, *Land of Zinj*, 155.

13. Sheldon, *Sultan to Sultan*, 56–57.

14. Gary, "Furniture Found in Kenya," 148. A German businessman living in Pangani commented on the high prices European collectors of antique porcelain were willing to pay for old ceramics from the Swahili coast. Meinecke, *Aus Dem Lande Der Suaheli*, 62.

15. Connah, *African Civilizations*, 178.

16. For a synthetic study of the porcelain world system see Finlay, *Pilgrim Art*.

17. Ibid., 3.

18. Drawing on Arjun Appadurai's formulation of the "social life of things," Horton and Middleton discuss porcelain as an important symbol of status for patricians. They emphasize that ceramics "lost any commercial value but became representations of *uungwana* status and civilization." Horton and Middleton, *Swahili*, 112.

19. Finlay, *Pilgrim Art*, 237

20. Ibid., 24.

21. For an overview of modern chinaware in Zanzibar, see Aldrick, "Painted Plates." Other objects of material culture once the exclusive purview of patricians became accessible to the larger community. Especially certain items of dress, once regulated under sumptuary laws, became common symbols of Swahili identity. For a discussion of this shift in personal adornment see Fair, "Remaking Fashion."

22. Allen, " Swahili House," 17.

23. Mathew, "Culture of the East African Coast," 56; Ingrams, *Zanzibar*, 68; Donley-Reid, "Power of Swahili Porcelain," 49–50.

24. Playne and Gale, *East Africa (British)*, 111.

25. From the mid–nineteenth century onward the east African ivory trade was shipped almost exclusively to North Atlantic markets.

26. John Haggard to his father, 29 September 1884. Quoted in Romero, *Lamu*, 40 and 252.

27. Rene Bravmann suggested it was based on nineteenth-century Anglo-Indian furniture and James De Vere Allen traced its form and method of construction to Egytian Mamluk chairs. Bravmann, *African Islam*, 109–111; Allen, "Kiti Cha Enzi" 56–58.

28. *Mombasa Times*, 23 December 1903.

29. Krapf, *Dictionary*, 59.

30. Stuhlmann and Stern, *Handwerk und Industrie*, 130; Marett, "Siwa in East Africa."

31. Glassman has argued that the trading boom of the second half of the nineteenth century led to the commodification of daily life on the Swahili coast. Glassman, *Feasts and Riot*. Prestholdt presents this commodification in largely positive terms, as a form of "rebirth" and "remaking" of the self. Prestholdt, *Domesticating the World*.

32. Becker, "Materials for Understanding of Islam," 51.

33. On scholarly exchanges along the east Africa coast, see Bang, *Sufis and Scholars*.

34. Ruete, *Memoirs of an Arabian Princess*, 19–20.

35. Currently it is unknown which newspaper published the photograph with this byline. An original of the newspaper page and the photo's caption are in the collection of Torrence Royer. Mr. Royer, a collector and historian of colonial-period Zanzibari photography, has generously shared his knowledge and the materials in his archives with me over the years. Versions of the same photograph are in the Zanzibar National Archives and in Rautenstrauch-Joest Museum in Cologne, Germany.

36. On the role and meaning of photography in Zanzibar see also, Prestholdt, *Domesticating the World*, 95–96.

37. Jackson, *Early Days in East Africa*, 17–18.

38. Bunn, "Aesthetics of British Mercantilism," 303–321. On the staging of Africa in European interiors see Roberts, *Dance of Assassins*, 157–173.

39. Rahima Ali, author interview, 10 May 2005.

40. Mwalimu Mohammad Matano and Aziz Ahmed, author interview, 25 January 2005. Interestingly, according to the historian Margaret Strobel, women enacted the most vital transformation of coastal culture at the turn of the twentieth century by trespassing the seemingly inviolable divide between waugwana (patricians) and watumwa (slaves, bondsmen). Women reshaped traditional dance competitions and wedding festivities by increasingly merging the cultural traditions once demarcated as "slave" and "patrician" in the decades following the abolition of slavery. Strobel, *Muslim Women in Mombasa*.

41. Sheib Khamis and his wife, author interview, 24 January 2005.

42. Stuhlman, a German ethnographer and zoologist who collected large quantities of cultural objects for German museums in 1893–1894, noted the importance of what he considered Arabian Peninsula metalwork and ornaments along the Swahili coast. His book features photographs of the most popular "representative" material culture of the Swahili coast, including *dele* plates.

43. The two ivory and brass masiwa from Pate Island are the most famous examples. They are now on view in the National Museum of Kenya in Nairobi and Lamu.

44. Sheikh Abdullahi Nasser, author interview, 25 January and 7 February 2005. The *hanbali madhab* is one of the four schools of law in Sunni Islam. It is associated with Saudi wahabism. Swahili coast Muslims have historically followed the shafi'i madhab. Yet many local young people study at and are supported by Saudi religious institutions. Saudis are also renovating mosques in Mombasa.

45. Fatuma Mbwana Amiri and Hadija Mmwana Amiri, author interview, 21 March 2005. Fatuma Mbwana Amiri claims chakacha originated in her area of mainland Mombasa. Chakacha is usually considered to be a musical tradition from the Manyema area of present-day Tanzania. Many Manyema came to the Swahili coast from the nineteenth century onward.

CONCLUSION

1. This door, however, was likely made by a junior or even self-taught carver. The carving style does not exhibit the three-dimensional depth practiced by master carvers. Athman Hussein Athman, conversation with author, 15 August 2015.

2. This way of seeing the world was supported by new scientific disciplines such as geography and anthropology. Lewis and Wigen, *Myth of Continents*, 119.

3. My point here draws on Deborah Poole's analysis of the role visual images, especially photography, played in the making of racial difference in colonial South America. Poole, *Vision, Race, and Modernity*.

4. Pierre, *Predicament of Blackness*, xii.

5. M. Jackson, *Lifeworlds*, 3–4.

6. For critiques of Eurocentric ways of studying African art, see Blier, "Enduring Myths"; Coombes, "Containing the Continent"; Kasfir, "African Art and Authenticity"; Kasfir, "One Tribe, One Style?"; Okoye, "Tribe and Art History."

7. Cooper, *Colonialism in Question*, 83.

8. Young, *Colonial Desire*. For an analysis of how "hybridity" is used as a racialized cultural concept in art history, see Dean and Leibsohn, "Hybridity and Its Discontents."

9. Frederick Cooper's and Ann Stoler's critique of the colonizer-versus-colonized binary and the discourse of racial fixities also informs this present work. Cooper and Stoler, *Tensions of Empire*. See also Fabian, *Time and the Other*, and Trouillot, "Otherwise Modern."

10. Of course, today much popular expressive culture, especially music and dance, is called Swahili by locals (especially in Tanzania), but this is a reflection of recent processes of postcolonial nation-building. The key study of this phenomenon is Askew, *Performing the Nation*.

11. Mama Hadija Abdul Rahman, conversation with author, 15 September 2005.

BIBLIOGRAPHY

Abdulaziz, Mohamed H., and Muyāka ibn H̲ājjī, al-Ghassānī. *Muyaka: 19th Century Swahili Popular Poetry*. Nairobi: Kenya Literature Bureau, 1979.

Aldrick, Judith. "The Painted Plates of Zanzibar." *Kenya Past and Present* 30 (1998): 26–28.

Allen, James de Vere. "The Kiti Cha Enzi and Other Swahili Chairs." *African Arts* 22, no. 3 (1989): 54–63, 88.

———. "The Siwas of Pate and Lamu: Two Antique Side-Blown Horns from the Swahili Coast." *Art and Archeology Research Papers* 10 (1976): 38–47.

———. "Swahili Culture and the Nature of East Coast Settlement." *International Journal of African Historical Studies* 14, no. 2 (1981): 306–334.

———. "Swahili Culture Reconsidered: Some Historical Implications of the Material Culture of the Northern Kenya Coast in the Eighteenth and Nineteenth Centuries." *Azania* 9 (1974): 105–138.

———. "The Swahili House: Cultural and Ritual Concepts Underlying Its Plan and Structure." In *Swahili Houses and Tombs of the Coast of Kenya*, edited by James de Vere Allen and Thomas H. Wilson, 1–32. London: Art and Archaeology Research Papers, 1979.

———. "Swahili Ornament: A Study of the Decoration of the 18th Century Plasterwork and Carved Doors in the Lamu Region." *Art and Archaeology Research Papers* 3 (1971): 1–14.

Alpers, Edward A. *East Africa and the Indian Ocean*. Princeton: Markus Wiener Publishers, 2009.

———. *Ivory and Slaves: Changing Pattern of International Trade in East Central Africa to the Later Nineteenth Century*. Berkeley: University of California Press, 1975.

———. "Recollecting Africa: Diasporic Memory in the Indian Ocean World." *African Studies Review* 43, no. 1 (2000): 83–99.

Appadurai, Arjun. *The Social Life of Things: Commodities in Cultural Perspective*. Cambridge: Cambridge University Press, 1986.

Askew, Kelly Michelle. "As Plato Duly Warned: Music, Politics, and Social Change in Coastal East Africa." *Anthropological Quarterly* 76, no. 4 (2003): 609–637.

———. *Performing the Nation: Swahili Music and Cultural Politics in Tanzania.* Chicago: University of Chicago Press, 2002.

Bang, Anne K. *Sufis and Scholars of the Sea: Family Networks in East Africa, 1860–1925.* London: Routledge, 2003.

Barbosa, Duarte, Fernão de Magalhães, and Mansel Longworth Dames. *The Book of Duarte Barbosa: An Account of the Countries Bordering on the Indian Ocean and Their Inhabitants.* London: Hakluyt Society, 1918.

Beaujard, Philippe. "The Indian Ocean in Eurasian and African World-Systems before the Sixteenth Century." *Journal of World History* 16, no. 4 (2006): 411–465.

Becker, C. H. "Materials for the Understanding of Islam in German East Africa." *Tanzania Notes and Records* 68 (1963): 31–61.

Bellingham, Beatrix L. *Mombasa: A Guide to Mombasa & Surroundings.* Nairobi: Mombasa Times, 1933.

Bennett, Norman Robert. *A History of the Arab State of Zanzibar.* London: Methuen, 1978.

Bennett, Tony. "The Exhibitionary Complex." In *Culture/Power/History: A Reader in Contemporary Social Theory,* edited by Nicholas B. Dirks, Geoff Eley, and Sherry B. Ortner, 122–154. Princeton: Princeton University Press, 1994.

Berg, Fred James. "Mombasa under the Busaidi Sultanate: The City and Its Hinterlands in the Nineteenth Century." PhD diss., University of Wisconsin, 1971.

———. "The Swahili Community of Mombasa, 1500–1900." *Journal of African History* 9, no. 1 (1968): 35–56.

Berg, Fred James, and B. J. Walter. "Mosques, Population and Urban Development in Mombasa." *Hadith* 1 (1968): 47–100.

Bissell, William Cunningham. "Conservation and the Colonial Past: Urban Planning, Space, and Power in Zanzibar." In *Africa's Urban Past,* edited by David M. Anderson and Richard Rathbone, 246–261. Oxford: James Currey, 2000.

———. *Urban Design, Chaos, and Colonial Power in Zanzibar.* Bloomington: Indiana University Press, 2011.

Blier, Suzanne Preston. *The Anatomy of Architecture: Ontology and Metaphor in Batammaliba Architectural Expression.* Cambridge: Cambridge University Press, 1987.

———. "Enduring Myths of African Art." In *Africa, the Art of a Continent: 100 Works of Power and Beauty,* 26–32. New York: Guggenheim Museum Publications, 1996.

Bose, Sugata. *A Hundred Horizons: The Indian Ocean in the Age of Global Empire.* Cambridge, MA: Harvard University Press, 2006.

Bravmann, René A. *African Islam.* Washington, DC: Smithsonian Institution Press, 1983.

Brennan, James. *Taifa: Making Nation and Race in Urban Tanzania.* Athens, Ohio: Ohio University Press, 2012.

Bunn, James H. "The Aesthetics of British Mercantilism." *New Literary History* 11, no. 2 (1980): 303–321.

Burton, Richard F. *Zanzibar: City, Island, and Coast.* London: Tinsley Brothers, 1872.

Cameron, Verney L. "Zanzibar: Its Past, Present and Future." *Revue Coloniale Internationale* 1 (1885): 417–430.

Campbell, Gwyn. *The Structure of Slavery in Indian Ocean Africa and Asia*. London: Frank Cass, 2004.

Casale, Giancarlo L. "The Ottoman Age of Exploration: Spices, Maps and Conquest in the Sixteenth-Century Indian Ocean." PhD diss., Harvard University, 2004.

Çelik, Zeynep. *Urban Forms and Colonial Confrontations: Algiers under French Rule*. Berkeley: University of California Press, 1997.

Chakrabarty, Dipesh. *Provincializing Europe: Postcolonial Thought and Historical Difference*. Princeton: Princeton University Press, 2000.

Chaudhuri, K. N. *Trade and Civilisation in the Indian Ocean: An Economic History from the Rise of Islam to 1750*. Cambridge: Cambridge University Press, 1985.

Chami, Felix A. "A Review of Swahili Archaeology." *African Archaeological Review* 5, no. 3 (1998): 199–218.

Cheah, Pheng. *Inhuman Conditions: On Cosmopolitanism and Human Rights*. Cambridge, MA: Harvard University Press, 2006.

Clifford, James. *The Predicament of Culture: Twentieth-Century Ethnography, Literature, and Art*. Cambridge, MA: Harvard University Press, 1988.

Connah, Graham. *African Civilizations: Precolonial Cities and States in Tropical Africa, An Archaeological Perspective*. Cambridge: Cambridge University Press, 1987.

Coole, Diana H., and Samantha Frost. *New Materialisms: Ontology, Agency, and Politics*. Durham, NC: Duke University Press, 2010.

Coombes, Annie E. "Containing the Continent: Ethnography on Display." In *Reinventing Africa: Museums, Material Culture, and Popular Imagination in Late Victorian and Edwardian England*, 129–160. New Haven: Yale University Press, 1994.

Cooper, Frederick. *Colonialism in Question: Theory, Knowledge, History*. Berkeley: University of California Press, 2005.

———. *On the African Waterfront: Urban Disorder and the Transformation of Work in Colonial Mombasa*. New Haven: Yale University Press, 1987.

———. *Plantation Slavery on the East Coast of Africa*. New Haven: Yale University Press, 1977.

Cooper, Frederick, and Ann Laura Stoler, eds. *Tensions of Empire: Colonial Cultures in a Bourgeois World*. Berkeley: University of California Press, 1997.

Crinson, Mark. *Empire Building: Orientalism and Victorian Architecture*. London: Routledge, 1996.

Crofton, Richard Hayes. *The Old Consulate at Zanzibar*. London: Oxford University Press, H. Milford, 1935.

Davis, Richard Harding. *The Congo and Coasts of Africa*. London: T. Fisher Unwin, 1908.

Dean, Carolyn. *A Culture of Stone: Inka Perspectives on Rock*. Durham, NC: Duke University Press, 2010.

Dean, Carolyn, and Dana Leibsohn. "Hybridity and Its Discontents: Considering Visual Culture in Colonial Spanish America." *Colonial Latin American Review* 12, no. 1 (January 6, 2003): 5–35.

von der Decken, Carl Claus, and Otto Kersten. *Reisen in Ost-Afrika in Den Jahren 1859 Bis 1865*. Leipzig: CF Winter, 1869–79. Reprint. Graz, Austria: Akademische Druck- u. Verlagsanstalt, 1978.

Desai, Gaurav Gajanan. *Commerce with the Universe: Africa, India, and the Afrasian Imagination.* New York: Columbia University Press, 2013.

Donley-Reid, Linda. "A Structuring Structure: The Swahili House." In *Domestic Architecture and the Use of Space: An Interdisciplinary Cross-Cultural Study,* edited by Susan Kent, 63–73. Cambridge: Cambridge University Press, 1990.

———. "The Power of Swahili Porcelain, Beads and Pottery." *Archeological Papers of the American Anthropological Association* 2, no. 1 (1990): 47–59.

Doris, David. *Vigilant Things: On Thieves, Yoruba Anti-aesthetics, and the Strange Fates of Ordinary Objects in Nigeria.* Seattle: University of Washington Press, 2011.

Elliot, J. A. G. "A Visit to the Bajun Islands. Part I: Brief Historical Sketch—Source of Origin of the Present and Past Population." *Journal of the Royal African Society* 25, no. 97 (1925): 10–22.

Fabian, Johannes. *Time and the Other: How Anthropology Makes Its Object.* New York: Columbia University Press, 1983.

Fair, Laura. *Pastimes and Politics: Culture, Community, and Identity in Post-Abolition Urban Zanzibar, 1890–1945.* Athens: Ohio University Press, 2001.

———. "Remaking Fashion in the Paris of the Indian Ocean: Dress, Performance, and the Cultural Construction of a Cosmopolitan Zanzibari Identity." In *Fashioning Africa: Power and the Politics of Dress,* edited by Jean Allman, 13–30. Bloomington: Indiana University Press, 2004.

Farsy, Abdallah Salih, and Randall Pouwels. *The Shafi'i Ulama of East Africa, c. 1830–1970: A Hagiographic Account.* Madison: University of Wisconsin–Madison, 1989.

Finlay, Robert. *The Pilgrim Art: Cultures of Porcelain in World History.* Berkeley: University of California Press, 2010.

Fitzgerald, William Walter Augustine. *Travels in the Coastlands of British East Africa and the Islands of Zanzibar and Pemba: Their Agricultural Resources and General Characteristics.* London: Chapman and Hall, 1898.

Fleisher, Jeffrey, and Adria LaViolette. "The Changing Power of Swahili Houses, Fourteenth to Nineteenth Centuries A.D." In *The Durable House: House Society Models in Archaeology,* edited by Robin A. Beck, 175–197. Carbondale: Center for Archaeological Investigations, Southern Illinois University, 2007.

Flood, Finbarr Barry. *Objects of Translation: Material Culture and Medieval "Hindu–Muslim" Encounter.* Princeton: Princeton University Press, 2009.

Frankl, P. J. L. "The Old German Consulate in British East Africa: A Mombasa Mansion and Its Carved Door." *British Journal of Middle Eastern Studies* 30 (2003): 137–153.

Freeman-Grenville, G. S. P. *The East African Coast; Select Documents from the First to the Earlier Nineteenth Century.* Oxford: Clarendon Press, 1962.

Garlake, Peter S. *Early Art and Architecture of Africa.* Oxford: Oxford University Press, 2002.

———. *The Early Islamic Architecture of the East African Coast.* Nairobi: Oxford University Press, 1966.

Gary, G. S. "Furniture Found in Kenya." *Old Furniture: A Magazine of Domestic Ornament* 8 (1929): 148–151.

Ghaidan, Usam. *Lamu: A Study of the Swahili Town.* Nairobi: East African Literature Bureau, 1975.

Gikandi, Simon. "Between Roots and Routes: Cosmopolitanism and the Claims of Locality." In *Rerouting the Postcolonial: New Directions for the New Millenium,* edited by Janet Wilson, Sandru Critina, and Sarah Wilson, 22–34. London: Routledge, 2010.

Giles, Linda. "Mbaraki Pillar and Its Spirits." In *Kenya Past and Present* 19 (1987) 44–49.

———. "Spirit Possession on the Swahili Coast: Peripheral Cults or Primary Texts?" PhD diss., University of Texas at Austin, 1989.

Glassman, Jonathon. *Feasts and Riot: Revelry, Rebellion, and Popular Consciousness on the Swahili Coast, 1856–1888.* Portsmouth, NH: Heinemann, 1995.

———. *War of Words, War of Stones: Racial Thought and Violence in Colonial Zanzibar.* Bloomington: Indiana University Press, 2011.

Gray, John Milner. *The British in Mombasa, 1824–1826: Being the History of Captain Owen's Protectorate.* London: Macmillan, 1957.

———. *History of Zanzibar, from the Middle Ages to 1856.* London: Oxford University Press, 1962.

Great Britain Admiralty. *A Handbook of Kenya Colony (British East Africa) and the Kenya Protectorate (Protectorate of Zanzibar).* London: H. M. Stationery Off., 1920.

Guillain, Charles. *Documents sur l'histoire, la géographie et le commerce de l'Afrique orientale, recueillis et rédigés.* Paris: A. Bertrand, 1856.

Hardinge, Arthur Henry. *A Diplomatist in the East.* London: J. Cape, 1928.

Hardt, Michael, and Antonio Negri. *Empire.* Cambridge, MA: Harvard University Press, 2000.

Hinawy, Mbarak Ali, and Abdallah bin Mas'ud bin Salim al-Mazrui. *Al-Akida and Fort Jesus, Mombasa.* Nairobi: East African Literature Bureau, 1970.

Ho, Engseng. *The Graves of Tarim: Genealogy and Mobility across the Indian Ocean.* Berkeley: University of California Press, 2006.

Hofmeyr, Isabel. *Gandhi's Printing Press: Experiments in Slow Reading.* Cambridge, MA: Harvard University Press, 2013.

———. "Universalizing the Indian Ocean." *PMLA: Publications of the Modern Language Association of America* 125, no. 3 (2010): 721–729.

Hofmeyr, Isabel, Preben Kaarsholm, and Bodil Folke Frederiksen. "Introduction: Print Cultures, Nationalisms and Publics of the Indian Ocean." *Africa* 81, no. 1 (2011): 1–22.

Horton, Mark. "East Africa." In *The Mosque: History, Architectural Development and Regional Diversity,* edited by Martin Frishman and Hasan-Uddin Khan, 194–207. London: Thames and Hudson, 1994.

———. "Islam, Archeology, and Swahili Identity." In *Changing Social Identity with the Spread of Islam: Archaeological Perspectives,* edited by Donald S. Whitcomb, 67–88. Chicago: Oriental Institute of the University of Chicago, 2004.

———. "Swahili Architecture, Space and Social Structure." In *Architecture and Order: Approaches to Social Space,* edited by Michael Parker Pearson and Colin Richards, 132–152. London: Routledge, 1994.

Horton, Mark, Helen W. Brown, and Nina Mudida. *Shanga: The Archaeology of a Muslim Trading Community on the Coast of East Africa.* London: The British Institute in Eastern Africa, 1996.

Horton, Mark, and John Middleton. *The Swahili: The Social Landscape of a Mercantile Society.* Malden: Blackwell Publishers, 2000.

Hoyle, Brian. "Urban Renewal in East African Port Cities: Mombasa's Old Town Water-front." *GeoJournal* 53 (2001): 183–197.

Huebner, R. F. Paul, and Herward Sieberg. *Zeitenumbruch in Ostafrika: Sansibar, Kenia Und Uganda (1894–1913): Erinnerungen Des Kaufmanns R.F. Paul Huebner.* Hildesheimer Universitätsschriften, Bd. 3. Hildesheim: Universitätsbibliothek, 1998.

Hunter, Matthew C., and Francesco Lucchini. "The Clever Object: Three Pavilions, Three Loggias, and a Planetarium." *Art History* 36, no. 3 (June 2013): 474–497.

Ingrams, William Harold. *Zanzibar, Its History and Its People.* London: H. F. and G. Witherby, 1931.

Ivanov, Paola. "Cosmpolitanism or Exclusion? Negotiating Identity in the Expressive Culture of Zanzibar." In *The Indian Ocean: Oceanic Connections and the Creation of New Societies,* edited by Abdul Sheriff and Engseng Ho, 209–237. London: Hurst, 2014.

Jackson, Frederick John. *Early Days in East Africa.* London: Dawsons of Pall Mall, 1969.

———. "The Ghost of Leven House." *Uganda Journal* 15, no. 23 (1951 [1888]): 159–164.

Jackson, Michael. *Lifeworlds: Essays in Existential Anthropology.* Chicago: University of Chicago Press, 2013.

Jaffer, Amin, and Karina Corrigan. *Furniture from British India and Ceylon: A Catalogue of the Collections in the Victoria and Albert Museum and the Peabody Essex Museum.* London: V and A Publications, 2001.

Johnston, Harry Hamilton. *The Kilima-Njaro Expedition: A Record of Scientific Exploration in Eastern Equatorial Africa; and a General Description of the Natural History, Languages, and Commerce of the Kilima-Njaro District.* London: Kegan Paul, Trench, 1886.

Juma, Abdurahman. *Unguja Ukuu on Zanzibar: An Archaeological Study of Early Urbanism.* Uppsala: African and Comparative Archaeology, Dept. of Archaeology and Ancient History, Uppsala University, 2004.

Kasfir, Sidney L. "African Art and Authenticity: A Text with a Shadow." *African Arts* 25, no. 2 (1992): 41–97.

———. "One Tribe, One Style? Paradigms in the Historiography of African Art." *History in Africa* (1984): 163–193.

Kindy, Hyder. *Life and Politics in Mombasa.* Nairobi: East African Publishing House, 1972.

King, Anthony D. *The Bungalow: The Production of a Global Culture.* London: Routledge, 1984.

Kirkman, James S. *Men and Monuments on the East African Coast.* London: Lutterworth, 1964.

———. "The Zanzibar Diary of John Studdy Leigh." *International Journal of African Historical Studies* 13, no. 2 (1980): 281–312.

Krapf, Ludwig. *A Dictionary of the Suahili Language.* London: Trübner, 1882.

Kress, Kai. *Philosophising in Mombasa: Knowledge, Islam and Intellectual Practice on the Swahili Coast.* Edinburgh: Edinburgh University Press for the International African Institute, 2007.

Kusimba, Chapurukha Makokha. "Kenya's Destruction of the Swahili Cultural Heritage." In *Plundering Africa's Past,* edited by Peter R. Schmidt and Roderick J McIntosh, 201–224. Bloomington: Indiana University Press, 1996.

———. *The Rise and Fall of Swahili States.* Walnut Creek: AltaMira Press, 1999.

Larson, Pier. *Ocean of Letters: Language and Creolization in an Indian Ocean Diaspora.* Cambridge: Cambridge University Press, 2009.

LaViolette, Adria. "Swahili Cosmopolitanism in Africa and the Indian Ocean World, A D 600–1500." *Archaeologies: Journal of the World Archaeological Congress* 4 no. 1 (2008): 24–49.

Lewcock, Ronald. "Architectural Connections between Africa and Parts of the Indian Ocean." *Art and Archaeology Research Papers* 9 (1976): 13–23.

Lewis, Martin W., and Kären Wigen. *The Myth of Continents: A Critique of Metageography.* Berkeley: University of California Press, 1997.

Lyne, Robert Nunez. *Zanzibar in Contemporary Times: A Short History of the Southern East in the Nineteenth Century.* London: Hurst and Blackett, 1905.

Marett, R. R. "The Siwa in East Africa." *Folklore* 25, no. 4 (1914): 499–500.

Mark, Peter. *"Portuguese" Style and Luso-African Identity: Precolonial Senegambia, 16th–19th Centuries.* Bloomington: Indiana University Press, 2003.

Mathew, Gervase. "The Culture of the East African Coast in the Seventeenth and Eighteenth Centuries in the Light of Recent Archaeological Discoveries." *Man* 56 (1956): 65–68.

McIntosh, Janet. *The Edge of Islam: Power, Personhood, and Ethnoreligious Boundaries on the Kenya Coast.* Durham: Duke University Press, 2009.

McPherson, Kenneth. "Port Cities as Nodal Points of Change: The Indian Ocean, 1890s–1920s." In *Modernity and Culture: From the Mediterranean to the Indian Ocean,* edited by Leila Tarazi Fawaz, C. A. Bayly, and Robert Ilbert, 75–95. New York: Columbia University Press, 2002.

Meinecke, Gustav. *Aus Dem Lande Der Suaheli: Teil 1.* Berlin: Deutscher Kolonial-Verlag, 1895.

Middleton, John. *The World of the Swahili: An African Mercantile Civilization.* New Haven: Yale University Press, 1992.

Mignolo, Walter. *Local Histories/Global Designs: Coloniality, Subaltern Knowledges, and Border Thinking.* Princeton: Princeton University Press, 2000.

Mitchell, Timothy. *Colonising Egypt.* Berkeley: University of California Press, 1991.

Müller, Fritz Ferdinand. *Deutschland, Zanzibar, Ostafrika; Geschichte Einer Deutschen Kolonialeroberung, 1884–1890.* Berlin: Riitten and Loening, 1959.

Myers, Fred R., ed. *The Empire of Things: Regimes of Value and Material Culture.* Santa Fe: School of American Research Press, 2001.

Myers, Garth Andrew. "Sticks and Stones: Colonialism and Zanzibari Housing." *Africa* 67, no. 2 (1997): 252–272.

———. *Verandahs of Power: Colonialism and Space in Urban Africa.* Syracuse, NY: Syracuse University Press, 2003.

National Archives of Rhodesia and Nyasaland, and Centro de Estudos Históricos Ultramarinos. *Documents on the Portuguese in Mozambique and Central Africa, 1497–1840.* Vol. 1, Lisbon, 1962.

New, Charles. *Life, Wanderings and Labours in Eastern Africa: With an Account of the First Successful Ascent of the Equatorial Snow Mountain, Kilima Njaro, and Remarks Upon East African Slavery.* London: Hodder and Stoughton, 1874.

Nimtz, August H. *Islam and Politics in East Africa: The Sufi Order in Tanzania.* Minneapolis: University of Minnesota Press, 1980.

Okoye, Ikem Stanley. "'Hideous Architecture': Mimicry, Feint and Resistance in Turn of the Century Southeastern Nigerian Building." PhD diss., Massachusetts Institute of Technology, 1994.

———. "Tribe and Art History." *Art Bulletin* 78 (December 1996): 610–615.

"On the Track of the Germans in East Africa." *Pall Mall Gazette* vol. 41 (June 3, 1885).

Parkin, David J., and Stephen Cavana Headley. *Islamic Prayer across the Indian Ocean: Inside and Outside the Mosque.* Richmond: Curzon, 2000.

Pearce, Francis Barrow. *Zanzibar, the Island Metropolis of Eastern Africa.* London: T. F. Unwin, 1920.

Pearson, M. N. *The Indian Ocean.* London: Routledge, 2003.

———. *Port Cities and Intruders: The Swahili Coast, India, and Portugal in the Early Modern Era.* Baltimore: Johns Hopkins University Press, 1998.

Pels, Peter. "The Spirit of the Matter: On Fetish, Rarity, Fact, and Fancy." In *Border Fetishisms: Material Objects in Unstable Spaces,* edited by Patricia Spyer, 91–121. New York: Routledge, 1998.

Pels, Peter, and Oscar Salemink. *Colonial Subjects: Essays on the Practical History of Anthropology.* Ann Arbor: University of Michigan Press, 1999.

Pierre, Jemima. *The Predicament of Blackness: Postcolonial Ghana and the Politics of Race.* Chicago: University of Chicago Press, 2013.

Pietz, William. "The Problem of the Fetish, I." *Res* 9 (1985): 5–17.

Playne, Somerset, and Frank Holderness Gale, eds. *East Africa (British): Its History, People, Commerce, Industries, and Resources.* London: Foreign and Colonial Compiling and Publishing, 1908.

Poole, Deborah. *Vision, Race, and Modernity: A Visual Economy of the Andean Image World.* Princeton: Princeton University Press, 1997.

Pouwels, Randall. *Horn and Crescent: Cultural Change and Traditional Islam on the East African Coast, 800–1900.* Cambridge: Cambridge University Press, 1987.

———. "Sh. Al-Amin B. Ali Mazrui and Islamic Modernism in East Africa, 1875–1947." *International Journal of Middle East Studies* 13, no. 3 (1981): 329–345.

Prestholdt, Jeremy. *Domesticating the World: African Consumerism and the Genealogies of Globalization.* Berkeley: University of California Press, 2008.

Rappaport, Erika, ed. "Sea Tracks and Trails: Indian Ocean Worlds as Method." *History Compass* 11, no. 7 (2013): 497–502.

Reese, Scott Steven. *The Transmission of Learning in Islamic Africa.* Leiden: Brill, 2004.

Reichard, Paul. *Deutsch-Ostafrika: Das Land und Seine Bewohner, Seine Politische und Wirtschaftliche Entwickelung.* Leipzig: O. Spamer, 1892.

Risso, Patricia. *Merchants and Faith: Muslim Commerce and Culture in the Indian Ocean.* Boulder: Westview Press, 1995.

Roberts, Allen F. *A Dance of Assassins: Performing Early Colonial Hegemony in the Congo.* Bloomington: Indiana University Press, 2013.

———. "Is 'Africa' Obsolete?" *African Arts* 33, no. 1 (Spring 2000): 1, 4–9.

Romero, Patricia W. *Lamu: History, Society, and Family in an East African Port City.* Princeton: Markus Wiener, 1997.

Ropes, Edward D. *The Zanzibar Letters of Edward D. Ropes, Jr., 1882–1892*. Boston: African Studies Center, Boston University, 1973.

Ruete, Emilie. *Memoirs of an Arabian Princess from Zanzibar*. New York: Markus Wiener, 1989.

Ruete, Emilie, and E. J. van Donzel. *An Arabian Princess between Two Worlds: Memoirs, Letters Home, Sequels to the Memoirs: Syrian Customs and Usages*. Leiden: E. J. Brill, 1993.

Salim, A. I. *The Swahili-Speaking Peoples of Kenya's Coast, 1895–1965*. Nairobi: East African Publishing House, 1973.

Sassoon, Hamo. "Mosque and Pillar at Mbaraki: A Contribution to the History of Mombasa Island." *Azania* 17 (1982): 79–97.

Schmidt, Karl Wilhelm. *Sansibar: Ein Ostafrikanisches Culturbild*. Leipzig: F. A. Brockhaus, 1888.

Sheldon, Mary. *Sultan to Sultan: Adventures among the Masai and Other Tribes of East Africa*. Boston: Arena, 1892.

Sheriff, Abdul. "An Outline History of Zanzibar Stone Town." In *The History and Conservation of Zanzibar Stone Town*, edited by Abdul Sheriff, 8–29. Zanzibar: Department of Archives, Museums, and Antiquities, 1995.

———. *Dhow Culture of the Indian Ocean: Cosmopolitanism, Commerce and Islam*. New York: Columbia University Press, 2010.

———. "Mosques, Merchants and Landowners in Zanzibar Stone Town." In *The History and Conservation of Zanzibar Stone Town*, edited by Abdul Sheriff, 46–66. Zanzibar: Department of Archives, Museums, and Antiquities, 1995.

———. *Slaves, Spices, and Ivory in Zanzibar: Integration of an East African Commercial Empire into the World Economy, 1770–1873*. London: James Currey, 1987.

———. "The Spatial Dichotomy of Swahili Towns: The Case of Zanzibar in the Nineteenth Century." *Azania* 36–37 (2001): 63–81.

Sheriff, Abdul, and Engseng Ho. *The Indian Ocean: Oceanic Connections and the Creation of New Societies*. London: Hurst, 2014.

de Silva, Chandra Richard. "Indian Ocean but Not African Sea: The Erasure of East African Commerce from History." *Journal of Black Studies* 29, no. 5 (1999): 684–694.

Simpson, Edward, and Kai Kresse. *Struggling with History: Islam and Cosmopolitanism in the Western Indian Ocean*. New York: Columbia University Press, 2008.

Siravo, Francesco. *Zanzibar: A Plan for the Historic Stone Town*. Geneva, Switzerland: Aga Khan Trust for Culture, 1996.

"Sketches of Zanzibar. Written During a Sojourn on That Island, from May 20th to August 10th, 1843." *American Review* 2, no. 2 (1885): 154–162.

Spear, Thomas. "The Shirazi in Swahili Traditions, Culture, and History." *History in Africa: A Journal of Method History in Africa* 11 (1984): 291–305.

Spyer, Patricia. *Border Fetishisms: Material Objects in Unstable Spaces* (Zones of Religion). New York: Routledge, 1998.

Stanziani, Alessandro. *Sailors, Slaves, and Immigrants: Bondage in the Indian Ocean World, 1750–1914*. New York: Palgrave Macmillan, 2014.

Stewart, Susan. *On Longing: Narratives of the Miniature, the Gigantic, the Souvenir, the Collection*. Baltimore: Johns Hopkins University Press, 1984.

Stigand, Chauncey Hugh. *The Land of Zinj, Being an Account of British East Africa, Its Ancient History and Present Inhabitants.* London: Constable, 1913.

Strandes, Justus, and James S. Kirkman. *The Portuguese Period in East Africa.* Nairobi: East African Literature Bureau, 1968.

Strobel, Margaret. *Muslim Women in Mombasa, 1890–1975.* New Haven: Yale University Press, 1979.

Stuhlmann, Franz, and R. Stern. *Handwerk und Industrie in Ostafrika; Kulturgeschichtliche Betrachtungen.* Abhandlungen Des Hamburgischen Kolonialinstituts. Bd. 1. Reihe B. Völkerkunde, Kulturgeschichte und Sprachen, Bd. 1. Hamburg: L. Friederichsen, 1910.

Thomas, Nicholas. *Entangled Objects: Exchange, Material Culture, and Colonialism in the Pacific.* Cambridge, MA: Harvard University Press, 1991.

Thomson, Joseph, Henry W. Bates, John G. Baker, and E. A. Smith. *To the Central African Lakes and Back: The Narrative of the Royal Geographical Society's East Central African Expedition, 1878–1880.* London: S. Low, Marston, Searle and Rivington, 1881.

Topan, Farouk M. T. "Swahili and Isma'ili Perceptions of Salat." In *Islamic Prayer Across the Indian Ocean,* edited by Stephen Headley and David Parkin, 99–115. Surrey: Curzon Press, 2000.

Trouillot, Michel-Rolph. "The Otherwise Modern: Caribbean Lessons from the Savage Lot." In *Critically Modern: Alternatives, Alterities, Anthropologies,* edited by Bruce M. Knauft, 220–240. Bloomington: Indiana University Press, 2002.

Um, Nancy. *The Merchant Houses of Mocha: Trade and Architecture in an Indian Ocean Port.* Seattle: University of Washington Press, 2009.

Vizetelly, Edward. *From Cyprus to Zanzibar by the Egyptian Delta: The Adventures of a Journalist in the Isle of Love, the Home of Miracles, and the Land of Cloves.* London: C. A. Pearson, 1901.

Willis, Justin. *Mombasa, the Swahili, and the Making of the Mijikenda.* Oxford: Oxford University Press, 1993.

Willoughby, John C. *East Africa and Its Big Game; the Narrative of a Sporting Trip from Zanzibar to the Borders of the Masai.* London, New York: Longmans, Green, 1889.

Wilson, Thomas H. "Swahili Funerary Architecture of the North Kenya Coast." In *Swahili Houses and Tombs of the Coast of Kenya,* edited by James de Vere Allen and Thomas H. Wilson, 33–41. London: Art and Archaeology Research Papers, 1979.

White, Luise. *Speaking with Vampires: Rumor and History in Colonial Africa.* Berkeley: University of California Press, 2000.

Wynne-Jones, Stephanie. "It's What You Do With It That Counts: Performed Identities in the East African Coastal Landscape." *Journal of Social Archaeology Journal of Social Archaeology* 7, no. 3 (2007): 325–345.

Wright, Gwendolyn. *The Politics of Design in French Colonial Urbanism.* Chicago: University of Chicago Press, 1991

Young, Robert. *Colonial Desire: Hybridity in Theory, Culture, and Race.* London: Routledge, 1995.

INDEX

Page numbers in italics refer to figures.

Abungu, George, 21

Africa, 8, 14, 51, 109, 115, 152, 182, 183, 184, 185, 197n61; central, 16, 27, 34, 39, 149; coastal east, 5, 10, 111, 149, 152, 196n33; coastal west, 7; east, 1, 10, 16, 17, 18, 23, 39, 78, 86, 90, 92, 93, 96, 110, 112, 128, 141, 144, 148, 149, 150, 152, 161, 162, 182, 186, 192n22, 197n54; inland, 10, 26–27, 28, 141; mainland, 1, 13, 149; northeast, 93; south, 149; west, 4, 6, 17, 144

Africanists, 141, 183–184, 193n28

Afro-Asian Association, 202n71

agency, 155; collective, 101; in things, 5–6, 140

Ali bin Salim, 99, 201n62

Allen, James de Vere, 36, 195n25, 206n5, 207n27

Anglo-German Agreement, 110

Anglo-Zanzibar War, *20*

anthropology, 209n2; anthropologists, cultural, 192n15

Appadurai, Arjun, 140, 207n18

appropriation, 3, 19, 24, 27, 50, 110, 140, 166, 170, 196n41

Arab Administration, 63, 79, 99, 197n59

Arabian Peninsula, 8, 11, 29, 79, 111, 152, 160, 175, 193n27, 208n42

archeology, 17, 22, 23, 69, 92, 94; archeologists, 18, 21, 37, 90, 151

arches, 83, 84, 85; horseshoe, 116; ogee, 83, 84; pointed, 2, 37, 83, 84; South Asian, 85

architecture, 4, 11, 19, 21, 24, 26, 37, 47, 92, 105, 106, 111, 122, 123, 130, 184, 185, 186, 196n42; "Arab," 31; colonial, 59, 182; domestic, 93, 140; Islamic, 18, 23, 39; *makuti*, 13, 58, 113; merchant, 23, 114; mosque, 67, 70, 79, 99, 100; religious, 92, 150, 175; stone, 3, 4, 6, 10, 11, 13, 15, 16, 17, 19–20, 22, 23, 26, 27, 36–37, 39–41, 46, 47, 63, 66, 96, 125, 150, 153, 182, 186, 195n25, 196n41; Swahili coast, 2–3, 10, 18, 20, 22, 23, 24–25, 39, 47, 146, 192n19, 195n24; waterfront, 1, 10, 17, 50; wattle and daub, 22, 64, 106, 195n31. See also *nyumba ya mawe*; ornamentation: architectural; space: architectural

art historians, 5, 157, 179, 182, 183

artifacts, 3, 5, 23, 50, 140, 141, 166, 182; cultural, 15, 150; material, 184

Askew, Kelly, 192n20, 204n40

Middle East, 7, 26, 27, 28, 29, 30, 31, 32, 34, 35, 79, 91, 116, 119, 130, 141; Middle Eastern forms, 10, 61, 76, 90; Middle Eastern law, 97

Mignolo, Walter, 7, 191n10

migration, 3, 7, 8, 9, 10, 31, 32, 64, 70, 192n20, 194n10

Mijikenda, 31, 33, 34, 98, 177, 199n16

minarets, 18, 31, 79, 201nn39–41, 201n43; pillar, 23, 67, 69, 70, 72, 86, 87, 88, 90, 93, 96, 101, 201n44

mirrors, 24, 108, 132, 136–137, 143, 146, 154, 161

missionaries, 17, 42, 49, 51, 53, 122–123, 196nn45–46, 203n2. *See also* Church Missionary Society

mitaa (designations of neighborhoods), 31, 79, 171, 194n10; *mtaa ya mzungu*, 62, 63, 197n64

Mkisi, Mwana, 33–35

mobility, 3, 9, 10, 32, 36, 119, 170, 191n1, 192n20; in Islam, 70; mercantile, 1; oceanic, 41, 136, 167; social, 11, 141, 186

Mocha, 192n19, 194n3, 195n26

modernity, 2, 11, 19, 24, 60, 103, 118, 123, 139; capitalist, 8, 24

Mohammad (the Prophet), 120

Mombasa, 2, 3, 4, 9, 13, 16–17, 19, 20, 22, 26, 27–29, 31, 33–35, 39, 40, 41–42, 44–46, 47, 50, 53, 56, 59–65, 66, 67, 69, 72, 74–77, 79, 90, 92, 96, 98, 100, 101, 143, 146, 149, 152, 154, 155, 157, 160, 162, 164, 170, 171, 173, 175, 177, 179, 180, 186, 193n1, 194n3, 194n10, 194n17, 194n18, 195n31, 196n44, 197n59, 199nn8–9, 200n28, 200n34, 202n63, 205n55, 205n60, 208nn44–45; governance of, 64, 99, 149, 197n54, 197n59, 199n7, 201n62; Mombasans, 27, 29, 30, 31, 32, 34–35, 51, 64, 69, 70, 74–75, 77, 100, 129, 156, 177, 197n58, 199n9, 200n25; Mombasa Protectorate, 59; Old Town, 18, 23, 32, 43, 48, 49, 51, 64, 65, 78, 79, 93, 98, 99, 158, 170; waterfront, 36, 46, 53, 63. *See also* Mombasa Island; Mombasa Old Town Conservation Office;

Mombasa Public Works Department; *Mombasa Times*

Mombasa Island, 27, 29, 30, 32, 33, 34, 66, 67, 74, 76, 86, 89, 90, 96–97, 101, 177, 193n1, 194nn3–4, 197n59, 201n47

Mombasa Old Town Conservation Office (MOTCO), 65

Mombasa Public Works Department, 64

Mombasa Times, 53, 60, 61, 115, 197n64

monsoons, 9, 124

mosques, 1, 4, 7, 9, 18, 19, 34, 37, 66–67, 69, 70–71, 72, 74, 75, 77, 78, 82, 90, 92, 93, 99, 100–101, 143, 150, 177, 185, 199n13, 200n25, 200n35, 201nn40–41, 202n66, 202nn72–73, 208n44; Basheikh (formerly Tangana or Mnara), 18, 23, 67, 69, 78, 79, 82, 83, 84, 86, 88, 96, 98, 99, 100–101, 198n3, 200n28, 202n72; Friday, 37, 79, 99, 128; Juma, 205n57; Kizimkazi, 69; Malindi, 87; Mandhry, 18, 23, 67, 68, 69, 70, 78–79, 80, 81, 83, 84, 85, 86, 99–100, 101, 198n3, 201n37, 202n72; neo-Orientalist, 11, 31; Shela Town, 70, 72, 86

Mtwapa, 75

multiplicity, 3, 24, 36, 139, 154

Muscat, 104, 128, 160, 193n27, 203n2

music, 178, 209n10; *chakacha*, 177–178, 204n40, 208n45; musical instruments, 108, 175, 205n41; musical performances, 103, 118, 119, 205n41; musicians, 119; *taraab*, 118, 177, 204n40

Muslims, 4, 9, 23, 29, 31, 35, 37, 40, 41, 53, 63, 64, 66, 67, 69, 70, 71–72, 78, 91, 92, 93, 97, 98, 99–100, 107, 119, 130, 134, 150, 152, 154, 175, 176, 177, 187, 192n22, 198n6, 199n13, 202n68, 205n55; coastal, 29, 30, 74, 77, 91, 187, 191n11, 208n44; Muslim communities, 31, 51, 91; Muslim heritage, 30; Muslim identity, 63, 70, 141, 198n6; Muslim scholars, 69; urban, 15, 39. *See also* Islam; Qur'an; *umma*

Mutawa, 104

Muyaka bin Hajj, 33, 34, 194n17

Mvita, 33–34, 45

Mvita, Shehe, 35, 66

PRITA MEIER is Assistant Professor of Art History at the
University of Illinois at Urbana–Champaign.